ETHICS
In Hospitality Management
A Book of Readings

About the Educational Institute

The Educational Institute of the American Hotel & Motel Association was established in 1952 as a nonprofit foundation to provide essential training and educational resources for the expanding hospitality industry. The Institute's materials are now used by hotel companies, academic institutions, governmental agencies, and correspondence students in more than 120 countries. Nearly two million individuals have benefited from EI's programs, distinguishing the Institute as the world's largest educational resource center for the hospitality industry. All of EI's programs are regularly revised, with leaders from industry and academia assisting in each phase of development to ensure that the materials are relevant, useful, and completely up-to-date.

ETHICS
In Hospitality Management
A Book of Readings

Edited by

Stephen S.J. Hall

EDUCATIONAL INSTITUTE
of the American Hotel & Motel Association

Disclaimer

This publication is designed to provide accurate and authoritative information in regard to the subject matter covered. It is sold with the understanding that the publisher is not engaged in rendering legal, accounting, or other professional service. If legal advice or other expert assistance is required, the services of a competent professional person should be sought.

—From the Declaration of Principles jointly adopted by the American Bar Association and a Committee of Publishers and Associations

The authors or author of each chapter are solely responsible for its content. All views expressed herein are solely those of the authors and do not necessarily reflect the views of the Educational Institute of the American Hotel & Motel Association (the Institute) or the American Hotel & Motel Association (AH&MA).

Nothing contained in this publication shall constitute a standard, an endorsement, or a recommendation of the Institute or AH&MA. The Institute and AH&MA disclaim any liability with respect to the use of any information, procedure, or product, or reliance thereon by any member of the hospitality industry.

©Copyright 1992
By the EDUCATIONAL INSTITUTE of the
AMERICAN HOTEL & MOTEL ASSOCIATION
1407 South Harrison Road
P.O. Box 1240
East Lansing, Michigan 48826

The Educational Institute of the American
Hotel & Motel Association is a nonprofit
educational foundation.

Printed in the United States of America
1 2 3 4 5 6 7 8 9 10 96 95 94 93 92

Library of Congress Cataloging-in-Publication Data
Ethics in hospitality management : a book of readings / edited by
    Stephen S.J. Hall.
        p.   cm.
    Includes bibliographical references.
    ISBN 0-86612-067-X
    1. Hospitality industry—Management. 2. Business ethics.
I. Hall, Stephen S. J.
TX911.3.E84E84   1992
174'.9647—dc20   92-2704
                                                        CIP

Editors: Daniel T. Davis
              Marj Harless

Contents

Joseph W. Fischer, Director of Headquarters Purchasing;
Richard C. Hummrich, Director of Operational Supply—
all with ITT Sheraton

Foreword

A book dedicated to the consideration of ethics in the field of public hospitality is indeed welcome and long overdue. It is most refreshing to have this collection of readings made available to students, educators, and men and women of the hospitality industry.

The hospitality industry is unfortunately susceptible to dishonesty of all sorts—from petty thievery to major manipulations of finances. Computers are notorious for their lack of "audit trails," and temptations are manifold for people who are notoriously underpaid.

Hotel guests too do not necessarily set a good example for those who serve them. Is taking a bar of soap, an ashtray or a bath towel really stealing? Many guests rationalize this as "promoting" the hotel or restaurant. Purveyors to the industry may present other problems. Is a box of candy or a bottle of liquor given to the purchasing agent because of "friendship," or because the purchasing agent continues to buy the product? Where is the line dividing small gifts from "kickbacks," if indeed there is such a line?

Is overbooking rooms ethical? How does one compare the legal responsibilities of the innkeeper to the moral obligations?

This, of course, becomes a personal matter determined in part by one's conscience, upbringing, and values, and is certainly a matter of one's culture. What may be considered unethical in the Western world may be accepted as normal business procedure in the East.

To compound the situation further, what is a "fair" or "reasonable" wage? A "fair" or "reasonable" return on investment? Is it "fair" or ethical to underpay employees for the benefit of the investors? Is it "fair" or ethical to increase prices to the consumer for the benefit of the employees or the investors?

English Common Law left such decisions to the "reasonable man." "Was this the act of a reasonable man?" a judge would ask the jury. Thus it appears that questions of an ethical nature should be left to the "ethical man/woman" to decide.

Just what is "ethics"? In reading the papers of the authors in this book, many different definitions may be found. Ethics comes from the Greek work ethos which may be translated as "habit" or "custom." I prefer the definition of ethics as "the

science of behavior. . . the bit of religion that tells us how we ought to behave."
(William Barclay—*Ethics in a Permissive Society*)

Aristotle indicated, "Every art and every inquiry and similarly every action and pursuit, is thought to aim at some good; and for this reason the good has rightly been declared to be that which all things aim."

It appears, then, that ethical behavior is not easily understood in theory or practice. Each person has his/her own perception of what is "good" or "bad." Thus this collection presents, as it should, a multifaceted approach to the subject—a group of essays well worth reading.

As indicated earlier, such a book as this is long overdue. Stephen St. John Hall and IIQEST are certainly to be congratulated for bringing this to fruition.

—Robert A. Beck, PhD
Professor Emeritus
School of Hotel Administration
Cornell University

Preface

This book was conceived and produced by IIQEST—the International Institute for Quality and Ethics in Service and Tourism, a non-profit corporation established in 1989 and registered in the Commonwealth of Massachusetts.

While perfecting the teaching curricula in both quality and ethics, I found that the two concepts are virtually inseparable. It is as difficult to envision quality (defined as "conformance to standards" in some circles) existing in an unethical environment as it is to picture pure ethics (defined as "knowing what *ought* to be done and having the will to do it") applied in an inconsistent manner. But the basic reason that quality and ethics are mutually inclusive is that quality can only exist where there is an employee attitude of acceptance, and employee attitudes develop best in an environment of total ethics.

An IIQEST survey found that there are very few books that deal in any depth whatever with the concept of quality assurance for the service and tourism industries. And there are virtually no books that address in-depth questions of ethics in hospitality.

Our goal, thus, became obvious: produce a book of readings in ethics for the hospitality industry that would encourage schools to begin teaching ethics and authors to begin writing in greater depth about the subject.

Chapter headings were developed and the arduous task of finding qualified writers in each of the identified subject areas was begun. The entire project has taken almost two and a half years to complete, but the finished product has exceeded the expectations set forth when it was envisioned.

Ethics in Hospitality Management is a book that stimulates thinking, discussion, and debate. These three elements will produce the heightened awareness of quality and ethics sought in the mandate of IIQEST.

Many people made this book possible. Quite obviously, we are totally indebted to the authors who contributed the 24 chapters. We are also highly indebted to many industry leaders who led us to these authors as we sought to assemble the cast and who, like Pat Schappert of the Opryland Hotel, reviewed chapters and made suggestions. The membership of IIQEST who lived through quarterly reports on the progress of the book and lent their support to the effort were far more valuable than they can imagine. And to Shari and Alan Wasserman of The Office Annex and their staff who did the word processing, we extend our sincere appreciation. And, finally, to Gerard Guibilato, the Director of IMHI (the Institut de Management Hotelier International) in Cergy Pontoise, France, whose faith and foresight permitted me to use the final draft as a vehicle for teaching students from many diverse cultures, I am personally indebted.

In conclusion, *Ethics in Hospitality Management* is intended to stimulate readers to dedicate themselves to furthering the ideals of IIQEST by adopting ethics as a way of life, personally, and as a foundation upon which to build success in the business world. I am thus grateful in advance for whatever help readers can give us in reaching our goal.

—Stephen S.J. Hall

Dedication

To the Traveling Public of the World

"May the cup of hospitality be ever full . . .
. . . and the weary traveler's trust forever met"

—Stephen S.J. Hall

1

Ethics in the Hospitality Industry: An Overview

David L. Whitney

Hospitality Is Number One!

Our electronic world is powered largely by fossil fuel, clothed by manufactured textiles, and girded by steel and reinforced concrete. Yet, it is often a shock to realize that none of these elements represents the largest global industry. That industry is hospitality.

One of every 16 workers worldwide is employed in the feeding, lodging, entertaining, or transporting of guests. That means more than 101 million people, whose employment, investment, and productivity represent an economic force estimated at $2 trillion annually. That amount has recently been exceeded only by the gross national product (GNP) of the United States, the former Soviet Union, and Japan.

In developed countries, consumers spend as much for travel and tourism as they do for clothing or health care. Similarly, businesses spend as much on travel as they do on advertising, some spending more.[1] In developing countries, tourism is the number one generator of foreign capital and generally represents the brightest hope in an otherwise uncertain economic future. It is not difficult to believe that an industry which generates such enormous economic impact and touches the lives of so many people also experiences the whole gamut of concerns and opinions about the rightness and wrongness of human behavior.

Hospitality Is Ethics!

Hospitality is one of the noblest words in the English language, connoting welcome, friendship, comfort, and gracious service.

David L. Whitney, EdD, is Associate Professor of Marketing and Hospitality Services at Central Michigan University. He received his BA degree from Bryan College and his master's and doctorate in education from Pepperdine University. He has been widely published, and his article "Ethics in the Hospitality Industry: with a Focus on Hotel Managers" was selected by the Council on Hotel, Restaurant, and Institutional Education as one of the outstanding articles in 1989.

Hospitality is also an action noun that is abstract and empty until it is applied. In fact, the very words used to describe hospitality are action-based. "Welcome," for example, is meaningless without acts of receiving and expressions of acceptance. So, hospitality, by definition, requires hospitable acts, expressions of kindness, and the treating of others as we would like to be treated. It includes the idea of extending friendship to others and providing them with comfort.

As we view hospitality in these terms—as activities aimed at pleasing and enriching others—we are actually overlapping our definition of hospitality with that of ethics. "Ethics is the science of judging specifically human ends and the relationship of means to those ends. . . . It studies the impact of acts on the good of the individual, the firm, the business community and society as a whole."[2]

Certainly, a sense of well-being is an end to which humans strive, and the activities employed in that quest are part of what ethics consists of. Hospitality, as we have described it, is also a human end. Therefore, hospitable acts are a means to that end and are ethical in nature. Thus, we argue that the good of the individual, the firm, the community, and society as a whole cannot be maximized without the efforts and deeds of hospitable people—hospitality!

Hospitality Problems Are Ethical Problems

The link between hospitality and ethics is strengthened by the fact that virtually every critical issue in today's hospitality industry is strongly ethical in nature. For example, consider ethics in food and beverage management. In America, many politicians are sensing constituent support for legislation requiring "truth-in-menu," and a number of states already have such laws, although various restaurant associations oppose such legislation. It is a major issue, and, by definition, an ethical one because it is not possible to discuss "truth-in-anything" without considerations of rights, justice, fairness, and moral absolutes.

Also, there is the conflict between a hotel's need to sell rooms and facilities and the practice of overbooking: guaranteeing, in effect, a room or service that does not exist at the time of the guarantee. Certainly, overbooking is a financial issue in that revenue from unsold services is lost forever, but it is also an ethical issue if the availability of a room or service is misrepresented to the disservice of the guest. Overbooking is an issue of some importance in the airline business as well, and it is an ethical issue there, also.

The need for ethics in employment is obvious in such areas as sexual harassment, equal opportunity, and fairness in wage and promotion policies. Such employee considerations become crucial in this labor-intensive industry where managers feel the opposing pulls of profit versus employee benefits, of efficiency versus worker exploitation. The *right* (an ethically loaded word) of the firm to maximize its productivity confronts labor's right to freedom from exploitation head-on every day.

Any discussion of ethics in the hospitality industry demonstrates that, except in instances which are wholly technical in nature (and relatively easy to solve), the problems and critical issues confronting the hospitality industry worldwide all have strong ethical components in addition to being operational, technical, financial, or promotional in nature.

Are Hospitality Professionals Ethical?

The hospitality industry is no different from other endeavors in that its people constantly feel the stress of marketplace reality. That is, they realize that making a profit is necessary for survival, but, at the same time, so are product quality and customer satisfaction.

Ethical strain results when short-term opportunities to maximize profit come at the expense of long-term quality concerns. It has been said that "the relationship between ethics and profits is a rather tenuous one," and in many instances "corporate responsibility, rather than being the cause of increased profitability, may instead be a consequence of it."[3] So, we may draw the conclusion that being ethical does not always pay, at least not in the short run, and only the financially secure can afford to be ethical.

Does that mean that hospitality professionals are inherently unethical? By no means. A recent study of the ethical orientations of American hotel managers showed them as having very strong traditional values plus a fundamental respect for law as their orientation toward ethical issues.[4] In addition, the study found these managers to be somewhat skeptical of the ability of the hospitality industry to police itself ethically. These research results are simply another demonstration of the ethical tug-of-war managers are experiencing. With their strong values, most managers want to hold high ethical ground, but they often find it difficult because profit-making is still the bottom line in business.

Add to this the fact that international hospitality represents a very broad spectrum of beliefs and ethically acceptable behavior. This diversity should encourage us to maintain an open mind to cultural, racial, and religious differences as they affect what people believe and how they express hospitality. Beliefs and behavior do not always appear to be consistent from an ethnocentric viewpoint. We need a global understanding of right and wrong behavior.

Perhaps the conflict between value-based beliefs and practices is clarified when we consider that an ethic is composed of two elements, the ideological and the operational. Ideological refers to what we believe—the values we hold and our convictions. Operational alludes to what we do—our actions and practices.

When our beliefs are consistent with our actions, we experience ethical consonance or harmony. When this is not the case, when we hold values that are being undermined by contradictory behavior, we experience ethical dissonance.

This concept of ethical consonance and dissonance helps us understand why good people behave unethically. It also explains why unethical behavior is so stressful: we are splitting our belief system from our behavior system, creating a state of "ethical schizophrenia." The hospitality manager experiences this stress daily. In fact, "this may constitute his major challenge: how to be efficient, make profits, *and* observe moral values . . . the technical *must* versus the ethical *ought*."[5]

Further, there are two compounding factors that affect hospitality managers—ethical ignorance and professional cynicism. The first, ethical ignorance, is not meant as a criticism, but simply refers to the fact that most businesspersons are not sophisticated with regard to the philosophical aspects of ethics. Ethics is, after all, a branch of moral philosophy, and knowledge of moral philosophy is hardly on any manager's list of critical business competencies. Thus, when managers find themselves in an ethical dilemma, they turn to what they know best—financial figures, performance data, customer counts, occupancy rates, labor costs, and so forth. They do not generally scrutinize the ethical aspects of a problem, and that is simply because they lack the tools to determine whether a particular act is ethically sound or ethically unacceptable.

Among the many enemies of ethical behavior, few are more harmful to the individual than cynicism. Just as its counterpart, optimism, affirms the value of taking a risk, of trusting people to be ethical until they prove themselves otherwise, cynicism denies the value of taking a risk. It tells us to not trust others and to expect unethical behavior of them. Cynical people enter into ethical situations expecting betrayal and therefore come pre-justified for their own unethical behavior. Their paraphrase of the Golden Rule is, "Do others before they do you."

The effect of a manager's cynicism upon organizational climate and overall team spirit is counterproductive. In one international food service organization, a department head kept on his desk a paperweight with the words engraved, "Trust everyone, but always cut the deck." His staff concluded that the motto really meant, "Trust no one." One staff member then carried the thought to its logical conclusion by observing, "'Trust no one' means he doesn't trust me, and if that's the case I don't trust him, either."

Putting Ethics to Work

Applying ethics to business is similar to some people's approach to cooking. They enjoy good food but are so intimidated by culinary jargon that they rarely cook at home. "That's for the professionals to do," they say and head for a restaurant. In business we tend to respond similarly. "Ethics? that's for the professionals." That does not have to be so. What follows are some key ethical principles that will enable individuals to weigh the issues and draw sound, defendable conclusions. After all, at the heart of ethics is the desire to justify and defend our actions. Many managers have slid into questionable practices because somehow they felt defenseless; they couldn't justify doing what they believed was right.

The Utilitarian Principle

Basically, utilitarianism asks the question, "What action or policy will provide the greatest amount of good for the greatest number of people?" To see how this works, consider how hospitality service providers walk a fine line between providing quality of service and maintaining profitability. This fine line is evident in the area of staffing, where they must determine how many employees are necessary to handle the needs of their guests. Having too many servers is unprofitable; having too few results in poor service. Quality of service is not just a matter of profitability. It is also an ethical issue addressing this principle of utilitarianism: providing the most good for the greatest number of people. It means the provider must ask, "What level of service will most benefit my customers without endangering the basic profitability of the company?" And conversely, "How much profit can I make without depriving my customers of adequate service?" Where is the greatest good for all? That question represents the ethical aspect of what is otherwise a personnel and profitability issue.

In the hospitality industry, this utilitarian principle is extremely important because it is the most universally applied standard of ethics. That is, considerations of "what's the most good for the greatest number of people" drive a very large percentage of decisions, such as the staffing example. Most of the time, when confronted by ethical issues, decision-makers defend their actions by claiming that the overall good is best served by what they have done.[6] They are actually claiming justification. In their minds, their actions are ethically justified because they meet the utilitarian principle of providing the greatest good.

However, one can always prove a case by arguing the greatest good because the greatest good is nearly impossible to measure and certainly depends on one's personal perspective. It is not that the principle of utilitarianism is flawed, but rather that it is limited in its applicability and lacks objectivity. Fortunately, utilitarianism is only the first of three ethical litmus tests managers are applying to business activity. The other two are rights and justice. Together, these three principles provide great insight into ethical decision-making.

The Principle of Rights

Rights and justice are part of corporate values that "help establish and maintain the standards that delineate the 'right' things to do and the things 'worth doing'. . . [they] influence individuals' choices and lead to actions that are desirable to organizations."[7]

Approaches to ethics based on rights assert that human beings have certain moral entitlements that must be respected at all times regardless of race, creed, or economic status. For example, every guest at a hotel has the right to security, freedom from fear of life-threatening danger. That right is not based so much on the individual's guest status as it is upon the fact that the guest is a human being, and life itself is a moral entitlement. Naturally, there are many fundamental human rights, but within organizations, primary consideration is generally given to the right to free consent, right of privacy, freedom of conscience, right of free speech, and the right of due process.[8]

Clearly, this second principle, rights, throws a very different light on ethical issues. Whereas utilitarianism takes the overview by seeking the greatest good for the greatest number of people, rights looks after the individual. Minority status cannot be brushed aside under the principle of rights. A great strength of the American Constitution is its Bill of Rights, which consists of guarantees to the individual that moral entitlements exist and must be honored. Still, consideration of rights often produces conflict. For example, an employer has the right to protect the company against theft, but does that entitle management to administer lie-detector tests to employees? Whose rights prevail?

In conjunction with rights is the principle of duty. That is, if an individual has rights, other individuals have a duty either to protect those rights or not to interfere with the exercise of them. Rights and duty, two sides to the same ethical coin.

The Principle of Justice

Justice simply means that everyone should have access to the playing field of life, and that the field should be level. Whatever the benefits and burdens may be, justice requires that they be equitably distributed. That does not mean some will win and others lose, but it does insist that, win or lose, the game be played fairly. Justice does not insist that each employee be manager, but that each have access to the process whereby managers are chosen. It means that ethically one cannot discriminate against an individual by using an irrelevant criterion as a condition for hiring or promotion or pay.

There are three main canons of justice that are particularly relevant to organizational behavior: equal treatment, consistent administration of rules, and restitution.[9]

Basically, equal treatment means treating equals equally and unequals unequally. That is, when the job is similar, workers should be treated similarly in terms of pay, promotion, working conditions, and so forth. But if market conditions or job responsibilities differ, then treatment of the individuals involved may also differ without being unethical.

Consistent administration of rules denotes fairness of management, clarity of communication regarding job descriptions, and impartial application of performance requirements.

Restitution is the other face of justice by which injustice is punished fairly and impartially. Those guilty of rule violations are held responsible for their acts, except in cases where they were ignorant of the rule or powerless to avoid the violation. Further, under restitution, victims are recompensed for their loss.

Although justice is a critical criterion for ethical behavior, it is also difficult to apply. This is because the rules of justice are themselves subject to ethical debate; the facts may be difficult to ascertain; and responsibility may be diffused among a number of individuals. Still, justice poses questions that must be asked when assessing ethical behavior.

Utilitarianism, rights, and justice are complementary and fairly comprehensive principles that make it possible for individuals to defend their actions ethically. While ethical justification may often support a manager's decisions, it is also obvious that these high principles will not always be enough. Sometimes, as the saying goes, "a six-gun beats three aces." That "six-gun" may consist of threat of dismissal if an unethical practice is not performed, loss of competitive advantage, career derailment, or even the positive prospect of gain as a result of unethical practice.

While the "three aces" of ethical principles may serve to clarify the issues, they may not always be able to replace a lost paycheck, competitive advantage, or financial windfall. Under such conditions, it is very wise to keep in mind the moral ambiguity of all individuals and policies, to remember that we are all subject to ethical temptation, and even when we think we are doing the right thing there may be new questions that trouble us. Many see this ambiguity as the fatal flaw of ethics. After all, so many issues are gray that even when we think we are right we may be wrong. However, instead of being a fatal flaw of ethics, that reality is its dynamic strength, humbling us and opening our lives to the possibility that others also have legitimate points of view.

Extenuating Circumstances

A final word must be said about conditions under which individuals may claim unethical behavior to be unintentional or unavoidable. Except when people deliberately keep themselves ignorant, or fail to take reasonable steps to be informed, they must assume some level of responsibility for behaviors that occur within their sphere of activity. Managers who tell subordinates, "I don't want to know how you do it, just do it!" are thus acting unethically by attempting to avoid responsibility through deliberate ignorance.

Sometimes, however, people find themselves powerless to prevent a questionable act from occurring. It may be that they lack resources to alter the situation, or do not have the organizational position to take a stand. Perhaps threats and duress cause them to remain silent while an injustice or crime is committed. When powerless to stop the act, or when the cost of dissent is justifiably too high, individuals may find relief from ethical responsibility. However, who is to say when the cost is too high? How does one know that his or her dissent would be totally ineffective? Like so many aspects of ethics, considerations of extenuating circumstances are extremely subjective and difficult to apply.

Holding High Ground

By its nature, the hospitality industry is subject to ethical constraints and opportunities. Of all industries, it is the most intensely interactive: people serving people and providing comfort, sustenance, conviviality, transport, amusement, enlightenment, employment, and more. In this maelstrom of human behavior, concerns of right and wrong can be neither ignored nor hidden. For that reason, perhaps the most challenging of all hospitality industry problems is that of ethics. And, unfortunately, all who serve are on the front line. So excellence in service requires men and women who are technically skilled in their craft, experienced, educated, mature, and have the ability to hold high ethical ground under fire. More than any attribute, the latter distinguishes the true professional.

Endnotes

1. American Express Travel Related Services Company, Inc., "The Contribution of the World Travel and Tourism Industry to the Global Economy: Executive Summary," 1989.

2. Thomas M. Garret, *Business Ethics* (New York: Appleton-Century-Crofts, 1966), pp. 4–5.

3. David Vogel, "Ethics and Profits Don't Always Go Hand in Hand," *Los Angeles Times,* Dec. 28, 1988.

4. David L. Whitney, "Ethics in the Hospitality Industry: with a Focus on Hotel Managers," *International Journal of Hospitality Management* 9, no. 1, 1990.

5. Benjamin M. Selekman, "Cynicism and Managerial Morality," *Harvard Business Review,* September–October, 1958, p. 55.

6. David J. Fritzche and Helmut Becker, "Linking Management Behavior to Ethical Philosophy—An Empirical Investigation," *Academy of Management Journal*, 1984, pp. 166–175.

7. Shelby D. Hunt, Van R. Wood, and Lawrence B. Chonko, "Corporate Ethical Values and Organizational Commitment in Marketing," *Journal of Marketing* 53, July 1989, p. 80.

8. Robert A. Cooke, *Ethics in Business: A Perspective* (Boston: Arthur Anderson, 1988).

9. Manuel Velasquez, Dennis J. Moberg, and Gerald F. Cavanagh, "Organizational Statesmanship and Dirty Politics: Ethical Guidelines for the Organizational Politician," *Organizational Dynamics,* Autumn 1983, p. 71.

Discussion Topics

1. From your work in the hospitality industry, consider an ethical problem you or someone you know has experienced. Discuss how the principles of utilitarianism, rights, and justice might influence or clarify your concerns about what was the right thing to do.

2. In a brainstorming session, list as many critical hospitality industry issues as you can. Then discuss the extent to which each issue is ethical in nature.

3. Discuss the question, "Do hospitality companies have the right to require ethical behavior of their employees?" Isn't ethics a matter of personal conscience?

4. There are two components in ethics: ideological (what we believe) and operational (how we behave). Give some examples of basic beliefs that might conflict with business behavior. For example, "Honesty is the best policy."

Term Paper Topics

1. Trace the historical roots of the ethical schools of thought presented in this chapter, e.g., utilitarianism, rights, and justice. Discuss how the hospitality industry might demonstrate each of these philosophies in positive or negative ways.

2. Develop a hospitality industry ethical case study and analyze it using the principles of utilitarianism, rights, and justice. Also discuss the principle of diminished ethical responsibility.

2

The Emergence of Ethics in Quality

Stephen S.J. Hall

Excellence is not an event, it is a habit.
—Aristotle

Quality Defined

In 1981, the American Hotel & Motel Association, under the leadership of Doug Fontaine, retained my company to develop and implement the "Quest for Quality" program throughout the association. We conducted a comprehensive survey to determine the level of awareness and understanding of quality among the membership.

One question in the survey simply asked, "What is the definition of 'Quality'?" The responses were varied. However, some 34% of the respondents used what we called superlative definitions: "Quality" is providing the "best," the "finest," the "most outstanding," the "highest level," etc. While that approach to defining quality sounds good to the ear, it is not particularly helpful because it relies too heavily on the experience, mood, and perception of the evaluator. It is simply too vague. "Finest" for the gourmet might well be pheasant under glass, but for the production-level employee on a limited budget, "finest" could be pot roast. To be sure, there could be good and bad pheasant and good and bad pot roast, but consumers' perceptions will vary as well. A good definition should consist of words that are universally understood. It then becomes a solid platform for all users and can be easily measured.

There were other examples of "right sounding" but unusable definitions. For example, "Quality is service." The finest service available cannot make a poorly prepared steak taste good; nor will the most animated and spectacular tableside preparation result in a quality Caesar salad if the ingredients are improper.

Stephen S.J. Hall is a graduate of the School of Hotel Administration at Cornell University, holds an MBA from Michigan State University, and a master's in divinity from Harvard University. Following thirteen years of service with ITT Sheraton Corporation, culminating in the position of Director of Operations Support Worldwide, he spent five years as Vice President for Administration of Harvard University, leaving in 1976 to form his own companies, one of which developed the "Quest for Quality" program for the American Hotel & Motel Association. In 1988 he formed the International Institute for Quality and Ethics in Service and Tourism (IIQEST), and serves as its Executive Director. Mr. Hall is the author of Quality Assurance in the Hospitality Industry *and is an adjunct professor of Quality and Ethics at the Institut de Management Hotelier International in Cergy-Pontoise, France.*

Only 9% of the AH&MA respondents came close to what has been the traditional definition of quality—"conformance to standards." Far from being an indictment of the hospitality industry, the lack of consensus is more a failing of the American educational system to concentrate on and include quality in its curriculum. On the other hand, the United States never seemed to believe that the quality of American products and services needed improvement until the Japanese showed the way following World War II.

The definition "conformance to standards" permits us to view quality aside from economics. Pheasant under glass may cost more than pot roast, but both may be quality if the standards at each level are met consistently. So, too, can the budget motel and the luxury hotel be quality—each at its own economic level—if the standards governing each hospitality facility are met without exception. The "conformance to standards" definition of quality assumes that the market level has been well-defined and that the standards appropriate for that market level are well-documented and communicated. Assuming we are correct in our market judgment, consistent delivery of our standards will ensure success. That, in essence, is quality.

Today's trend is to focus on the guest or customer as the judge of quality. One approach is to "give the customers what they want when they want it." To be sure, the customer is the final judge, but behind every product or service there is a process and there are standards governing that process. Offering a guest steaks to-order does not eliminate the need to buy properly, trim professionally, store correctly, cook with expertise, and serve properly—each and every time an order is received. "Conformance to standards" is the definition we will use for this discussion.

We are now faced with a dilemma of sorts. Assume for the moment that we are the "Rip Off Muffler Company." Our standards are to use scare tactics on an unsuspecting customer to upgrade a simple tailpipe problem into a complete exhaust system overhaul, plus new front and rear brakes. And we do it well! We meet our standards all the time; our employees are well-trained and well-managed. Do we have quality? Yes—by definition. Do we have excellence? Hardly. But why? What is the definition of excellence? In the area of quality, "excellence" is usually defined by example. Company "A" or Company "B" has excellence. This is fine if we are in the same business and business environment as companies "A" and "B." But if we are not, how can we model ourselves after them? How can we define excellence? What is missing? Could it be ethics?

The Case for Ethics

In 1989, at the 44th Annual International Congress of the American Society for Quality Control held in San Francisco, General Systems Co. President Armand Feigenbaum gave the keynote address. Dr. Feigenbaum, head of this international quality consultancy, introduced ten benchmarks for total quality control:

1. Quality is company-wide.
2. Quality is what the customer says it is.
3. Quality and cost are inseparable.
4. Quality is a way of managing.
5. Quality involves both the individual and teamwork.

6. Quality and innovation are mutually dependent.

7. Quality is an ethic.

8. Quality involves constant improvement.

9. Quality is the most cost-effective and least capital-intensive route to productivity.

10. Quality is implemented with total systematic integration of customers and suppliers.

The list was intriguing to me because he identified quality as an ethic in item #7. Twelve months earlier at a quality conference in New York City, I had listened intently as Dr. Feigenbaum delivered a keynote speech on quality without mentioning the word "ethics." I am in no way criticizing him; he has made too great a contribution to the advancement of quality for that. I only note the trend toward relating quality and ethics. It is long overdue and still has a long way to go, but quality is slowly and steadily changing in perception—from a systematic approach to the management of people toward a humanistic approach to the implementation of systems. Even the words are changing. "Control" (as in quality control) is giving way to assurance, or management, or performance.

Americans Lag Behind

The Europeans and Japanese are well ahead of Americans in their understanding of the inseparable nature of quality and ethics. At an international conference sponsored by the Institute for Moral Re-armament in Caux, Switzerland, in July 1990, a full week was dedicated to "Quality and Ethics in Today's World." More than 600 persons from 32 countries attended the conference. These delegates represented a wide variety of professions. The importance of ethics in the attainment of quality was never questioned; the basic premise was that quality without people is impossible, and properly motivated and managed people without ethics is equally impossible. Americans need to pick up speed!

It is interesting to note that at the 1989 Francisco Congress, Horst V. Lammermeyer's book *Human Relations—The Key to Quality*[1] was described by the publisher as "a major new book which unveils the 'human aspects' of Quality and provides new insight on how interpersonal communications, effective management, and employee motivation can result in the successful application and maintenance of total Quality."

The Human Side of Quality

The human side of quality is, of course, not new. Edward Demming, Joseph Juran, and Phillip Crosby—three highly recognized modern "prophets" of quality—have preached teamwork for many years. And Tom Malohn, president of North American Tool and Die, has advocated human relations as the key to quality since acquiring the company in 1978. Profits have soared as he practices his particular brand of human relations, promoting flexible work hours, pushing decisions to the lowest levels possible, empowering employee problem-solving groups, and stopping the entire plant to call employees together for instant rewards and recognition. Production is up, turnover is down, and North American Tool and Die has carved a secure market niche in the tool and die industry. Yet, Malohn is considered a bit of a maverick even today.

That's the point! The relationship of basic human relations to quality is still considered a bit unique but that perspective is changing fast and nothing could be more exciting to the hospitality industry.

The hospitality industry and the manufacturing industry view quality from widely divergent perspectives. The manufacturing industry places its emphasis on multiple regression analysis, standard deviations, probability sampling, and discussions of alpha-beta calculations and theories. Hospitality places its emphasis on human relations.

Hoteliers must recognize that ethics and morality are the fundamental forces underlying wholesome human relationships. The ethics and morality practiced by individual hoteliers, expanded to a global scale through international tourism, hold the potential for shaping not only hospitality quality but world relationships as well.

The service and tourism industries are on the brink of a most exciting era. It is almost as if the process of quality control had passed them by, then refined and redefined itself more in human terms, and finally returned to include the industries in a new wave of quality progress. During a period of increasing public demand for quality (a period that began in the late 1950s and intensified in the early 1980s), attention was focused on manufacturing because of concern over the growing exodus of manufacturing operations to countries with cheaper labor. The worldwide success of Japanese manufacturing was also a large factor. In the mid-1980s, attention began to shift to the service sector as leaders realized the size of the service industries and also began to see foreign interests—English, French, Japanese, and Australians—moving into the American hospitality industry.

As I state in Chapter Three of my book *Quality Assurance in the Hospitality Industry,* I believe that quality and ethics are inseparable.[2] However, even though excellence now waits with open arms for the hospitality industry to embrace its principles, there are no guarantees that this will happen. What must occur is for the service and tourism industries to open themselves to the meaning and understanding of ethics and morality and how they relate to quality, and to begin treating ethics as a required part of good business rather than an abstract ideal.

To simplify our discussion, we can talk about hospitality as embracing the broader context of tourism. We also can assume that ethics and morality, viewed as separate by most ethicists, are still close enough in definition so that we can talk only in terms of ethics. If we can accept the premise that excellence equals quality plus ethics, how can we make ethics a more meaningful element in hospitality operations?

Ethics Defined

In a 1988 survey of 1,000 AH&MA-member hotels of 300 rooms or more, hoteliers were asked to define ethics.[3] Responses were varied, but essentially they had one thread in common—that of treating others in a fair and equitable manner, the Golden Rule. In fact, many ethicists, especially those in schools of theology, use the Golden Rule as their definition of ethics. While I concur with their logic, I believe that "treating others as you would like to be treated" permits some persons to view ethics in manipulative terms; i.e., "do unto others *so that* they will do unto you." Therefore, for this discussion I prefer to define ethics as "knowing what ought to be done, and having the will to do it." As is the case in all definitions, certain terms must be defined. For example, who decides what "ought to be done," that is, what is "right"?

The Five-Step Test for Ethics

A simple but effective test consists of answering the following five questions:

1. Is the decision legal?
2. Is the decision fair?
3. Does the decision hurt anyone?
4. Have I been honest with those affected?
5. Can I live with my decision?

Is the Decision Legal?

This question is not as simple as it seems. Sometimes a choice that seems ethical is in conflict with the law. For example, American attitudes about the Vietnam War were turned around basically by those people who believed ethically and morally that the war was wrong. Therefore, they broke laws by sit-ins, protests, refusing to fight, etc. The more one appreciates the need for ethics and morality, the more ready one is to break the law if forced to do so, rather than sacrifice one's own self-esteem. Yet, gifts to building inspectors, under-the-table payoffs for gaining business, withholding tips and not reporting them are illegal in every sense of the word.

Is the Decision Fair?

Is there a sense of justice involved?

Management is responsible for managing in the best way possible to provide for the common good of owners, customers, and employees. But failing to promote minorities or women simply because of prejudice is unfair. (Yes, it is also illegal but often impossible to prove.) The American hospitality industry must ask itself why the percentage of female general managers is so low when 40 to 50% of all hotel school graduates are women. Even counting out those women who leave the work force cannot explain the disparity.

Does the Decision Hurt Anyone?

Like the question of legality, this test is difficult to apply. Often, the application of utilitarian principles seems to provide a basis for the decision; i.e., the "right" decision is the one that results in the most "good" and least "pain."

Laying off ten good people during a recession-generated cutback so that 50 employees can remain employed will minimize the "pain" and maximize the "good." Yet, this same issue has ethical components. What if all employees were asked to take a small cut in pay? Were the ten severed fairly, with ample notice, ample severance pay, and sufficient help finding alternative work? Or, did we terminate ten higher-paid people who were just short of qualifying for retirement? Sometimes, despite our greatest attempts to be ethical, we still hurt people. The question is whether we really care.

Have I Been Honest with Those Affected?

Honesty is the cornerstone of ethics. It is never "right" to lie, no matter what the circumstances. We must begin with this fundamental fact. Yet, there are situations in which the "little white lie" hurts fewer people, causes fewer problems, and does more good than telling the entire truth. It does no good to tell a small child that he or she is terminally ill if the child is not prepared to handle it. Nor does it necessarily serve any useful purpose to tell employees that negotiations are under way to sell the property, or that the manager is transferring to another property—at least not until all of the consequences have been identified and analyzed.

Such events can sometimes cause great anxiety and harm unless they are properly presented. However, the fact that in rare situations something short of the truth seems to be the best course does not, in itself, make dishonesty ethical or open doors for misuse of truthfulness. Approached in this manner (i.e., honesty is always the right course), honesty becomes a good and proper test of ethics.

Can My Conscience Live with This Decision?

This question is but one of the five tests. It is not *the* test, although some view it as such, taking the position that as long as the decision-maker can live with the decision it must be a correct one. The "my conscience only" approach to ethics is too narrow, too subjective, and it often results in a poor decision. The underpaid, overworked, stressed-out desk clerk who embezzles a few thousand dollars to cover family medical costs may well be able to live with his or her conscience—if that were the only test. Yet, conscience is not to be taken lightly. It is a very important test.

According to my national survey on hospitality ethics, the prime source of ethics comes from family, with school, church, and "self-taught" being distant inputs.[4] The fact is that, regardless of origin, most humans have a sense of right. They do not always follow it, but it is there. Throughout history all social systems have tried to make order out of chaos and build fundamental tenets of ethics and morality. Theologians credit God. Sociologists credit the natural instinct that believes structure is better for survival than unchecked individualism. Regardless, there is an innate sense that separates right from wrong, "ought" from "ought not," good from bad, and just from unjust.

Applying the Tests

The five tests must be taken as a group. Applied to our behavior, they will elevate our ethical and moral conduct. Applying the tests to newly created standards in our hotels, motels, and motor inns will lift these standards to a higher level. And if the elevated standards are then met consistently, the result is excellence.

It is possible, of course, to apply all five tests diligently and still arrive at a decision that can be criticized as less than ethical. I would argue in such cases that the fault lies more in judgment than in ethics. The fact remains, however, that the application of the five tests constitutes a process of evaluation which, when applied in good faith, results in improved ethics. And, improved ethics is the goal we seek as we work toward excellence.

The need to consider long-term consequences of our decisions is also very important in the practice of ethics. What seems proper at the moment often becomes improper over time. This was the case in the Love Canal hazardous-waste-disposal and contamination case in Buffalo, New York. Of course, the classic example is the decision to drop atomic bombs on Hiroshima and Nagasaki. The long-term effects of nuclear radiation were never thoroughly considered.

Getting back to the hospitality industry, it may be considered highly ethical to promote the hotel manager who has achieved a significant operating profit turnaround. However, unless the reasons for the turnaround are carefully analyzed, you may find that profits were achieved short-term by depleting inventories, deferring maintenance, and reducing quality of product—actions destined to have a negative impact over time.

If ethics is such a meaningful part of quality, why then has the application of proper ethics been so difficult to achieve?

The Obstacles to Ethics

On the surface, practicing ethics makes eminently good sense. Set aside for the moment the fact that properly applied ethics may avoid costly legal settlements. Ethics, properly applied, provides the foundation for employee pride and motivation—two crucial elements in achieving quality. The proper application of ethical analysis transforms the workplace from mediocre to excellent. Why would not every hospitality leader, from supervisor to most senior executive, want to practice the highest level of ethical validation? These are factors that must be addressed.

Time

Two characteristics of the service and tourism industries are heavy workloads and stressful environments. Because the industries are people-intense (i.e., consistently have more people-to-people interactions than most industries) and because people have a seemingly infinite variety of needs, those in service industries' leadership tend to work long hours and face the responsibility of on-the-spot decisions, without adequate time in many cases to thoroughly analyze the situation. Service industries' managers complain about "18-hour days of constant pressure." Such an environment imposes a handicap to making good ethical decisions. Yet, it is estimated that as much as 50 to 80% of an executive's time is spent undoing or doing over the work of others. In short, the hoteliers' problems of long hours and intense pressure often result from lack of organization; that is, they are self-inflicted.

Management time must be spent supervising well-structured standards, correcting variances, and rewarding compliance. Hospitality management must begin to recognize the all-too-prevalent negative cycle that says, "I have to spend so much time putting out fires that I'm too busy to properly organize my area of responsibility." It's a descending spiral, which perpetuates the myth that hospitality management is mostly an art, that having "hospitality" in your blood means you will work long hours under conditions of great stress. Yes, inadequate time is an obstacle to higher ethical performance, but a laissez-faire attitude about ethics will only result in the use of more management time to undo and remake.

Ego

At times, all of us tend to hear and see only what we want to. Managers with large egos seem to live their lives that way! The mere mention of the word ethics sends them into a frenzy. They hear their integrity being questioned. It can be a waste of time explaining to them that ethics is not an event but a way of life, which is characterized by the constant attempt to become better. They only hear what they perceive as an attack on their management style. Imagine being a department head trying to upgrade a process or an event so as to be more ethical and taking your idea to the egocentric general manager who implemented the original process three years prior! The essence of both improved quality and ethics—i.e., excellence—is the willingness to view life with an open mind. A big ego will not permit it to happen. Such managers are characterized by "Do as I say, not as I do." And your normal response is: "I will do as you say when you're looking—otherwise, I'll do as I darn well please, just as you do!"

Unreliable Information

Good decisions rely on good information. Some years ago, IBM distributed to its work force a saying that highlighted this need for good information: "No one can ever take the weight of decision-making from your back. But, the more you know about the way things really are, the lighter the burden will be." This is very true, but it is not always so easy to know how "things really are." One need go no further than the Iranian arms scandal to illustrate this point. Americans still do not know if Lt. Col. Oliver North is guilty or not, and, if so, of what? After millions of words of testimony, we still do not know who was involved and why.

Propaganda provides a classic example of how poor ethical decisions can result from unreliable information. It has been hypothesized, for example, that the anti-German propaganda machine of the U.S. Government during World War I caused many respected clergy in America to speak out against German atrocities that never actually happened. Thus, when World War II broke out 20 years later, many American clergy, among others, remained silent while the Holocaust gathered full steam. Good ethics begins by questioning the validity of the information upon which choices are based and insisting upon correct information as a basis for ethical judgments.

Ignorance

Ignorance is the parent of most unethical judgments. I am not speaking of lack of knowledge per se, for a person can lack knowledge without being ignorant. As the saying goes: "A smart person is one who doesn't know and knows he doesn't know and tries to learn. An ignorant person is one who doesn't know, and doesn't know that he doesn't know and refuses to learn."

Often, ethical ignorance is environmentally based. For example, the manager who was raised in a sexist environment often cannot see sexual harassment when it is all around him. A manager raised in a highly prejudiced environment might be hard-pressed to appoint a minority to a department-head position, no matter how qualified that person may be. Managers who were taught that the only path to success is along the bottom-line road are often oblivious to ethical issues that do not have positive bottom-line impact. This point is important. Ignorance and intelligence can be mutually inclusive. To be a brilliant artisan of the bottom line but ignorant of the human side of enterprise is to court problems in the arena of ethical judgment.

Stratifying Ethics in Hospitality

To structure our examination of the inseparable relationship of ethics and quality in hospitality, we must identify four major areas of interaction.

1. **Promotional Ethics**—Ethics dealing with the presentation of the chain or individual hospitality unit's image to individuals or the public at large.
2. **Transactional Ethics**—Ethics involved in the interaction of the guest with employees of the hospitality unit or the physical unit itself.
3. **Hierarchical Ethics**—Ethics dealing with the interaction of employees at every level of the hospitality unit and/or with employees and the physical unit itself.
4. **Contractual Ethics**—Ethics dealing with contracts, real or implied, between the hospitality unit and others not employed directly by the unit.

Examples of promotional ethics are all media advertising and promotion, brochures, sales and marketing activities, public relations activities, reservation interactions, and customer relations following departure.

Transactional ethics begins with the booking of a guest reservation and ends with the collection of the guest's debt at departure or afterwards. It includes everything in between that takes place between the property, its personnel, and the guest.

Hierarchical ethics covers interactions among all employees. It is not limited to verbal or written interaction but includes the physical environment as well.

Examples of contractual ethics are general and subcontractors' projects; all relationships with inspectors and other enforcement officials; transactions with all vendors, consultants, entertainers, and temporary labor not carried as taxable employees. In the case of inspectors and other enforcement officials, there is no contractual relationship in the conventional sense, but there is an implied contract in that the property is licensed to operate in certain areas in return for compliance with lawful requirements.

Ethics Is an Absolute

Do not allow the stratification of ethics to mislead you into believing that there are different types, forms, and intensities of ethics. "Doing what is right" is the solid bottom line of ethics and is not mitigated by the fact that we are talking about interactions with the public, the guests, the employees, and those who support these interactions. The stratification is intended only to identify in which part of the hospitality process the ethical analysis is taking place. I recall discussing ethics with a high-level manager of a major U.S. auto manufacturer. He described a process whereby every executive in the company was required to read and sign off on the company's code of ethics each year. That process, he confided, was for public consumption. The company followed a different philosophy of ethics in dealing internally with personnel. A company that concentrates on promotional ethics and ignores hierarchical or contractual ethics cannot claim to be seriously in the hunt for excellence, and the public will discover the deception eventually.

Exhibit 1   Paradigm of Excellence

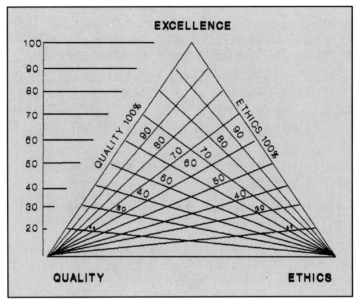

The Paradigm of Excellence

The paradigm of excellence (Exhibit 1) is useful as a visual symbol of the insepa-rable relationship between quality (being consistent) and ethics (being right); the para-digm is not an accurate index of achievement in the quest for excellence. The proper process to follow is to establish standards consistent with the market level sought. Standards would then be certified by testing them against the five tests for ethics. This is then followed by the quality assurance process to achieve one hundred percent com-pliance. The result is excellence at the market level selected. Measuring quality compli-ance is often difficult but is certainly not an impossible task. Judging the extent to which ethical thinking has been diffused throughout the organization is far more diffi-cult. A well-structured survey of employees, such as the quality index[5] and occasional surveys among guests, will give a good measure of the effectiveness with which ethics has been diffused within the work force.

Monitoring Excellence

The models for the administration of excellence range from dependence upon quality circles alone to the property's most senior executive taking on the task of man-aging excellence. As most persons dealing with quality would do, I propose that the model of a top-level quality assurance committee, chaired by a dedicated quality assur-ance director, is the most efficient and successful approach. The committee consists of from three to seven members, depending on property size, and meets for one hour each week.

The nature of excellence is that it is a journey, not a destination. That means the quest for excellence is ongoing. The committee has the primary function of reviewing all job titles and job tasks and creating meaningful standards for each task. If the quality assurance committee is responsible for overseeing ethics as well, it will test every standard for ethical compliance before establishing the standard as finite.

But the question of ethics goes beyond specific job-task standards. For example, there is the issue of sexual harassment (covered in greater detail in a later chapter). The quality assurance committee represents an excellent non-threatening environment in which to discuss problems in this and other sensitive areas so that the senior management members of the committee can produce a policy statement covering the problem. One of the characteristics of a good quality assurance director is that he or she is politically astute—that is, knowledgeable about what is or is not relevant to the committee's work and aware of issues of sensitivity to be respected and trusted among all employees. Respect and trust are, of course, crucial to the question of ethics as well. Thus, the quality assurance director becomes a very logical person to administer both areas effectively.

Will Ethics Pay?

We cannot leave the subject of ethics without addressing the question of cost. One common belief is that in today's hard-nosed business world the term "caveat emptor" (let the buyer beware) should prevail. Generally, this means that if the buyer accepts what is being sold, the seller is not being unethical. In short, those who operate under this philosophy believe that there is a cost associated with being ethical. If possible, this cost should be avoided.

According to David Freudberg in his book *The Corporate Conscience—Money, Power and Responsible Business*, Johnson and Johnson Chairman James Burke became intrigued with the question about whether being ethical (in a corporate sense) was an expense or actually contributed to profitability.[6] To answer Burke's question, the Johnson and Johnson accountants studied major companies that had been in existence for at least 30 years and that had maintained a written set of principles specifying their public-service policies and for which there was "solid evidence that these ideas had been promulgated and practiced for at least a generation."[7]

The Johnson and Johnson accountants found 26 companies that met these criteria: AETNA, Allied, American Can, AT&T, Coca-Cola, Dayton-Hudson, General Foods, Gerber Products, Hewlett-Packard, IBM, JCPenney, John Deere, Johnson and Johnson, Johnson's Wax, Kodak, Levi Strauss, McDonald's, McGraw-Hill, 3M, Pitney Bowes, Pittsburgh National Corp., Procter and Gamble, Prudential, R.J. Reynolds, Sun Company, and Xerox.

Further analysis eliminated 11 of these companies, either because they did not have stockholders or a code of ethics in effect for the full period. The remaining 15 companies had outstanding results. Their average profit growth over the 30-year period ending in 1982 was 11%. The figure for all 26 of the companies was 10.3%. Comparably, the other Fortune 500 companies over the same period had a 6.1% profit growth. No one had to convince James Burke and Johnson and Johnson of the value of ethics. As a result of this study, Johnson and Johnson initiated an ethics review of the company's operations, asking "what if" questions. By pre-determining their ethical responses to situations that could occur, the company was prepared for virtually every contingency.

Not long after, someone sabotaged an unknown number of bottles of Tylenol, one of the company's leading products, with arsenic. Several Tylenol users died. Without a moment's hesitation, Johnson and Johnson recalled all Tylenol, acknowledged the problem, offered a large reward, and redesigned the Tylenol containers to prevent future tampering. Nevertheless, most people predicted that Tylenol was finished as a product. But this did not happen. People trusted Johnson and Johnson because of their honesty and fast corrective action. When reintroduced some months later, Tylenol once again moved to the top of the sales charts. More proof that ethics pays dividends!

Hoteliers seem to agree that becoming more ethical would increase profits. In my 1988 study of 1,000 U.S. hotels of 300 rooms or more, 39% of the 102 general managers who responded thought ethics would increase profits, in contrast to only 10% who felt ethics would decrease profits. The remainder, about 51%, were not certain what effect ethics would have. Another finding in the study was that hoteliers want more information and training in ethics, a fact that should not be ignored by the associations of which they are members.

Conclusion

I have shown that conformance to mediocre standards, however consistent, results in a mediocre image. In order to raise standards, ethics must be applied and then coupled with conformance. This will result in compliance at a high level of excellence. I have discussed how ethics can be tested and how it can be administered by the quality assurance committee. To add greater weight to my conclusions, here are excerpts from my study of ethics in hospitality completed in 1988:

Excerpts from 1988 Study of
1000 U.S. Hotels of 300 Rooms or More[8]

1. In general, hoteliers consider themselves to be ethical. When asked to rate 18 industries in terms of ethics, one relative to the others, the results were as follows:

Area	Rating (avg 1–10)
1. Hotel Industry	7.44
2. Medical Profession	6.71
3. Restaurant Industry	6.63
4. Motel Industry	6.52
5. Retail Clothing	6.52
6. Airlines	6.47
7. Religious Leaders	6.46
8. Travel Agents	6.41
9. Food and Beverage Suppliers	5.98
10. Funeral Directors	5.85
11. Consultants	5.64
12. Municipal Inspectors	5.44
13. Government Inspectors	5.33
14. Print Media (Press)	5.17

Area	Rating (avg 1–10)
15. Construction Industry	5.17
16. Stock and Bond Brokers	5.14
17. Auto Dealerships	4.34
18. Trade Unions	3.44

Further studies as to whether or not the consumer shares the hoteliers' ratings seem to be in order.

2. Hoteliers believe that ethics does have a positive impact on profitability. When asked if becoming more ethical would increase, decrease, or have no effect on profits, they said:

Increase	39%
No Effect	37%
Decrease	10%
Don't Know	14%

Higher ethical behavior seems to pay dividends.

3. Hoteliers believe that their ethical behavior can be improved. When asked if hotel executives can be taught to be more ethical, 80% responded "yes."

4. Hoteliers believe schools of higher education can do a better job in teaching ethics. When asked, "In terms of teaching ethics, do you believe that America's hotel, restaurant, and institutional schools are doing a good job, an acceptable job, not enough?" they replied:

Doing a good job	5%
Doing an acceptable job	24%
Not doing enough	36%
Don't know	35%

5. Hoteliers want more training in ethics. "Does the need exist for the American Hospitality Industry to develop a program to promote greater ethical and moral responsibility and understanding?"

Yes	61.7%
No	19.1%
Don't know	19.1%

6. Hoteliers resolve most ethical issues after the fact. When asked about when they felt most ethical issues are resolved, they responded:

As they arise	48%
Only if they arise and appear to threaten the image of the operation	26%
Before they arise	26%

It is always true that it is easier to prevent unethical decisions than to undo the results of bad ethical judgment.

In summary, the industry is ready for more knowledge and understanding of ethics. Now that the relationship with quality is noted, there is a great opportunity for the American hotel industry to effectively combine the two and add even more strength to the perception that America provides leadership in the world of service and tourism.

Endnotes

1. Horst V. Lammermeyer, *Human Relations—The Key to Quality* (Milwaukee, Wis.: ASQC Quality Press, 1990).

2. Stephen S. J. Hall, *Quality Assurance in the Hospitality Industry* (Milwaukee, Wis.: ASQC Quality Press, 1990).

3. Stephen S. J. Hall, "The Role of Ethics in Quality," Master's Thesis, Harvard Divinity School, Cambridge, Mass., 1988.

4. Ibid.

5. Stephen Hall Associates, *Quality Index*, 1986.

6. David Freudberg, *The Corporate Conscience—Money, Power, and Responsible Business,* (New York: American Management Association, 1986).

7. Ibid.

8. Stephen S. J. Hall, National Survey on Hospitality Ethics, 1988 (on file at the Harvard Divinity School, Harvard University, Cambridge, Mass.).

Discussion Topics

1. In the final analysis, quality is what the customer says it is because the customer pays the bills. Discuss.

2. Quality in hospitality occurs when the entire organization performs like a well-oiled machine. It is management's responsibility to keep every employee in place and focused totally on his or her tasks. Discuss.

3. It is *always* wrong to lie—but sometimes more harm will result from telling the truth. Give examples and discuss decision criteria.

4. The 1988 ethics survey at the end of the chapter included a question not presented earlier in this chapter. It asked, "Where did you get your foundation for ethics?" The most important answer was "from parents." Is this true? Should it be true? What can we expect in the future?

Term Paper Topics

1. "Morality (Ethics) is an invention of the weak to neutralize the strength of the strong."

2. You are the new manager of a 15-year-old 500-room commercial mid-rate hotel. You decide to introduce a program to improve ethics. You call your eight department heads together and you present your case. In eight double-spaced pages or fewer, write out the speech you will give to your department heads and first-line supervisors.

CODE OF ETHICS
HOSPITALITY SERVICE AND TOURISM INDUSTRY

1. We acknowledge ethics and morality as inseparable elements of doing business and will test every decision against the highest standards of honesty, legality, fairness, impunity, and conscience.

2. We will conduct ourselves personally and collectively at all times such as to bring credit to the service and tourism industry at large.

3. We will concentrate our time, energy and resources on the improvement of our own product and services and we will not denigrate our competition in the pursuit of our own success.

4. We will treat all guests equally regardless of race, religion, nationality, creed or sex.

5. We will deliver all standards of service and product with total consistency to every guest.

6. We will provide a totally safe and sanitary environment at all times for every guest and employee.

7. We will strive constantly, in words, actions and deeds, to develop and maintain the highest level of trust, honesty and understanding among guests, clients, employees, employers and the public at large.

8. We will provide every employee at every level all of the knowledge, training, equipment and motivation required to perform his or her tasks according to our published standards.

9. We will guarantee that every employee at every level will have the same opportunity to perform, advance, and will be evaluated against the same standard as all employees engaged in the same or similar tasks.

10. We will actively and consciously work to protect and preserve our natural environment and natural reources in all that we do.

11. We will seek a fair and honest profit, no more, no less.

3

Morality—the Right of Guests, the Responsibility of Management

Eric F. Nusbaum

Almost all the chapters in this book have the word "ethics" in their title, as does the book itself. This chapter, however, starts with the word "morality."

While many people think of ethics and morals as being equivalent, there is a fine distinction that must be drawn between the two. Ethics deals with what is good and bad or duty and obligation from a perspective of culturally or generally accepted standards of conduct. Morality is a system of principles of right and wrong as they apply to both beliefs and actions. What is culturally acceptable on an ethical basis may not be morally correct (see Chapter 23, "Hospitality, Travel, and the Theory of the Mean," regarding ethics and the international tourist). Also, some suggest that ethics is based upon actions and that one who has not actively participated in a wrongful act cannot be held accountable. This notion is rejected on two counts: first by the legal principle "estoppel by silence," which may be interpreted as saying that failure to speak or act is inconsistent with honest dealings; and second by biblical teachings, which hold that there are two types of sins—those of commission (active participation) and those of omission (failing to act when action was morally required).

This chapter examines the origins of morality in Western Civilization. It will attempt to show that each of us has the power to develop our own standards of morally correct conduct and that these standards can then be applied to our daily lives and business dealings. We will review moral dilemmas that may confront the hospitality executive, and we will examine the moral implications of different courses of action so that the reader may see how morality can be applied to business decisions.

Eric Nusbaum, CHA, is a lecturer in the Department of Hotel, Restaurant and Travel Administration at the University of Massachusetts. He received his bachelor's degree in hotel administration and his master's degree in environmental engineering and hotel administration from Cornell University. He is currently studying for his doctorate in industrial engineering at the University of Massachusetts. Mr. Nusbaum has had a decade of experience in the hospitality field, in both staff and line positions, and has published several articles, most of which deal with the general area of systematic management.

Biblical Example

Few of us are students of ancient history or the Bible. Yet, most Americans could probably identify the Ten Commandments as being a statement of moral principles and actions. However, it is erroneous to think that the Ten Commandments are the first codification of moral conduct.

The Exodus of the Israelites from Egypt took place during the thirteenth century B.C., and it was during their wanderings in the desert that Moses handed down the Ten Commandments to the Israelites. Ancient Babylonian writings contain two overlapping codes of conduct, the Code of Hammurabi (circa 1700 B.C.) and the writings known as Shurpu (1500–1100 B.C.). Both contain some of the moral ideas expressed in the Ten Commandments and some of the specific additional laws given in the biblical book of Exodus. It is also worth noting that in Chapter 125 of the Egyptian *Book of the Dead* there is a plea for the soul of the deceased. This plea contains, in the same order, five of the Ten Commandments. This work, which predates the Exodus from Egypt by several hundred years, was probably known to Moses and may have served as a partial model for the listing of the Ten Commandments.

Ten Commandments

The Ten Commandments are listed twice in the Old Testament: first in Exodus 20:1–14 and again in Deuteronomy 5:6–18. Jewish biblical scholars indicate that the repetition of the text is a measure of its importance as a central tenet of Judaism. In both cases, the Ten Commandments are given as part of a charge for moral behavior and conduct that is addressed to the individual members of society. The reward for observing these statutes is a long and fruitful life. It is worth noting that the two versions differ slightly in their general language and significantly in the wording of the Fourth Commandment, which deals with the observation of the Sabbath. The version in Exodus says that the reason for the Sabbath observance is that it commemorates the six days of creation, whereas Deuteronomy cites the redemption from servitude as the reason for the sanctification of the seventh day. In either case, this is one of the longest and most detailed of the Commandments, which includes a precept for proper treatment of both servants (employees?) and strangers within the house (guests?).

Biblical scholars interpret these detailed descriptions as being reserved for important points that must be understood and complied with and not left to interpretation and inference. Hence, we are led to the conclusion that including a standard of treatment for our servants and guests is an essential part of a code of moral conduct. Conceivably, this could be construed as imposing the responsibility for moral treatment of both the staff and guest upon the hospitality executive who has both servants and strangers in his or her establishment.

Interpersonal Relationships

The first three Commandments deal with the interaction of humans with the deity: first is the affirmation of and singularity of God, then the prohibition of idol worship, and finally the injunction against profanity. The remaining seven Commandments are devoted to interpersonal relationships. The number and specificity of these commandments—the day of rest, honoring parents, and proscriptions against murder, adultery, theft, bearing of false witness, and envy—must lead us to conclude that our relationships with each other form a large and significant portion of a moral code of conduct. It would be unwise to think that these commandments represent the entire code of moral conduct (the Mishnah, which is a compilation of the ancient Jewish laws, contains 613 precepts), for they are merely the foundation and provide guidance for the development of a larger system of positive and negative precepts of action.

It is interesting to realize that the Ten Commandments are given in the second and fifth of the Five Books of Moses. The first book, Genesis, does give an indication of the moral codes that are deemed important by God. For example, Adam and Eve's failure to honor the wishes of their parent by eating of the tree of knowledge resulted in their expulsion from Eden. The serpent bore false witness against Eve by advocating that she eat of the tree of knowledge. Cain rose up against his brother and slew him, for which he was marked for life. Sodom and Gomorrah were destroyed for their wickedness. Yet, while a cause-and-effect relationship between the doing of evil and punishment is evident, there was no systematic code that people could use to guide their actions during the many years predating the Ten Commandments. It is the codification and definition of a moral course of action that gives the Ten Commandments their preeminence in western morality.

New Testament Themes

The themes of the New Testament echo those of the Old. Jesus Christ taught that we are all brothers and that we have a responsibility to each other. The teaching that one should love thy neighbor as thyself requires that equal and moral treatment be given to all; it is an exhortation to morally correct behavior. Who among us desires to be treated unfairly, to be robbed, or to be defamed? The New Testament also recognizes the importance of acts of kindness and mercy toward others, as in Matthew 25:31–40, where the passage into the heavenly grace is granted to those who have shown kindness to God. The righteous question the admission of these people because they have not tended the needs of God and are told, "Inasmuch as ye have done it unto one of the least of these my brethren, ye have done it unto me." It is doubtful that a simpler or more eloquent call for moral behavior in our dealings with our fellow man could be written.

Who has the right to interpret actions and make moral judgments? Is this solely the right of religious leaders? Or is there a responsibility incumbent upon all of us to examine and judge our own actions? Again, a bit of history and definition sheds some light on these issues.

Terms of Recognition

Each branch of Judeo-Christian religion has a preferred term of recognition and respect for its religious leaders. The Hebrew word "rabbi" means teacher, and the Catholic title "father" also recognizes an educational role for the person so titled. The titles of minister, pastor, and rector are all derived from French or Latin words and respectively mean agent, to feed, and to direct. These terms indicate that these individuals are supposed to assist us in the interpretation of theology. By definition, theology is "the rational interpretation of religious faith, practice, and experience" (*Webster's Seventh New Collegiate Dictionary*). There is room for different religious interpretations, which is why the ancient Hebrews established rabbinic courts in which questions of religious interpretation were (and still are) discussed by several rabbis.

The language of Deuteronomy preceding the repetition of the Ten Commandments states: "The LORD made not this covenant with our fathers, but with us, even us, who are all of us here alive this day." This puts the onus for moral actions upon the individual. An even more powerful charge to the individual to act in a morally correct manner is given in the Book of Micah (6:6–8), where the prophet rhetorically asks how shall man come before the Lord and what is it that will please the Lord. The answer quite simply instructs each of us to assume the obligation for our own conduct: "It hath been told thee, O man, what is good, and what the LORD doth require of thee: Only to do justly, and to love mercy, and to walk humbly with thy GOD."

Note that as in the Ten Commandments, the interpersonal relationships here account for the majority of required actions. The fact that in this recitation these relationships are given precedence over the human-deity relationship may be interpreted as suggesting that it is our code of personal conduct and action that is viewed as most desirous and meritorious by the Lord. This view is strengthened by previous passages indicating that the offering of a thousand rams or ten thousand rivers of oil or the life of the firstborn is not what will please the Lord. Instead, it is performing justly and loving mercy, or living a moral life, that is valued most highly.

Secular Writings

Lest the reader believe that it is only religious writings that set up moral obligations and responsibilities, it should be noted that there are secular writings and laws which also call for moral action. Historians report that the young men of ancient Athens were required to pledge the following oath upon turning age 17:

> We will never bring disgrace on this our City, by an act of dishonesty or cowardice.
>
> We will fight for the ideals and Sacred Things of the City both alone and with many.
>
> We will revere and obey the City's laws, and will do our best to incite a like reverence and respect in those above us who are prone to annul them or set them at naught.
>
> We will strive increasingly to quicken the public's sense of civic duty.
>
> Thus in all ways we will transmit this City, not only not less, but greater, and more beautiful than it was transmitted to us.

The Middle Ages are sometimes referred to as the Age of Chivalry. The name comes from the code of the chevalier, or mounted knight, and it originally referred to a regimen of training and preparation for combat. It was later expanded to include a code of conduct for both the battlefield and life. To be considered a worthy or true knight, the individual had to be brave and skillful in combat and be pious, respectful, generous, and courteous. The championing of the poor, the oppressed, and the downtrodden became a way of life for the true knight. Perhaps the most widely recognized writings of this period center on the legendary King Arthur, whose Round

Table welcomed all true knights who pledged their "might for right," rather than the then-prevalent "might makes right." Legend holds that it was a lack of marital fidelity that caused the dissolution of the Knights of the Round Table and the death of Arthur. Yet, the ideals of self sacrifice and devotion to good and just causes is the enduring theme of the legend.

Somewhat later, Cervantes wrote of Don Quixote, a slightly befuddled old man who thought himself a knight and whose goal was to travel around righting wrongs and protecting the unprotected. This story was popularized in the musical *The Man of La Mancha.*

Even today, there are organizations like the Boy Scouts that have made moral conduct a part of their creed. Traditionally, Scouts begin each meeting with a reaffirmation of the Scout Oath and Law, each pledging himself to "do my best . . . to help other people at all times; to keep myself . . . morally straight." Because service to others is a high calling, it has become not only a part of the Scout Oath but also the central tenet of Scouting's honor society, the Order of the Arrow.

Many of our civic and fraternal organizations are founded upon the concept of service to others and community: an implicit, but very tangible, affirmation of the moral duty of individuals to better their local community and the world. The motto of Rotary International is "Service above self."

The basis of the justice system of the United States is the belief that each individual is born with an unalienable set of rights. Some of these rights are enumerated in the Declaration of Independence and protected by our Constitution and the Bill of Rights, whereas others are implied. It does not take a very deep probe into these rights to see that many have a relationship with a moral code of behavior. Only a few examples are needed to demonstrate the fact that morality is the foundation of law:

The right to life	Proscription against murder
Property rights	Proscription against stealing
The right to trial	Facing an accuser lessens the likelihood of false witnesses

Does this mean that morality can be legislated? A similarly brief review of our legal history will show that attempts to legislate morality have failed to produce the desired results. Witness the American experience with Prohibition and illicit drugs, gambling, and prostitution.

The course of our legal history has been to define the scope of individual rights, enumerated and implied, and to establish boundaries to prevent the rights of different individuals or groups from coming into conflict. At the same time, our system has built on the rich history of English Common Law and has established that there are certain responsibilities which are incumbent upon all individuals in general and to certain classes of individuals in particular, including the innkeeper. Herein lies the second part of the title of this chapter, for the guest has certain rights of action and privacy that are his by entitlement, and the innkeeper has certain statutorily established limits on his rights that have been enacted for the protection of the guest. The guest entrusts his or her care to the innkeeper, and the innkeeper is legally required to uphold that trust. A common summary of the innkeeper's responsibility to his or her guests is to "keep safe premises and to keep the premises safe."

Hospitality Industry Morality

Recall that the word morality requires that the teaching of right and wrong courses of thought and action be done in a systematic manner. This simplifies our task, as there will be a framework that allows decisions to be made in a consistent and reasonable manner. The same principles will be called into action each time a decision must be made, and there will be a uniformity of action that will also serve to protect the establishment from charges of discrimination and bias. The basic building blocks of such a system of hospitality morality are:

- That service is an honorable profession, worthy of and deserving of respect and a code of moral conduct

- That a consequence of entering the service industries is that our guests are entrusting themselves to our care and that we willingly and knowingly accept the responsibility to protect them

- That we have a moral as well as statutory obligation to our guests that can be drawn from the basic foundations of the Judeo-Christian concept of morality—the Ten Commandments

- That we have a similar responsibility to our employees and its source may also be the Ten Commandments

- That we have a responsibility to protect and enhance the values of the assets belonging to those who employ us

- That we have the capability to evaluate the moral consequences of our own choices and courses of action based upon whether or not the outcomes of these actions are just

- That our decisions must be made in a reasoned and consistent manner because this simplifies the task and protects us from charges of discrimination

The topics covered in this book can be discussed either in terms of ethics or morality. One topic that frequently comes up in such discussions is the hotel industry's association with prostitution. It is an interesting topic because it involves a potential conflict between the rights of the guest and the responsibility of the innkeeper. It also may be used to show the difference between an ethics decision and a moral decision. We do not in any way condone prostitution, but it is a useful topic for discussion purposes.

The Example of Prostitution

Prostitution is illegal in the vast majority of states. So, too, is procuring prostitutes and operating an establishment for the purpose of encouraging prostitution. Some states also have statutes that prosecute the patrons of prostitutes.

The legal prohibition may be viewed by some as an attempt to legislate morality, and like other attempts to legislate morality, in many respects it has failed. Struggling under a burden of insufficient resources, law enforcement officials frequently put a low priority on enforcing the laws prohibiting prostitution. This is especially true where prostitution involves expensive and discreet liaisons. While prostitution is a crime, some within the judicial system may be inclined to view it as a victimless crime, and therefore punishment may be restricted by some to fines and short jail sentences.

Prostitution sometimes occurs in hotels because the primary purpose of the hotel is to rent private bedrooms for the use of guests. Guests who are traveling far from home may desire the companionship and sexual services of prostitutes. Prostitutes, recognizing the existence of this market, are attracted to hotels. Local residents who patronize prostitutes seek hotel rooms because they offer a safer and more discreet rendezvous. The other activities occurring at a hotel, such as meetings and conferences, may give local patrons a viable excuse for being in the hotel if they happen to be recognized by friends or associates.

The Guest's Rights

Legal precedent indicates that once a room key has been issued to a guest, access to that room is generally the exclusive right of the guest. The hotel operator can enter that room only under certain circumstances, such as to provide customary housekeeping services or requested food and beverages or in an emergency. The hotel operator can be penalized if the premises are used for illegal purposes. Given the violence in American society today, it could be dangerous for a hotel operator to seek entrance to guestrooms where illegal activities are occurring without the assistance of law enforcement officers. It is often difficult to discover the occurrence of illegal activities because the guest's right of privacy is essentially guaranteed (another reason why hotels may be sought as the location for illegal activities), and also because the short-term occupation of the guestroom makes it difficult for law enforcement agencies to obtain warrants allowing them to search the premises. As any innkeeper who has tried to track down a guest who has left without paying their bills knows, the departed guest is an elusive target.

While detecting occurrences of prostitution in a hotel guestroom may be difficult, hotel operators must try because in some states hotels may be liable for the failure to detect such illegal acts. But there are those who suggest that the hotel should not have any responsibility for interfering with the guest who brings a prostitute into the room. They contend that the guest is exercising a Constitutional right of freedom of association and perhaps the right to the pursuit of happiness.

Hotel Practices

This discussion is not meant to condone the illegal practice of prostitution. But in reality, there are some hotels that condone or become actively involved with prostitution. In the latter cases, employees (either hourly or managerial) may assist the guest in obtaining the services of a prostitute. Generally, some sort of consideration, typically monetary, is given in return for the referral. Some hotels take note of the fact that the guest had companionship and then change the room rate to reflect the double rather than single occupancy. In some establishments, the hotel advises its guests if the particular prostitute accompanying them has caused a "problem" for other clients in the past. On the other hand, some hotels actively discourage the use of their facilities by prostitutes and their clients in a number of discreet ways.

Ramifications

In addition to the illegality of prostitution in most states, there are other ramifications to its occurrence in hotels. To begin with, many prostitutes may be involved in other illegal activities, and the guest and hotel may be exposed to various risks. It is not unknown for prostitutes to rob their clients. Disputes may arise about the compensation for services, in which case one of the parties involved may get injured or worse. There is also a high risk of sexually transmitted diseases, including AIDS, being passed from one party to the other.

The worst-case scenario might include a guest suffering serious bodily injury, even death, as the result of a dispute over compensation, or the guest's contracting AIDS. If the guest is assaulted by either the prostitute or one of the prostitute's associates, the event will become public knowledge through police or emergency services' reports. It is likely that the event will be reported by the local media. In these types of situations, the guest, or his or her survivors, may institute legal action against the hotel and its management. In the event of the guest's death, charges for wrongful death may be filed. This will certainly make the local news reports. While all this may sound far-fetched, it is not outside the realm of possibility or inconsistent with some recent legal actions brought against hotels.

The hotel's management must be careful in what it does in trying to prevent prostitution from occurring in the hotel. Suspicions about activities of the guest must be communicated in a careful manner. Unfounded allegations may subject the hotel to legal actions such as those for defamation of character or for slander.

Rightness of Standards

So a dilemma exists. The manager does not want to expose the hotel to the risks of guest injury, either physical or medical. In addition, the hotel does not want to condone or encourage prostitution. The innkeeper has a duty to protect the guests and their rights to make their own choices, but the innkeeper must also act reasonably in trying to prevent illegal activities from occurring at the hotel. And what responsibilities do the guests have for protecting themselves? Is the dilemma an ethical one, involving issues of duty and obligation from a viewpoint of what is a generally accepted standard of conduct? (Note that the accepted standards of conduct might be different in New York, New Orleans, or Los Angeles than those in Salt Lake City.) Or is it a moral issue: a matter of establishing a standard of right and wrong? In Chapter 2, Steve Hall lists five questions to be used in determining if a standard is right:

1.   Is the standard fair?

2.   Is the standard legal?

3.   Does the standard hurt anyone?

4.   Have we been honest with those affected by the standard?

5.   Can I personally live with a clear conscience with the standard or action?

Perhaps we should add another question to this list—one that transforms the issue from one of accepted ethical behavior to that of moral behavior:

6. Would I want the issue to be made public knowledge to my family, friends, business associates, and community?

Some hotels may choose to ignore the fact that prostitution is illegal because of economic benefits it may bring to a hotel. What are the legal and ethical considerations of this? Does turning our heads when high-class prostitutes use the hotel's facilities represent a fair standard? Is setting an economic measure of the acceptability of prostitution any different than setting an economic standard of the desired guest, a standard we set by selling our rooms at high prices? Possibly not. Is setting an economic standard of "acceptable prostitution" legal? Well, no, but some law enforcement authorities have found it difficult to stop this type of prostitution. If they are unable to enforce the law, should the hotelier be expected to do so? Does the standard of acceptability hurt anyone? Possibly not. The prostitute in this market has made a conscious career choice and may be less likely to be subjected to exploitation than those practicing the trade on a lower economic level. Have we been honest with those involved in the situation? If they can afford the charges, the guests are probably entering into the situation with full knowledge of their actions. "Can I live with the consequences?" The high-class prostitute may be unlikely to cause problems and may even bring in revenue to the hotel. If society cannot legislate morality, why should the innkeeper try?

For discussion purposes, putting aside the illegality of prostitution, an economic "standard of the acceptability of prostitution" might pass ethical tests, provided we are willing to allow a little equivocation in the application of those tests. Adding the moral question may change the answer. Would I want my family to know that this hotel condones these actions? Would the hotel place a sign at the entrance saying, "This hotel accepts business from high-class prostitutes"? When individuals must stand up and publicly declare what they believe is right and wrong rather than what they will accept, the issue is one of morality. It is likely that individuals or organizations will find that taking a moral stand requires some deep and uncomfortable assessment of their values. They may also find themselves alienated from others who adhere to a different set of values.

Other issues in our industry may be subjected to the same type of scrutiny. There are conflicts between the guest's right to purchase liquor and the establishment's requirement to protect the guest and others from actions of the inebriated. There may be issues concerning to whom you rent meeting space, or the costs, features, and amenities of the guestroom, or the quality and portions of food and beverages served. The overbooking policies of a hotel require a hotel to make moral judgments both in establishing the basic overbooking policy and in determining how the hotel will respond when it finds itself in the position of having to refuse to accommodate guests with reservations. The guests have the luxury of only having to be responsive to themselves for their actions, but the hospitality executive is responsible to the guests, employees, owners, and the community. We must be willing to bare our actions to the scrutiny of others. We need to have a system within which to make these judgments so that they demonstrate a logical and moral answer to the issues.

Duties and Responsibilities

This chapter has taken the position that the hospitality industry has a moral duty to treat its guests fairly and to protect them. It has also taken the position that employers have a moral responsibility to their employees. These two responsibilities are deeply intertwined; for how can the hospitality industry live up to its obligations unless it has honest, dedicated employees? And how can there be honest, dedicated employees if they are not treated in a morally correct manner? Is the high level of turnover of hospitality employees and managers related to the lack of a moral relationship between the organizations and their employees? Relationships that are frequently characterized by long hours, low pay, and, for managers, frequent relocations. Do we not have a moral responsibility to provide our employees with reasonable working conditions, wages that permit them to maintain acceptable standards of living, adequate benefits, and involvement in the operations?

It is difficult to make decisions, especially ethical or moral ones, without having a commonly accepted set of facts. For purposes of this discussion, let us accept the following "facts":

- The industry is experiencing an unacceptably high level of hourly staff turnover.

- Management staff also has a high rate of turnover.

- Many of our hourly employees are recent immigrants, and many are from the lower socioeconomic classes.

- Some perceive a stigma attached to service workers, and many employees are rarely encouraged to think of themselves as professionals.

- Because of low profit margins, the industry tries to keep the costs of wages and benefits low.

- Approximately 50% of the graduates of college-level hospitality management programs will leave the industry within five years of graduation.

- Hospitality managers average fewer than two years in a given position or city.

It is true that there are a lot of legal statutes and codes which regulate employment. There are equal employment opportunity standards, minimum wage standards, workers' compensation codes, unemployment codes, occupational health and safety codes, and others. These codes establish **minimum legally acceptable standards** of employment practice. They are the legal, not the ethical or moral, floor. Until now, I have refrained from bringing personal experiences into this discussion. I should like to change that now and sketch out the employment policies of a hotel where I worked from 1978 until 1982.

Personal Example

The hotel believed that the most important people in the building were the guests and the employees. Most companies say this as part of their recruitment and public relations policy, but for this hotel it was an honest and deep-seated belief. Care was taken in the selection, training, and employment of the staff. A few examples will show the high level of commitment to its staff that the hotel actually practiced:

- All prospective employees were interviewed twice, once by the personnel director and once by their future immediate supervisor.

- At least two references were checked for each employee.

- When hired, the employee was given an orientation session, introduced to all management personnel, and given a copy of the employee handbook.

- No employee was hired at minimum wage; unskilled or entry-level employees were paid $.25 per hour more than minimum, and skilled employees were paid 110% of the going rate for their positions.

- All regular employees received company-paid health, dental, and disability insurance.

- All employees were eligible for a company-paid retirement program.

- All employees were reviewed twice a year for performance with an annual salary adjustment.

- The general manager, executive committee, and chef ate their meals in the employee cafeteria.

- No employee could be discharged or disciplined without the involvement of the personnel director.

- Employees were provided with quality uniforms and had a say in uniform selection and similar decisions.

- The hotel reached out to the local community and hired the developmentally or physically disabled in competitive positions at competitive wages.

- Managers were regularly required to work with their staffs during busy time periods and were prohibited from being in their offices when their staffs were busy.

- The performance of the hotel in terms of revenue and operating cost was shared with the employees on a quarterly basis.

- Promotion from within was practiced as the first source of personnel.

Results

The results of these simple and morally correct policies were wonderful to see. The staff had excellent tenure at the hotel, with most employees remaining more than three years. Some bellstaff had fourteen years of seniority; there were cooks, dishwashers, waitstaff, bartenders, and housekeepers with six, eight, and more years of seniority. They viewed themselves, their associates, and their managers as part of a professional team. More than half of the management team had more than three years of service at the hotel. Employees took pride in their ability to perform well and to control operating costs. In one case, a new cook was hired who started taking home costly items like shrimp and steaks. The other cooks turned him in because he was impinging on their professional reputation by causing *their* food costs to go up. Employees were proud to tell friends and family where they worked. And the community recognized the hotel and its facilities as being the best in the area.

Were the guestrooms always properly cleaned? Did the TVs always work? Was the orange juice always freshly squeezed? Was the Beefeater martini always made with Beefeater? Did employees recognize regular guests? Did employees show up for work as scheduled? Yes, yes, yes, yes, yes, and again, yes.

This hotel satisfied its moral responsibility to its employees who then fulfilled the hotel's responsibility to the guests. In turn, the guests fulfilled management's responsibility to the owners. This hotel had an average room occupancy 10 percentage points higher than any of its competitors; at the same time, the average rate was $10 higher as well. The per-room sale of food and beverages in 1981 was more than three times the 1988 national average for hotel food and beverage revenues. The net income before mortgage and taxes was almost twice the national average.

Quality

A single word summarizes what this particular hotel offered to both its employees and its guests—quality. The employees were treated with the respect that is due professionals of premier quality. In turn, they gave the guests a quality experience in every sense of the word. Food and beverage products were made from high-quality ingredients that were properly prepared to yield a high-quality end product; service was proper, and the standards of guestroom cleanliness and presentation were also those of a quality establishment. The guest appreciated the high standards of the hotel and willingly paid the additional price necessary to obtain products and services of this quality.

John Donne, in *Devotions upon Emergent Occasions,* Meditation XVII, wrote: "No man is an Island, entire of it self; . . . because I am involved in Mankind." This certainly holds true for the hotel manager, for it is not the manager acting alone who fulfills the hotel's or restaurant's responsibility to the guest. Rather, it is the staff who are responsible for performing various tasks and functions that make up the products and services needed to satisfy the guest's desires and our responsibility to accommodate (where morally appropriate) those desires. Without fulfilling our duties to our staff—duties that include providing them with proper training, proper tools and equipment, and a morally correct employment and compensation package—they will be unwilling and unable to perform to the best of their ability.

If we cannot expect our employees to perform correctly without proper training, tools, equipment, and compensation, what can we expect if we provide them with these items? To begin with, we can expect that they will perform their job functions at or above the minimum levels of performance that we set. At least part of those performance levels will be standards of quality in service: the number of rings before a phone is answered, the effectiveness of reservations records, the use of proper service techniques in the restaurant, etc. Others will be concrete standards of product quality: the orange juice will always be freshly squeezed and served in an 8-ounce glass on an underliner with a doily, the baseboards in guestrooms will be cleaned daily, and the credit card voucher will be properly filled out and the card's validity will be checked. Performance at or above some minimum standard establishes the quality of an organization. When every employee provides guests with the same standard of service and performance, the guest receives a quality experience that can be valued according to the price paid.

Nothing we have written thus far should give the reader the impression that only operations which provide freshly squeezed orange juice can be considered quality establishments. It is the relationship of price to value that establishes the quality of an operation. It is quite possible for a budget motel to provide a quality lodging experience, provided that minimum standards appropriate to the cost are met. Similarly, the quality of fast-food restaurants cannot be compared with gourmet dining. It is the adherence to set standards of performance that are the hallmarks of a quality product or service. Inconsistency is equivalent to a lack of quality.

One more comment must be made about the benefits of operating a quality establishment. It is far easier to come to work every day knowing the operation is giving the guest a quality experience commensurate with the price charged. There is less stress involved in responding to situations involving guests when one knows that few complaints are likely to be received. Similarly, it is easier to discuss the desired level of performance with an employee when one knows that the standards are reasonable, given the level of training, equipment, and compensation available to that employee. I remember reading an article in which the author asked if it was more appropriate to lower our standards to those that were easily obtained or to challenge our suppliers and employees to do better. In the absence of a quality, morally correct work environment, it is not possible to provide this challenge to our staff and suppliers, and so it is impossible to provide our customers and guests with a quality product or service.

Responsibility

Nor is any business enterprise an island. It exists as part of the greater community and therefore has a moral responsibility to the community. If necessity is the mother of invention, then the need for food and lodging is the mother of our industry. But the father of our industry must be the community that provides us with financial backing, staff, and the goods and services we require to successfully conduct our business. As Adam and Eve were expelled from Eden and no longer could depend upon the abundance of Eden to support them, so, too, the business that fails to honor its responsibility to its parent community must eventually find that the parent withdraws its support and patronage. Without that support where will we obtain the resources we need to satisfy our responsibilities to our guests? If we are to be successful in business, then as businesspeople we must, as the Fifth Commandment dictates, honor our parents.

In respecting our community, we must pay attention not only to giving something back to our community but also to recognizing how our operations impact upon the reputation of the community. Recall that in the pledge of the young men of Athens they vowed: "We will never bring disgrace on this our City, by an act of dishonesty or cowardice."

Providing a level of quality less than that which is paid for is, in fact, dishonest as well as immoral. So part of the respect shown our parent community is to provide quality for value received. We should also remember that we are part of the greater hospitality community and our actions should not discredit the industry as a whole. Recall that the learning and practicing of a standard of conduct based upon what is correct is what separates morally correct behavior from that which may be ethically correct. Even if the general business community in which your operation exists does not practice providing quality for value received, it is your obligation as part of the larger community of hospitality providers and mankind in general to provide your guests with quality service and products.

Conclusion

Only recently have we started to take a long and serious look at business ethics. There are still those who are opposed to the concept that ethical actions are consistent with good business management and profitability. Under the circumstances, the suggestion that business has an obligation to act and operate in a morally responsible manner is likely to be contemptuously cast aside. This chapter has advanced the idea that moral conduct is not only the responsibility of business, but in fact it can contribute to a business's success. Choosing to recognize a link between the Fourth and Fifth Commandments and the hospitality industry is the reader's choice. But even when one sets religion aside, one finds that society keeps discovering a need for morality. The recognition of individual rights, which carry with them responsibilities for moral actions, is the hallmark of both ancient and modern civilizations. This recognition and the enumerated individual rights are based largely upon moral precepts. Historically, societies that have lost their moral fortitude have failed and disappeared. The same must happen to individual business enterprises and even to whole industries that do not recognize the moral implications of their actions and those that fail to provide their customers with a quality product or service. Let us hope that the present contemplation of ethics in business in general, and in our industry in particular, is the first step toward our recognition that morality, the teaching of a system of right and wrong, must be the foundation of any business or industry that hopes to prosper and survive.

Discussion Topics

1. Obtain a copy of the mission statement or service objective of your employer. Determine whether there is a moral imperative in that document; if there is, relate it, and discuss how it is carried out.

2. Describe a morality issue facing college students and the hospitality industry today. What do you feel is the "morally correct" course of action?

3. In the United States there is supposed to be a separation of church and state. Discuss whether the moral basis of laws violates this separation.

4. How does morally correct behavior contribute to product or service quality?

Term Paper Topics

1. Describe circumstances relating to either a company's employment policies or community relations, where the company has acted in either a morally correct or incorrect manner. Discuss how the company's actions affected the attitudes of guests and the local community and how this affected the profits of the operation. It may be appropriate to examine how competing operations act and to do a comparison.

2. Describe a situation in the hospitality industry where the rights of the guest are in conflict with management's responsibility to operate in a morally correct manner. Trace the development of this conflict by doing such things as finding legal cases which define the limits of action of the guest and management. Discuss how you would react in this situation and what you believe is the morally correct action (that is, justify your thought process).

4

Ethically Empowering Others to Win in the 1990s

Tarun Kapoor and
Sandy Kapoor

Today, newspapers are filled with stories about white-collar crime, whereas just a few years ago the term was practically nonexistent. So what has changed? Did career criminals discover a new, more profitable field? Of course not. If they had, all hard-core criminals would have converted to white-collar crime. Rather, the cause of this increased emphasis is the business-world culture we so carefully cultivated during the 1970s and 1980s that says to do quickly whatever it takes to get the job done and make a profit. American business encouraged new managers to cut corners. Even business schools taught the need for maximizing profits and recognizing that success meant making profits regardless of cost. The movie *Wall Street* epitomized this national hunger. It supported the theory that it is OK to make a quick buck and get away with it.

This cultural virus, if one can call it that, spread rampantly. It can now affect the very core of a business. This theory says that because cutting corners is acceptable, simple white lies are acceptable. And, because white lies are acceptable, simple manipulation of rules and regulations is also justifiable.

Anytime individuals can take it upon themselves to break or bend the rules, control becomes impossible. Without control, no business can ensure consistency of product or service. As a result, quality suffers. This eventually affects the financial viability of the business.

Only now that the business community is being affected financially has it begun doing some soul-searching. The better-managed companies have begun to question their current business policies. They are examining the ethics of their organizations at

Tarun Kapoor, CHA, is Coordinator of Food & Beverage and Associate Professor for Hotel Operations at the School of Hotel and Restaurant Management at California State Polytechnic University. His experience includes being General Manager of a 600-room five-star hotel. He earned his bachelor's degree in hotel and restaurant management from the University of Wisconsin-Stout and his MBA from Michigan State University.

Sandy Kapoor holds MPH and PhD degrees in the field of nutrition and food science. She is a trained chef from the Culinary Institute of America and is a registered dietitian. She is currently on the faculty of the School of Hotel and Restaurant Management at California State Polytechnic University. Previously, she served on the faculties of the Culinary Institute of America and Michigan State University.

the company level as well as the ethics of their individual employees. Ethics is fast becoming the hot, new concept in business management.

While the preceding scenario may be an oversimplification of current American business practices, it does help to explain the lack of ethical behavior and demonstrates the need for a new look at ethics.

What Is Ethics?

According to Webster's *New World Dictionary* (1987), ethics is the study of standards of conduct and moral judgment, and it is the system of morals of a particular person, religion, group, etc.

Because standards, judgment, and codes of morals are all subjective terms, the meaning of ethics is different for each individual. This is true because individuals are inherently different. In addition, one's interpretation of ethics is influenced by environmental factors such as family background, ethnic community, and religion. For this reason, it is likely people in the workplace will have different standards, judgments, and moral codes. Thus, creating an ethical work environment is a difficult challenge.

What Are Morals?

Notice that the word "morals" appeared in both definitions of the word "ethics." Ethics is created by society, while morals are an individual's personal beliefs of what is right or wrong. Therefore, as individuals interact with persons holding different beliefs, their own beliefs are affected. Thus, to create an ethical workplace one has to balance differences not only within the work force but also between the work force and society.

One also has to be sensitive to the fact that a company's moral standing is generally affected by a few individuals (the owners and/or top management, for example). This suggests that an organization's code of ethics can be established based on the morals of a few individuals. If the morals of these individuals are good, the morals could set the tone for a superior code of ethics. On the other hand, if the morals of the individuals with influence are poor, the reverse could occur.

An organization's code of ethics is also influenced by management practices. Quite often, leadership says: "Do whatever it takes to get the job done. Make money. Satisfy the customer." This may call for bending or breaking the rules or the company's code of ethics. For example, the last guest in the restaurant asks for a refill on a cup of coffee. Without informing the guest, the manager directs the server to give the guest decaf instead of regular coffee because the pot of regular coffee is empty. The manager justifies this decision by rationalizing that this was the last customer of the day. In this situation, the server is getting the job done while doing what the manager believes will benefit the business. But, is the server really doing what is best for the business?

In another scenario, the menu states, "We serve prime beef." Yet, when the price of prime beef increases by 25%, the manager substitutes choice beef without recording the change on the menu. The chef is aware of the substitution but ignores it. He has to consider his job. This is not only unethical, but illegal; the operation could be liable under false advertising statutes.

Why Is Ethics Important?

To begin with, ethical behavior is expected. Guests, employees, and the industry-at-large assume that an organization is ethical. They believe it will adhere to the ethical parameters defined by society. Return again to the coffee situation. In that scenario, the guest expected the server to serve her regular coffee when she requested it. The server should have asked if it was acceptable to substitute decaf coffee for regular. At the same time, the server expected the manager to allow serving regular coffee when it was ordered. When the manager told the server to do otherwise, she asked the server to compromise his own ethics.

It is understood that an organization will serve the product it promotes. Only then can it earn the public's trust. Consider the reputation of the used car industry. Because of a few unscrupulous used car salespeople, the entire industry has been branded. According to Suzie Stephenson, "Each day, food service executives and managers are faced with temptation. What is ethical and what is practical is a balancing act for the conscience."[1]

The American public is learning to recognize unethical behavior. People are no longer willing to tolerate that which does not live up to their expectations. Today, Americans are asking organizations questions about their business practices and they are demanding promises, more frequently written ones. They are requiring organizations to share their code of ethics with them and to make their policies available. On this basis, Americans are developing trust in the quality of services provided by organizations. Many organizations are losing customers due to breaches of this trust.

Another reason organizations should develop a code of ethics is to inform their employees how to act and make decisions in their daily job situations. Often, employees do not know house policies. Therefore, they act in the manner they deem most appropriate.

Types of Ethics

Any business is affected by two types of ethics, the community's and those of the employees. When there is a conflict, whose ethics should an individual follow, his or her own or the community's? Perhaps businesses should practice the ethics of their target markets. It is possible that ethical values differ among target markets. This requires careful consideration when one is developing a code of ethics. For example, bargaining is customary in many Asian countries. Consider India where it is common for owners of highway budget motels to bargain over room rates. Thus, most Indians operating this type of lodging establishment expect to do some negotiating with their guests. On the other hand, bargaining by operators of luxury hotels is unheard of in India. Such behavior would create distrust among guests.

Communicating Ethics

The success of an ethics policy depends upon how effectively it is communicated to the entire organization. This communication must convey to all employees both the policy's moral intent and its parameters. The policy should be in writing, and all employees should be given a copy when they are hired. To emphasize the policy's importance, the company's mission statement should appear in the same document. A written policy statement is essential. In addition, it must be communicated verbally.

Equally important is the implementation of an organization's ethics policy. Without consistent enforcement at all levels, the policy will be meaningless. For example, the policy might state that alcohol consumption is prohibited on the job. Yet, every evening the manager has two glasses of wine with dinner. This double standard sends mixed messages to the staff. It appears that the organization's policy is discriminatory. How can such a policy be ethical? What is ethical for one should be ethical for all.

Empowering Others to Be Ethical

For a code of ethics to be successful, every member in an organization must follow it. All employees must be aware of the code of ethics; they must understand it; and they must be allowed to practice it in their jobs. Everyone in the organization must be empowered to do their jobs ethically. Empowerment is often overlooked when companies develop their ethics policies.

Empowerment is the level or degree to which owners/managers allow their employees to act within their job descriptions. It is the ultimate extension of the authority-responsibility dilemma. It occurs when all employees have the appropriate authority to perform all the tasks for which they are responsible. They are given the power to make all decisions relevant to their respective jobs. The key words are "all decisions relevant to their respective jobs." Thus, the server who was faced with having to serve decaf coffee instead of regular should have been empowered to do his job—satisfy the guest. He could have accomplished this in a number of ways. He could have made a new pot of regular coffee, poured the decaf coffee with the guest's permission, dropped the charge for the single cup of regular coffee, or provided a complimentary dessert in lieu of a refill on the regular coffee. The server should have been able to make the decision. He should have been empowered to act without the manager's approval in this instance.

Why is empowerment important? It serves several functions:

- It is essential for an effective code of ethics.
- It saves the company time and money.
- It increases guest satisfaction.
- It gives employees a sense of worth and ownership.

Code of Ethics

The effectiveness of a code of ethics depends on empowerment. A code of ethics cannot be truly effective unless all employees are empowered to implement it.

Time and Money

Time can be saved by allowing employees to handle most job problems by themselves. When an irate guest has waited too long for his or her food, the server should be allowed to make adjustments for the inconvenience rather than having to consult the manager. This could include "comping" food. Empowering employees to act saves the manager time. Saving time means saving money. In addition, nipping the problem in the bud is usually cheaper than resolving it after it becomes full-blown. If, in the preceding situation, the server were allowed to resolve the problem expeditiously, all parties could benefit. Empowerment here could prevent an already irate guest from becoming even more disgruntled while waiting for the manager to solve the problem. It could eliminate the imposition on the manager (who may not have the information to make a better decision than the server), and the server could have the satisfaction of doing a good job.

Guest Satisfaction

Empowerment can increase guest satisfaction if it is administered properly. The time span between the point at which the problem begins to become serious and when it is solved can be reduced through employee empowerment. Prompt handling minimizes the problem and optimizes damage control. Proper administration requires training employees how to act and make decisions. It is also necessary for companies to provide their employees with the resources for handling situations in an effective manner.

Worth and Ownership

Empowerment provides a sense of "I can make a difference." It gives employees the responsibility to get the job done along with the authority to do it. This attitude helps employees feel that they can make a difference and are contributing to the organization. This feeling of accomplishment fuels a sense of self-worth and employees begin to act and behave like owners.

How Much Empowerment?

How much empowerment is too much? Should all employees be empowered equally? These are the concerns raised most often by skeptics. The answer is simple. The amount of empowerment is dictated solely by the job description. Each employee should be empowered to make all decisions relative to his or her responsibilities. In other words, employees should be given the appropriate authority to successfully perform their responsibilities. More important, though, is the need to properly train every employee to exercise this authority. Do not forget that, historically, employees have not been empowered. They have had to rely on management for decisions. Effective training with continuous retraining will produce results. In this light, the question of equal empowerment becomes mute. Empowerment is based on each employee's job description, not on equity among workers.

Current Industry Practices

Empowerment is the new buzzword in our industry. Everyone is talking about it. Yet, not everyone is practicing it. Even the companies that have implemented an empowerment program are not practicing it completely. In many ways, empowerment is still a foreign idea. It will take time before all companies buy into the concept of empowerment and completely implement the process in their organizations.

The Marriott Example

Leading the way in the lodging industry is the Marriott Corporation. Long recognized as an industry leader, Marriott recently implemented a company-wide empowerment program. According to Greg Behm, Marriott's director of human resources, "The foundation of empowerment is the belief that outstanding service requires front-line employees who are trained, equipped, authorized and trusted to meet or exceed customer expectations and needs."[2] He believes that "the barriers to employee performance must be removed and appropriate boundaries or limitations established and understood through a collaborative effort with managers and employees."[3]

Marriott is phasing in empowerment over a three-year span. Employees are no longer referred to as such. Instead, they are called associates. Slowly, it is becoming apparent that this is not just another management program. Rather, it is a business philosophy that fits within the company's moral outlook toward both its guests and its employees.

Marriott's empowerment program (which is still under way) involves training its associates area by area from the top down. Each level in the organization removed the barriers hindering progress and simultaneously established new boundaries. In training, each associate learns the how, why, when, where, and who of empowerment. They then practice it through role playing. Once in place, associates are rewarded for their empowerment-related work. Noteworthy acts of empowerment are posted on the Wall of Fame and acknowledged in the company newsletter.

The consensus within Marriott is that the program is a success, although it is too early to measure any monetary gains. Satisfaction, both guests' and associates', appears to have increased. At the same time, associates' mistakes and turnover seem to have decreased.

Ironically, three realities have begun to consistently surface throughout the company:

1. Initially, employees are hesitant to exercise their newly given power. They must be convinced that management will support their decisions (good or bad), and, more important, will not punish them for making decisions.

2. The number of mistakes may not decrease. However, the cost of giveaways and/or resolutions of mistakes has been reduced. This is reasonable. When a guest complaint is resolved in a timely manner, it requires less compensation than one that is not resolved promptly. And, who can do it faster than a front-line associate?

3. The properties that were better managed previously appear to have become more successful in the program than those that had less effective management. Good managers/leaders tend to accept the program better and more willingly than weak ones. In addition, good managers do a better job of implementing the program. This includes training the associates. At some point, employees are able to determine whether management believes in the program and wants them to be empowered.

Marriott logs all acts of empowerment performed by its employees. This allows them to monitor the program, spot trends, and decide on future training needs and/or changes. The following examples show how Marriott's employees have actually used their empowerment.

- A female guest was working late one night on a report in the hotel lobby. Around 4:00 a.m., the security officer brought her a cup of coffee and a light snack. Without being asked, he prepared and delivered the items to her.

- A guest approached the hotel front desk to ask where he could borrow a tie for the evening. The airlines had lost his luggage and he was required to wear a tie to dinner. The front desk supervisor offered the guest the one he was wearing.

- The room service operator received a call from a very distraught guest. The guest wanted to cancel an order she had placed a few minutes earlier. Noticing her distress, the operator asked the guest if she was OK. The guest told the operator she had just received a call from her brother. Her mother in California had suffered a massive stroke and was not expected to survive the night. She had called the airlines to schedule a flight. They told her that there was only one flight out and it was leaving in 35 minutes. Realizing that she could not make it to the airport in time, she made a reservation for the next morning. She was canceling her room service order because she was too upset to eat.

  The room service operator jumped into action. She called the restaurant hostess, briefly informed her of the problem and forwarded the room service phones to the restaurant. She hurried to the guest's room, greeted her with a hug, told her to quickly pack and that she would take her to the airport. While the guest was packing she called the airline, changed the flight reservation, called the front desk to prepare the guest's bill and the bell desk to get her bags.

  Because of the operator's actions, the guest was able to arrive at her mother's bedside before she passed away that night.

Satisfaction Guaranteed Eateries

Another pioneer in the field of empowerment is a Seattle-based company called Satisfaction Guaranteed Eateries. It operates four restaurants. Timothy W. Firnstahl, president of the company, discussed a strategy in a *Harvard Business Review* article that worked exceptionally well in his operation, and he is convinced it will do the same in others like his.[4]

A few years ago, when the book *In Search of Excellence* became popular, Firnstahl instituted its "Ten Tenets of Excellence" in his own operation.[5] However, over time both he and his staff forgot the tenets. It was at this point that Firnstahl discovered an easier and more compelling strategy to direct his company—the guarantee. His operations expressed it as a promise: Your Enjoyment Guaranteed Always (YEGA). For about a year, YEGA dominated the company's consciousness. But as time passed, Firnstahl grew increasingly uncomfortable with YEGA. His operations were receiving complaints at rates equivalent to those in previous years. He could see that the guarantee was being implemented here and there, now and then, but not on a regular company-wide basis.

Thus, he realized the guarantee by itself was not enough. His employees had been given responsibility without any authority. As a result, they tried to bury mistakes or blame others. This, of course, was not unique to either his company or the industry in general. Americans had learned to delegate responsibility over the years. Delegating authority was another story.

Firnstahl believed it would not be possible for hospitality organizations to make a guarantee that would be truly effective unless they gave workers the power to make good on the guarantee—at once and on the spot. Initially, his staff was skeptical of the process and afraid to exercise its authority. But eventually the guarantee became immensely successful.

Firnstahl suggests the following steps to formulate a successful strategy:

1. Make the guarantee simple and easy to understand—a striking acronym helps.

2. Make sure employees know how to use their new authority—provide training.

3. Make progress visible.

In addition to Marriott Corporation and Satisfaction Guaranteed Eateries, other companies, both large and small, have implemented similar programs. Sheraton Hotel Corporation and Taco Bell Incorporated are two examples. Although the nuances of each company's program may be different, any effort at all in this direction is a welcome change.

Developing a Code of Ethics

Today, businesses must be ethical if they are to be successful. Ethics also helps create structure in a company. It defines the extent to which employees can act within their jobs to please the guest and maximize profits.

When developing a code of ethics, one must take into consideration a number of variables. They include: employees, guests, competitors' policies, and the owner's moral values. The code must also conform to the local community's standards. Once established, it must be adhered to as the gospel. The following discussion presents a step-by-step process for developing a code of ethics.

1. Survey Both Employees and Guests

When developing the policy, consult your employees first. They deal daily with situations that management may not be aware of. In a large organization, a random sample of employees should be surveyed. The sample should include representatives from all levels of the hierarchy and every department. In a small organization, all employees can be surveyed. Employees should be asked which areas in the operation they believe need improvement and how the company's standard operating procedures could be revised to help them perform their jobs better.

Guests should also be surveyed. Many companies use comment cards to solicit guest feedback on an ongoing basis. Some companies conduct random phone surveys of their regular guests. Others rely on guest focus groups for feedback.

The success of a code of ethics is contingent on this research. It should serve as a basis for modifying existing standards and formulating new policies.

2. Develop the Code with a Guarantee

A framework for the company's code of ethics can be developed from the research findings. This framework should address the concerns of both guests and employees. Guests' concerns generally focus on their satisfaction with the company or the quality of the company's products and/or services. If the company can guarantee its guests' satisfaction, it is likely to have addressed its guests' concerns.

Meanwhile, employees are concerned with their ability to do their jobs well. This means providing their guests with both quality products and service. If the company can empower its employees to perform these functions, it will likely have addressed its employees' concerns.

The following is a proposed code of ethics:

- We shall obey all the laws of the community when conducting business.

- We shall guarantee complete satisfaction of both our products and service.

- We shall not refuse anyone our products or services on the basis of race, creed, color, sex, or other personal traits.

- We shall empower all our employees to serve our guests as they deem appropriate within the parameters of their job descriptions.

- We shall offer all our employees equal working conditions and opportunities to advance within the organization.

- We shall continually strive to improve our products and services through employee and guest feedback.

This code is not intended to be all-inclusive. Rather, it is designed to serve as a model. Other organizations may refer to it when creating their own personalized codes.

3. Communicate the Code of Ethics

The success of a code of ethics greatly depends on how well it is communicated and implemented. A code's effectiveness is less dependent on its content. The code should be easy to read and understand. Once it is created, employees and guests must be made aware of it. For employees, the code can be posted on an employee bulletin board, listed in their company handbook, or discussed during training programs or at staff meetings.

The code can be shared with guests by posting it in a location they frequently visit or by printing it on company promotional materials such as menus, table tents, or in-room collateral. A well-communicated policy will inform guests that the company is actually adhering to its code.

Over a period of time, a long code of ethics is easily forgotten. This can be avoided by promoting the "satisfaction guarantee" in the code. Creative acronyms can help both guests and employees remember the code, too. The successful operator of Kadie's Diner in Southern California used the acronym KADYS (Kadie Always

Demands Your Satisfaction) in her establishment. It is listed on her menus and table tents, in her employee manual, and worn on buttons by her servers.

4. Provide Follow-Up and Feedback

Generally, innovative programs like this one do not work immediately. They require patience and continuous revision. Often, both managers and staff are initially skeptical of the process. Staff employees are frequently convinced that they will not be allowed to make decisions and if they are, their decisions will not be honored. At the same time, many managers are reluctant to relinquish their control. They fear the consequences will be disastrous. As a result, they sabotage the program. It is important for managers to understand that their continuous and consistent support of the empowerment program is essential for it to succeed. The empowerment program is destined to fail without their support.

Employees can be motivated to make decisions independently, when appropriate, through positive feedback. For example, Marriott Corporation recognizes its employees monthly with an empowerment award called "Empowered to be the Best." Hilton Hotel Corporation has the "100% Club" and Sheraton Hotel Corporation is currently pilot-testing a "Gain Sharing" program. Training can also help employees build confidence in their ability to make sound decisions.

Conclusion

For a company to succeed in the 1990s, it must be ethical. For a company to be ethical, each of its employees must be informed of its policies and then empowered to implement them. Implicit in this empowerment is the mandate that all employees take responsibility for guest satisfaction. At the same time, if a company's guarantee of satisfaction is to be appreciated by guests, it must be honored immediately.

Through an effectively transmitted empowerment program, an environment can be created for the long-term success of a business.

Endnotes

1. S. Stephenson, "A Sense of Right and Wrong," *Restaurants & Institutions*, 98, no. 22, 1988, pp. 81–83.
2. Greg Behm, personal interview, 1990.
3. Ibid.
4. Timothy W. Firnstahl, "My Employees Are My Service Guarantee," *Harvard Business Review*, 67, no. 4, 1989, p. 28.
5. T. J. Peters and R. H. Waterman, Jr., *In Search of Excellence* (New York: Harper & Row, 1982).

Discussion Topics

1. What relationship does ethics have to empowerment?

2. Should everyone in the organization have the same amount of empowerment? Why?

3. Develop a code of ethics for an international hotel chain. Should it be the same for all countries? How would you implement it?

4. Unethical behavior is rampant in the hospitality industry. True? False? Trends? Discuss.

Term Paper Topics

1. Identify two hospitality companies that have instituted empowerment programs. Discuss the strengths and weaknesses of their programs. Do their programs nurture ethical behavior?

2. Historically, has the hospitality industry been more or less ethical than the rest of American business? Why do you think this is the case?

5

Sexual Harassment in the Hospitality Industry

Martha E. Eller

Sexual harassment in the workplace is the epitome of unethical behavior. It is perpetrated at all levels of organizations, most often by an individual, frequently acknowledged or supported by the immediate work group, and sometimes condoned by even top management. This chapter discusses what we know and what we do not know about sexual harassment, what we know about ethics in organizations, examples of sexual harassment in the hospitality industry, and what management can do to ensure more ethical reasoning and the prevention of sexually harassing behavior.

What We Do Not Know About Sexual Harassment

There is no easy description of sexual harassment or a complete list of behaviors that form a comprehensive definition. Many people argue that, since sexual harassment cannot be so defined, it must just be the result of romances gone sour, or evidence that women cannot handle themselves in a group, or an example of vindictive women unfairly using their "ultimate weapon" against unsuspecting men.

We also do not know the actual extent of sexual harassment in American society because research studies have varied considerably in their definitions, sampling procedures, and measurements of incidents. We cannot even project an accurate assessment of the problem based on the number of complaints filed because very often victims put up with abuse for fear of losing their jobs or simply quit to avoid both the problem and the personal consequences of complaining.

Martha E. Eller is Director of the President's Council of Cornell Women, Cornell University. She holds a bachelor's degree from Duke University and a master's from Cornell. Her articles have appeared in the Training and Development Journal *and in the* Cornell Hotel and Restaurant Administration Quarterly. *A member of the Council on Hotel, Restaurant, and Institutional Education, the author is a former lecturer at Cornell's School of Hotel Administration and a former restaurateur. She also has experience in personnel.*

What We Do Know About Sexual Harassment

We do, however, know that sexual harassment is illegal. The Equal Employment Opportunity Commission's *Final Guidelines on Sexual Harassment in the Workplace* sets forth the current legal definition:

> Unwelcome sexual advances, requests for sexual favors and other verbal or physical conduct of a sexual nature constitute sexual harassment when (1) such conduct is made either explicitly or implicitly a term or condition of an individual's employment, (2) submission to or rejection of such conduct by an individual is used as the basis for employment decisions affecting such individual, or (3) such conduct has the purpose or effect of unreasonably interfering with an individual's work performance or creating an intimidating, hostile or offensive work environment.

The Guidelines make a critical distinction between types of sexual harassment: situations (1) and (2), above, constitute *quid pro quo* harassment, while situation (3) is hostile environment harassment.

In its only ruling on sexual harassment, *Meritor Savings Bank v. Vinson,* the U.S. Supreme Court affirmed the concept of hostile environment sexual harassment and said the critical standard is whether the alleged sexual advances were "unwelcome." A recent article in the *Academy of Management Journal* suggests that, according to "expert and non-expert judges," there are three key elements in determining sexual harassment: a victim's reaction to the harassment, the existence of coercion, and job consequences.[1] It appears that the respondents in that study completely ignored hostile environment harassment. Employers today cannot afford such laxity.

Although the *Guidelines* are clear in assigning employer responsibility, subsequent case law has clouded the issue. Strict employer liability applies in cases of *quid pro quo* harassment, but there is much confusion regarding hostile environment cases. What is certain, however, is that both types of sexual harassment are illegal and that employers cannot depend merely on the existence of written policies and procedures to avoid responsibility for sexually harassing behavior within their organizations.

A Serious Problem

What we do know is that sexual harassment is a serious problem in American workplaces. Working Women United, *Redbook* magazine, the *Harvard Business Review,* the U.S. Merit Systems Protection Board, *Working Woman* magazine, and various researchers and authors have provided strong evidence that sexual harassment in workplaces in this country is a widespread, pervasive phenomenon. Although it is not possible to compare their results because of differences in methodology, researchers from industry, feminist organizations, and academia have contributed irrefutable collective evidence. In research it was found that the percentage of female respondents who reported they had experienced sexual harassment in their workplaces ranged from 42% to 90%. In the same studies, 15% to 37% of the male respondents also reported having been sexually harassed.

In addition, research has established that sexual harassment is an expensive drain on the American workplace in terms of turnover, absenteeism, reduced productivity, and lowered morale and commitment to the organization, not to mention the legal expenses to companies involved in sexual harassment lawsuits. In fact, one study puts the cost to a typical Fortune 500 company at $6.7 million per year. Lest anyone think the public sector is immune, sexual harassment is said to have cost the federal government $267 million between May 1985 and May 1987. The problem is costly to individuals also, in terms of personal anguish, psychological damage, reduced concentration on performance, and lost wages.

Problem More Serious in Hospitality Industry

We also know that employees in the hotel industry are experiencing more sexual interaction in their workplaces than workers in society-at-large. Indeed, the entire hospitality industry may be particularly susceptible to incidents of sexual harassment given certain of its characteristics, such as the ambiguity of "hospitality service," the unusual hours and conditions of work, the interaction of persons in the delivery of service, and traditional personnel practices in the industry.

The hospitality industry is in the business of satisfying guests' needs. The fine line between service and entertainment can be misunderstood, leading to inappropriate expectations and awkward, unpleasant, and sometimes ugly situations among those involved in offering and receiving "hospitality." The widespread presence of alcohol and its altering effect on people's behavior cannot be underestimated.

Employees in this industry often work long, irregular hours with alternating peak and slack times; these long hours often involve night, evening, and even holiday shifts. Many employees have noted that they spend more time with their co-workers than they do with their families. In such working conditions, the line between appropriate and inappropriate familiarity may be crossed more easily than in an office setting.

Work in the hospitality industry often involves an employee with a number of different people in the course of delivering service. The others may be co-workers, supervisors, guests, and/or suppliers. Potentially, any of those persons can sabotage another's work performance given the integrated effort involved in some service delivery and the isolation of other service delivery situations. In addition, personnel practices in this industry have traditionally made physical attractiveness, physical attributes, and sociability the primary bases for hiring and placement decisions.

Finally, we know that most victims of sexual harassment are women. No other characteristic consistently identifies the target of this behavior.

What We Know About
Organizations and Ethical Behavior

Ethics includes the rules or standards that govern the conduct of the members of a group. Each member of the group brings to the situation his or her own values and ways of determining right and wrong. Different people may come to the same decision through very different thinking; likewise, different people may reason similarly but, in a given situation, may reach different conclusions.

Kohlberg has defined six stages of ethical thinking.[2] A person at stage 1 (the lowest level of ethical thinking) obeys a rule as a way to avoid punishment, whereas at stage 2 a person obeys a rule to gain approval for being obedient. At stage 3, a person feels the need to belong and acts ethically because of wanting to maintain membership in the group. At stage 4, a person behaves in a certain way because it is consistent with the rules and established practices of the group. The last two stages involve principled reasoning, not just obedience to rules. Stage 5 thinking weighs the "greatest good for the greatest number" above the group's particular needs, and stage 6 thinking is shaped by a sense of justice for all, drawing on universal principles that transcend particular cultures, nationalities, and religions.[3]

Intervening Factors

A person's stage of thinking about ethical dilemmas, however, does not ensure particular behaviors. As Blake and Carroll wrote, "Ethical thinking and ethical conduct are not one and the same thing."[4] They identify several factors that may intervene:

- **Rebellion against authority.** Despite agreeing with the correctness of the group's policy, some people so resent being told what to do that they will act otherwise just to prove that they can resist control.

- **Group pressures.** For others, the desire to preserve their membership in the group is so strong that they will act as they think the members expect them to, even if they are capable of higher ethical reasoning.

- **Group policy.** The absence of group policy or the presence of unclear, confusing policies can make it difficult for the individual.

- **Gambling or risk taking.** Other people may behave in a manner inconsistent with their ethical reasoning in order to experience the thrill of taking a risk.

- **Competition.** Circumstances in an industry, such as intense competition for survival, may lead some people to questionable or wrong actions.

- **Culture.** A final influence may be the culture of the group. If carelessness in adhering to policies is the norm, then members are likely to do whatever they want to do or what others are doing rather than following their own stages of ethical thinking.[5]

Other people may simply rationalize that what they want to do is actually the "right" thing to do. We need look no further than the current savings and loans debacle or the insider trading scandal to see rationalization being actively practiced by virtually entire industries. The four most common rationalizations are:

1. A belief that the activity is not really illegal or immoral, but actually within acceptable ethical limits

2. A belief that such activity is actually expected

3. A belief that the activity will never be found out

4. A belief that the group will condone the activity and even protect the person doing it because the activity helps the group

Different Moral Development

Individual values are thought to be the final standard; however, some people may be confused by cultural standards and uncertain about what is acceptable, particularly in terms of social etiquette, execution of authority, and social relations with the opposite sex. In today's multi-cultural and multi-ethnic hospitality work force, it is unrealistic to expect such a diverse group of workers to share a common philosophy, religion, and/or traditions, which are acknowledged to be the basis of ethics. In addition, in an industry that is so dependent on women as employees and that claims itself ready to serve the ever-growing number of women travelers, it is important to consider Carol Gilligan's theory that women's moral development differs significantly from men's.[6]

Management's concern must be with how to ensure throughout the organization understanding and commitment to higher-level ethical actions, not just mere allegiance to far-from-all-encompassing specific policies and lists of restrictions. At best, those policies and lists, and the law itself, provide only the lowest common denominator of acceptable behavior. Indeed, the behavior of one's co-workers and supervisors has been shown to be a stronger influence than anything else.

Sexual Harassment: Unethical Behavior

If unethical behavior in the workplace can be defined as conduct or actions within organizations that fail to support human welfare, then intimidating and/or threatening a person on the basis of his or her sex must be considered unethical behavior.

Sexual harassment in the hospitality workplace appears in many forms. A recent study of unionized workers in seven major Boston hotels revealed a variety of incidents of sexual harassment. Respondents described the problems waitresses encounter serving at all-male banquets, where many guests consider it "sporting fun" to try to touch a server's body in inappropriate places. Hotel guests make sexual demands on front desk clerks; others request room service and then disrobe in front of the server or the housekeeper. Bar patrons frequently assume that the server will not risk losing the potential good tip by resisting improper advances and demands for sexual favors. Numerous complaints dealt with chefs who berate their servers with sexual innuendoes and who suggest that preparation of orders in a timely fashion depends on sexual compliance.

In all of these cases, the offensive behaviors are unethical because they poison the workplace, they undermine the confidence of the victims, they focus on the person's sex rather than on job performance, they put the temporary pleasure of one person above the sanctity of another, and they misuse power. Such behaviors demean, distract, dehumanize, and demoralize. Each of the cases demonstrates an individual acting either alone or with support of the immediate work or social group.

Doris

A current case illustrates even more ethical dimensions as a corporation responds to a charge of sexual harassment. The complainant is a female kitchen worker, employed by a large corporate food service contractor in a corporate account's cafeteria. Doris (a pseudonym) is deaf and mentally retarded. Although she cannot comprehend complex abstract concepts, she has demonstrated convincingly that she does know right from wrong. She lip reads and signs to communicate.

The chronology of this case has been recorded by Doris's employment placement specialist from the community agency for retarded citizens; Doris has been their client for a number of years. Furthermore, she lives in a residential group home, and her well-being is monitored by a number of social service agencies and by the local restaurant workers' union of which she is a member.

The placement specialist was called by Doris's supervisor and told that Doris was being suspended for three days for refusing to mop a wet floor. It was known that the wet floor was a recurring problem due to a malfunctioning dishwashing machine, but Doris had never before refused to clean it. The placement specialist and two of the residence's managers met with Doris and asked her, "What things do you not like to do that Fred (a pseudonym for Doris's supervisor) asks you to do?" Doris answered that she did not like Fred to touch her breasts, to hug her, to press his groin area against her from the front and from the back, to squeeze her breasts until they hurt, and to touch her in other places through her clothes. She also explained that every Friday, Fred put her paycheck in his unzipped pants fly and told her to come and get it herself. She said that she always told him it was not nice of him to do these things, that it was wrong, and that she did not like it. Doris was able to give specific dates and times, as she had kept a diary of these incidents. They had started six months earlier, one month after she had started the job, and had occurred every day in the last two months. She said these incidents happened when she and Fred were alone on the elevator bringing the coffee truck up to the conference room, and also in his office and near her dishwashing machine station.

The food service contractor's district manager and human resources manager were contacted. They promised to investigate and asked that the matter be kept quiet because Fred was popular with the account's management and they feared that they would lose the account if such allegations became public. During the investigation, these district managers said that if Doris's story were corroborated, she would get her old job back with full back pay and that Fred would be severely disciplined. If it were not corroborated, they would place her in another account.

The employment specialist notified Fred that Doris was not feeling well and would not return to work for a few more days. She also contacted the Disabled Persons Protection Commission, her union, and eventually the district attorney's office. Shortly thereafter, Fred called to say he had already filled Doris's job; she, however, was never officially notified of her termination.

During the investigation, Fred denied all the charges, admitting only to an occasional hug and "horseplay." No witnesses were found to corroborate Doris's story. After consulting with his national office, the regional human resources director offered a package deal: no discipline for Fred and another job for Doris with a different local account, in exchange for her not pressing charges against Fred. The director pointed out to the placement specialists that, if this story went public, the agency's professionalism and effectiveness in protecting its clients would be questioned, thereby causing public embarrassment. He further stated that the corporation's legal staff would defend Fred, not Doris, and that Doris would be subjected to questioning by different interpreters.

One week later, the regional human resources director called to say that layoffs and shutdowns at the other two local accounts meant that there was no job available for Doris, other than her old one with Fred still as her supervisor.

Great care was taken in explaining this to Doris, but she adamantly refused to work in that situation again and insisted that Fred should be punished. At the present time, Doris is still not working and Fred has been charged by the state with assault and battery, as well as lewd and lascivious behavior. Doris will be a witness for the prosecution.

In this case, upper management has clearly put its own self-interest above the well-being of an employee and, in so doing, has failed to set the necessary moral tone for the organization. The negative repercussions of their irresoluteness may be far greater than had they shown more respect for the credibility of the victim and the seriousness of her complaint, conducted a farther-ranging investigation, followed their own established disciplinary guidelines and their contractual agreement with the union, and followed through on the reassurances they gave the victim. Suffice it to say, a properly developed and well-maintained contractual relationship with a corporate account should be able to withstand occasional personnel changes.

Steps Management Can Take

The ethics that govern the conduct of the members of an organization evolve from the policies of the corporation and from the standards set by the example of top management. In order to have a workplace free of sexual harassment, the commitment of upper management is critical. This commitment must be made known publicly to all employees and scrupulously adhered to and exemplified by every level of management. That requires managers to be not only committed to but also comfortable in dealing with matters of human behavior outside those required in task performance.

This is not easy for many managers. The responsibility for caring about employees goes against the grain of what most managers have been taught—remain aloof and do not get involved with employees as people. That distance is a societal norm taught by parents and reinforced by many social situations. It is one that can establish an environment of professionalism; but, when taken to extreme, this norm can allow inappropriate behaviors to go unabated.

Commitment Clearly Stated

Management's commitment should be clearly stated in a policy that defines sexual harassment in explicit terms, prohibits such behavior, and specifically states that the prohibition applies equally to the actions of supervisors and managers, co-workers, customers, and suppliers.

According to one author, "Consensus regarding what constitutes proper ethical behavior in a decision-making situation diminishes as the level of analysis proceeds from abstract to specific."[7]

Indeed, a stated policy needs to be supported by discussion of realistic case studies and believable situations to demonstrate the application of the policy. Conflicts and choices are inherent in the work world today; we must not separate ethics from business decisions. The policy should be reiterated in all literature and illustrations, in all facilities. In addition, meetings should be held, pamphlets distributed, and periodic surveys conducted to determine the existence and extent of the problem.

Procedures Formulated

Procedures for complaining about sexual harassment should be formulated and made known to all employees. In cases where the supervisor is the harasser, the employee should know to complain directly to the personnel director or a designated, credible person who has sufficient authority to deal effectively with all levels of the organization. If the employee is not satisfied with that person's response, he or she should go directly to the general manager. Given the organization's commitment to eliminating harassment, access to top management must be provided.

Grievance procedures for sexual harassment complaints need not be identical to other grievance mechanisms. A two-step mechanism may be appropriate, allowing for informal resolution, followed by formal procedures if the problem is not adequately addressed by informal resolution. In either case, the procedures for investigating complaints must be carefully followed and appropriate discipline administered. Thorough documentation must be recorded and included in the personnel files of those involved. In addition, positive behavior that supports the commitment to eliminating sexual harassment should be incorporated into the organization's reward structure.

Complaints Investigated

The policy should also guarantee that each complaint will be investigated thoroughly and that appropriate remedial and disciplinary action will be taken against anyone in the company who harasses another employee. The sanctions for non-compliance must be clearly stated and enforced.

In my recent research on sexual harassment in the hotel industry, I found that most sexual harassment in hotels originates with co-workers. This finding, together with the acknowledged powerful influence of peers, implies that the traditional approach of training only managers is not enough. The U.S. Merit Systems Protection Board, whose 1981 and 1988 studies on the extent of sexual harassment in the federal government are often cited, observed:

> . . . aiming sexual harassment training at managers and personnel officials . . . may have been appropriate initially, considering always-limited training resources, competing needs, and the imperative for initiating training focused on a problem newly recognized as serious . . . However, in view of the continued high level of alleged sexual harassment . . . and increasing attention to the possible existence of a "hostile environment," agency training programs should also be broadened to include the entire work force.

Maintain Balanced Distribution of Sexes

In addition, management should strive to achieve and maintain a balanced distribution of men and women within and among departments. It has been observed that wherever both sexes are present the workplace is sexualized. However, where there is a balance of power and an emphasis on work performance, sexual interaction is more often within acceptable boundaries and sexually harassing behavior is not as likely to occur.

Conclusion

Basically, management's responsibility is to commit to a strong code of ethics including a prohibition against sexual harassment; to publicize and discuss that code regularly among all employees; and to hold supervisors throughout the organization responsible for the behavior of employees in their areas. Such a course of action should prevent further erosion of the sanctity of our workplaces.

Endnotes

1. David E. Terpstra and Douglas D. Baker, "Outcomes of Sexual Harassment Charges," *Academy of Management Journal* 31, no. 1, 1988, pp. 185–94.

2. Lawrence Kohlberg, *The Psychology of Moral Development* (New York: Harper & Row, 1984).

3. Ibid.

4. Robert B. Blake and Deborah Anne Carroll, "Ethical Reasoning in Business," *Training and Development Journal*, June 1989, p. 104.

5. Ibid.

6. Carol Gilligan, *In a Different Voice* (Cambridge, Mass.: Harvard University Press, 1982).

7. Gene Laczniak, "Business Ethics: A Manager's Primer," *Business*, Georgia State University, January–March 1983, pp. 23–29.

Discussion Topics

1. What explains the apparent discrepancy between many men reporting having been sexually harassed and the author's (and other's) conclusion that most victims of sexual harassment are women?

2. "Most women use their femininity to get ahead in the workplace." Discuss.

3. Some studies have found that women with higher education are more likely to be victims of sexual harassment than are more poorly educated women. What would explain this finding?

4. As women move from the assembly line to the boardroom, sexual harassment does not stop; it just changes. Discuss.

Term Paper Topics

1. Write a code of ethical behavior regarding sexual harassment for a domestic U.S. corporation or for an American university. Devise an implementation plan. How should this code be enforced? How can it be evaluated?

2. Compare the role of women in American society to that of women in another culture (for example, Mexico) and design a training program on "Appropriate Social Behavior in the Workplace" for an American company with an equal number of American and (in this case, Hispanic) employees.

6

Equal Opportunity

Nicholas J. Hadgis

> In the competitive search for corporate excellence, business leaders who put to-
> gether winning teams will be those brave enough to be among the first to learn
> how to use fully the diverse talents of our racially and sexually diverse
> population.
>
> *—George Davis*

Introduction

The focus of this chapter is on equal opportunity for minorities in the management and executive ranks of corporate America and particularly in hospitality industry
companies. While much has been done to document the lack of minority progress in
this environment, this writer believes it would be useful to look at the issue in a proactive perspective and to explore the ethical dilemmas and corporate policies that must
be resolved on the path toward providing equal opportunity. Legislation passed over
the last 20 years has opened many of the doors to hourly positions for minorities;
however, it is within the managerial career ladder, through and including the executive
suite, that many complex, subtle, and not-so-subtle obstacles exist. These obstacles
must be removed if American corporations wish to be truly successful in a global
economy.

As American executives learn to manage in an age of diversity, they will come
to realize that ensuring minority success in business is more intimately related to business success in general than they thought.

The challenge to the hospitality industry and to corporate America is more than
hiring a greater number of minorities and women or assuring equal pay and equal opportunities. As Rutgers University professor George Davis wrote in his article "The
Changing Agenda," it is something much more subtle:

*Nicholas J. Hadgis is Dean of the School of Hotel and Restaurant Management at Widener University in
Chester, Pennsylvania. He holds a bachelor's degree and master's degree from Cornell University School
of Hotel Administration and a bachelor of arts degree from Colby College. He is a consultant to the hospitality industry and a frequent speaker at conferences for industry and education. Further, he is a recipient
of the Lindbach Foundation Award for excellence in teaching.*

Exhibit 1   Summary of Equal Employment Opportunity and Affirmative Action Laws

EQUAL PAY ACT OF 1963	Prohibits differences in pay between men and women who are performing substantially similar work under similar conditions.
TITLE VII OF THE CIVIL RIGHTS ACT OF 1964	Prohibits discrimination based on race, sex, color, religion, and national origin. Includes all aspects of employment—recruiting, hiring, training, promoting, terminating, etc.
EQUAL OPPORTUNITY ACT OF 1965	Requires companies with federal contracts to take positive steps toward eliminating effects of past discrimination against women and minorities. Requires annual affirmative action plans for units with more than 50 employees.
AGE ACT OF 1967	Prohibits discrimination based on age against individuals who are 40 years of age and above.
REHABILITATION ACT SECTION 503	Prohibits discrimination against qualified individuals because of a handicap or history of disability.
VIETNAM ERA VETERANS POSTED READJUSTMENT ASSISTANCE ACT OF 1974	Prohibits discrimination against qualified disabled veterans. All job vacancies must be filed with state employment offices to recruit veterans.

Source: Proceedings from the National Conference of Minority Hoteliers, Cornell University, March 3, 1990.

> The intrinsic problem is much more difficult to address directly—which is not to say that it can, with any reasonable justification, be ignored. It involves changing the culture of corporate America or changing the environment of a particular company so that minorities and women will be able to make the full contributions they are qualified to make and that companies sorely need them to make.[1]

Writing in the *Philadelphia Inquirer,* Robert Rankin, Washington bureau reporter, noted that population trends are profoundly changing America's work force.[2] Demographic trends leave corporate America no choice; women and minorities must be hired, and business is aggressively recruiting them.

In his article, Rankin quotes Rudolph Oswald, director of economic research for the AFL-CIO, as stating, "The question is, is there equal opportunity across the board, or equal opportunity for only the least desirable jobs?"[3] Although some researchers feel that changing demographics may render affirmative action moot in the 1990s, for the purpose of this article it is appropriate to begin with a summary of the main Equal Employment Opportunity and Affirmative Action laws (see Exhibit 1). This data provides background and a point of departure in exploring the ethical issues involved in providing equal opportunity in corporate America.

Exhibit 2   New Entrants to the Labor Force

**Most New Entrants to the Labor Force Will Be
Non-White, Female or Immigrants**

Legend:
- Native White Male
- Native White Female
- Native Nonwht Male
- Native Nonwht Female
- Immigrant Males
- Immigrant Females

Labor Force 1985: 47, 35, 5, 5, 4, 3

Increase 1985–2000: 15, 42, 7, 13, 13, 9

Source: Hudson Institute.

Composition of the American Work Force by the Year 2000

The demographic trends that are reshaping the American work force have been summarized in the Hudson Institute study entitled *Work Force 2000* by William Johnston and Arnold Packer.[4] The major trends identified in the study are as follows:

- Most new jobs will be in services and information.

- There will be more immigrants in the work force than any time since World War I. (From 1970 to 1980, there were 4.5 million; from 1990 to 2000, there will be 9.5 million.)

- Economic growth will depend more directly on increased demand for income-sensitive products such as restaurant meals, luxury foods, travel, tourism, and health.

- Labor markets will be tighter, due to the slower growth of the work force and the smaller reservoir of well-qualified workers.

- One-third of new workers will be minorities.

- Black women will comprise the largest share of the increase in the non-white labor force. By the year 2000, black women will outnumber black men in the work force.

As Exhibit 2 indicates, white males, thought of only a generation ago as the mainstays of the economy, will constitute only 15% of net additions to the labor force between 1985 and 2000. The challenge will exist for minorities to be prepared to succeed in the new job market as well as for corporations to manage this diversity.

Concerning the number of black employees in the hospitality industry, *Insights,* a publication of the National Association of Black Hospitality Professionals, quotes the April 1989 issue of *Black Collegian* magazine as stating that "there are only 8 black general managers of major properties in the country."[5]

According to the National Restaurant Association, the food service industry currently employs more than 8 million persons, about 66% of whom are women, 13% are black, and 9% are Hispanic. The total number of people expected to be employed in the food service industry by the year 2000 is 11.4 million.[6]

In an interview for the May 1989 issue of *Nation's Restaurant News,* Marcia Rafig, the black female general manager of the Penn Tower Hotel in Philadelphia, said there is a need for "more positive minority role models in management positions."[7] In discussing employment statistics, Rafig put affirmative action in a significant perspective: "I'm not talking about quotas or numbers; I'm talking about equal access."[8]

As stated earlier, the declining growth rate of the work force, combined with the significant change in its composition, will certainly increase the number of minorities in the hospitality industry. The question is whether the employees will have equal opportunity for all positions from entry-level hourly to chairman of the board.

In discussing the opportunities for women in the food service industry, Charles Bernstein, editor of *Nation's Restaurant News,* wrote: "The barriers to women advancing in the food service industry are falling gradually—but not nearly fast enough. There are all too few women who have made it to executive levels."[9] Bernstein added that "this is not a problem unique to the food service industry. Only three of the 500 chief executives of the highest volume U.S. corporations and only 3 percent of senior executives are women."[10]

According to Bernstein, a survey revealed that four-fifths of the 1,000 chief executives interviewed conceded that "stereotyping and preconceptions by men were blocking women from reaching top management."[11]

Characteristics perceived as leadership qualities in men are often perceived as negative attributes in women. This was the case when Ann B. Hopkins was denied promotion to a partnership by Price Waterhouse in 1983, after executives evaluated her as "too macho and abrasive."[12] After legal action in May 1990, a federal judge ordered Price Waterhouse to award Hopkins the promotion.

While it may prove a point, legal action will not create an environment of true equal opportunity in corporate America nor will it achieve significant progress for minorities or corporations. This will require structural change driven by a corporate culture that values diversity and rewards the skillful management and development of human resources by managers and executives at all levels.

Affirmative Action: A Double-Edged Sword

Many Americans support affirmative action as an essential component in providing equal opportunity in corporations. It appears to be a moral, fair, and corrective process; and it is certainly founded on good intentions. Much of the literature on human rights and many conferences on minority issues support affirmative action, legislation, and programs. During the first National Conference of Minority Hoteliers held at Cornell University in March 1990, a report was presented that stated, "Affirmative action is a vital human resource process that expands opportunity for everyone."[13]

Throughout industry and society, supporters of affirmative action focus on its good intentions while detractors emphasize its negative effects. Indeed, we need only look at recent industry surveys to hear everything from charges of reverse discrimination to complaints that not enough is being done for minorities. And both points of view have come from management within the same organization.

Johnson and Johnson President David R. Claire is concerned by inconsistencies in the perception of affirmative action:

> In instance after instance, people see the same situations and draw different conclusions. In an IBM survey printed earlier this year, the question was asked, "Is the company doing too much or too little?" Twenty-nine percent of the white males and females said "too much"; whereas 36% of the minority employees said "too little." Our own surveys bear out that same point. A significant number of white managers feel that black managers, by virtue of their race, receive more favorable treatment than white managers. At the same time, a significant number of blacks who left the company indicate that they feel they were forced out because they were black.[14]

After 20 years of implementation of affirmative action programs at Johnson and Johnson, David Claire is justified in feeling that greater progress should have been made.

Writing for the *New York Times Magazine,* Shelby Steele gets to the heart of the underlying problem with affirmative action as we enter the 1990s.[15] In focusing specifically on blacks, Steele, a black college professor himself, writes that they "now stand to lose more from affirmative action programs than they gain."[16] While many blacks would disagree with him, Steele makes a convincing argument, pointing out that the results-favored or outcome-based orientation of affirmative action is at once its objective and its downfall. As industry is called upon to produce results, quotas, set-asides, and other forms of preferential treatment, perceptions are reinforced that blacks and other minorities are indeed inferior and that too much is being given. The essential process for true equal opportunity, which is to change corporate culture to value diversity and develop human resources of all races, is never implemented. This is a consequence of focusing on results while neglecting the process.

Steele gives the reader a clear idea of where he is coming from:

> Even though blacks had made great advances during the 60's without quotas, the white mandate to achieve a new racial innocence and the black mandate to gain power, which came to a head in the very late 60's, could no longer be satisfied by anything less than racial preferences. I don't think these mandates, in themselves, were wrong, because whites clearly needed to do better by blacks and blacks needed more real power in society. But as they came together in affirmative action, their effect was to distort our understanding of racial discrimination. By making black the color of preference, these mandates have reburdened society with the very marriage of color and preference (in reverse) that we set out to eradicate.[17]

Steele points out several liabilities of affirmative action, including the idea that an implied inferiority is the quality which earns blacks preferential treatment and also that it encourages blacks to exploit their own past victimization. He writes: "Victimization is what justifies preference, so that to receive the benefits of preferential treatment one must, to some extent, become invested in the view of one's self as a victim. In this way, affirmative action nurtures a victim-focused identity in blacks."[18]

By deriving power from suffering, blacks are encouraged to expand the boundaries of what qualifies as racial oppression rather than to build on their achievements. This results in a rather shallow or tenuous form of what appears to be equal opportunity. Steele adds, "This situation can lead us to paint our victimization in vivid colors even as we receive the benefits of preference. The same corporations and institutions that give us preference are also seen as our oppressors."[19]

One of the worst prices blacks pay for preference has to do with what Steele perceives as an illusion. This illusion is exemplified by the mother of a middle-class black student telling her son as he sets off for his first semester in college, "They owe us this, so don't think for a minute that you don't belong there." True progress toward equal opportunity cannot be based on a relationship of one race owing something to another. This perpetuates an unequal situation and places blacks or any minority at a disadvantage. A far stronger argument for equal opportunity can be based on the United States Declaration of Independence proviso "that all men are created equal, that they are endowed by their Creator with certain unalienable Rights."

Steele correctly points out "that it is impossible to repay blacks living today for the historic suffering of the race . . . that concept of historic reparation grows out of man's need to impose on the world a degree of justice that simply does not exist. Suffering can be endured and overcome, it cannot be repaid. To think otherwise is to prolong the suffering."[20]

In spite of these arguments, many blacks remain in favor of affirmative action because of the subtle discrimination they feel they are subject to once they are on the job. Some refer to a "glass ceiling" in corporations through which they can see the top positions of authority but which they can never reach. Steele's response to this perspective is, "I don't think racial preferences are a protection against this subtle discrimination; I think they contribute to it."[21]

Later in his article, Steele explains that much of the subtle discrimination that blacks refer to is often discrimination against the stigma of questionable competence with which affirmative action marks blacks. He contends that preferences make whites look better than they are and blacks worse, while doing nothing to stop the very real discrimination.[22] In short, Steele contends that affirmative action may revive rather than extinguish the old rationalization for racial discrimination. Once again, we see that while seeking to achieve parity between races through affirmative action, we fail to achieve equal opportunity. Passing out entitlement does not educate, develop, motivate, or provide mentors to minority managers moving up the career ladder. As long as the means for climbing the ladder are ignored, the goals of equal opportunity cannot be reached.

Opportunities for Minority Managers: A Corporate Perspective

In 1985, Rutgers University Graduate School of Management Professors Nancy DiTomaso, Donna Thompson, and David Blake surveyed 808 of the top publicly owned U.S. companies to determine the circumstances in corporate America enhancing or hindering minority advancement in management careers.[23] Their questionnaire's structure was based on three categories of problem areas: problems concerning the policies and practices of organizations; problems concerning the relationship between minority managers and other people; and problems concerning the preparation of minority managers for corporate careers. Respondents were asked to indicate the extent to which various issues were problematic in hindering minority success within the three categories. Each question could be answered on a seven-point scale ranging from 1, "no problem at all," to 7, "a very serious problem."

They found that five factors relating to organizational policies and practices were rated as highly significant in hindering minority success. In the order of their significance, these factors were:

- Lack of promotion opportunities
- Lack of planning for minority career development
- Recent economic conditions
- Minority managers assigned to staff jobs
- Supervision received

The researchers were not surprised to find that a lack of promotion opportunities was perceived as the most significant problem facing minorities in organizational policies and practices. Closely related to the lack of promotion opportunities was the lack of planning for minority career development. The researchers agreed that "many companies do not do a very good job with any of their employees in planning career development."[24] In light of this, they felt that it was necessary that minority advancement be incorporated into the business plans of companies since it was not likely that this would occur inadvertently.

The second category of problem areas regarding obstacles to minority advancement examined by the Rutgers survey was the relationships of minority managers with other people in the organization. Respondents rated six factors as highly significant in this category. In the order of their significance, these were:

- Lack of other minority managers to provide support
- Lack of role models
- Lack of mentors
- Lack of social/business connections
- Ability to "fit in"
- Familiarity with company politics

These findings support the accepted wisdom of corporate life that networks, role models, and mentors are necessary for success. The researchers point out that the high ranking of the top three factors in the relationships category supports the view that minority managers can be successful once they have learned the rules of the game through contacts and experience—just as it is true for any manager.

The possibility for expanding minority opportunities that this conclusion implies is tempered by the other three factors in the ranking relationships. The researchers state:

Minority managers are also said to be hindered by "lack of social business con-nections," the "ability to fit in," and "familiarity with company politics" (or lack thereof). These items are of a different nature than networks, role models, and mentors. They have less to do with understanding the business world and more to do with having contact and experience outside of it. Social connections are clearly related to family and friends, and business connections may be. Similarly, the ability to fit in presumably has to do with life-style and culture more than with training and qualifications.[25]

In essence, this research points out that while familiarity with the norms of the corpo-rate world is a prerequisite for success, it must be coupled with social and business connections if minorities are to have equal opportunity.

The third problem area studied was the preparation for corporate careers of mi-nority managers themselves. The researchers recognized that the responses in this cate-gory of questions may be controversial and subject to the individuals' own biases and opinions, but the issues still had to be dealt with since they clearly play a role in the upward mobility of minorities.

In presenting their data, the researchers referred to one particular risk:

There is clearly a concern that even discussing issues like preparation, whether in education, training, experience, or attitude, may lead to "statistical discrimina-tion." That is, any open discussion of the preparation of minority managers, "on the average," will create difficulties for those minority managers who do have adequate or superior qualifications and relevant business background and expe-rience because it will be assumed that because they are minorities, they too fit the "average."[26]

Having so prefaced the presentation of their data, the researchers listed five factors that respondents identified as being problematic in the category of minority managers' preparation for corporate careers. In the order of their significance, these were:

- Insufficient number of qualified candidates

- Writing skills

- Educational preparation

- Technical competence

- Oral communication skills

The factor of insufficient number of qualified candidates is influenced by a num-ber of variables depending on which minority group is considered. Studies of educa-tional backgrounds have shown that blacks and Hispanics are substantially underrepresented in engineering, science, and business fields, while Asians are over-represented in engineering and science, and are proportionately represented in busi-ness. Hispanics and blacks may be at an educational disadvantage as a result of their choice of fields of study as well as the poor quality of the schools they attended.

When considering writing skills, it must be noted that poor mastery of writing skills by managers of all races may be indicative of a deficiency of an entire generation rather than any particular minority.

Oral communication skills will vary by minority group depending on the ethnic and socioeconomic backgrounds of the various subgroups within the minority categories. For example, managers themselves may speak English as a second language and might, therefore, speak with a foreign accent or use incorrect idiomatic English.

Depending on which segment of the black community they are from, blacks may use "black English." Researchers state that "even those blacks who learned standard English in their own homes and in their education may inadvertently use some elements of black English in their speech and be unaware of the distinctions and the assumptions associated with them."[27] Regardless of a manager's minority group or background, the level of communication skills has been equated with inherent levels of intellectual abilities, much to the detriment of minorities striving for upward mobility.

In reviewing the results of the Thompson, et al., study, it is evident that minority managers and organizations are responsible for finding ways to meet the multi-faceted challenge of achieving equal opportunity. Minority managers must take responsibility for their own career development by setting specific goals and determining what they need to do to achieve them. Corporations must be more proactive in developing their human resources, including assisting in goal setting for guiding managers.

The Need for Structural Change

The preceding section of this article summarized descriptive research concerning the current status of minorities in corporations. The following material explores courses of action that will aid in providing equal opportunities in organizations without attaching the implicit stigmas that are associated with the affirmative action preferences of any one group.

Some of the literature has suggested that now that the doors of opportunity in corporations have been opened to minorities, it is just a matter of time before occupational equality is achieved by all people, regardless of race, sex, or national origin. As mentioned earlier, the pressure of changing demographics may add some support to this argument. However, researchers have applied mathematical models to project the time required for minorities to reach equality in corporations without the interventions of either affirmative action or changes in organizational structure. One study found that it would take eight generations to reach equal employment opportunity while another concluded that closing the earnings gap would require at least 50 years.[28] Clearly, letting equal opportunity evolve without intervention is not an option.

Work done by Rosabeth Moss Kanter on structural theory and change provides useful insights into how equal opportunity can be achieved in corporations.[29] Kanter's model of structural theory contains three components: opportunity, power, and numbers. Each affects who succeeds in organizations.

The first component in a program of facilitating minority success is to ensure true opportunity, which derives from the placement of minorities in jobs that have advancement and development potential. Ironically, positions that have been created to foster equal employment opportunity and affirmative action programs are often dead-end positions themselves because they are not part of the traditional corporate career ladders. Without the chance for upward mobility, anyone in an organization would lose career ambition.

The second component of Kanter's theory is power. She states, "Like opportunity, access to power is a matter of the design of the organization, and the location of certain people in the structure."[30] Jobs seen as positions of power have high discretion, high visibility and relevance. People in these jobs are able to make their own decisions about what to do. They are able to develop their own track record and can deal with the problems relevant to the mission of the organization. People in these positions also derive power through the support of those above, below, and around them. Thus, their upward mobility is enhanced. People higher in the organization support their climb and trust them, while people below want to work for them because they can help in the career progression of subordinates.

The third component of the theory is the phenomenon of numbers. Kanter explains that numerous problems result from scattering too few members of any one group throughout an organization. When people from a group are placed in non-traditional roles for members of that group, they tend to be scrutinized more carefully and placed under distinctive pressures to overachieve—simply to hold their own. They are subject to battling the images and stereotypes attached to their group, and they find it difficult to be perceived purely as individuals trying to make it on their own merits. Creating isolates in organizations is dysfunctional and can lead to a perception of tokenism.

Having defined the structural theory of organizations as a prerequisite for understanding structural change, we must look at where corporations are in implementing change. While goodwill toward minority advancement exists at the top of many corporations, there is "a gap between the existence of a value and its manifestations in practice."[31] Recent studies have found that there are few mentor-sponsor programs in place that attempt to influence the underlying power dynamics of organizations. All too often, rigid segmentalist organizations result in environments that limit networking and collaborative efforts. There is little opportunity for people to move out of their boxes, work on task forces, communicate across levels, and simply learn more and develop. In fact, the corporate cultures and structures that limit growth for minorities tend to limit growth of all their people. Such organizations find it difficult to achieve productive change and to maintain business growth and success in a changing environment.

A much more productive model for corporations is described in *The Change Masters* by Rosabeth Moss Kanter.[32] This model is called "integrative" and is exemplified in the hospitality industry by companies such as Marriott, ARA, and many smaller organizations. Kanter characterizes such companies as having much more open opportunity and empowerment:

> Their job assignments are broad rather than narrow. They focus less on dividing up the territory (giving everybody their box) and focus more on getting people oriented toward results and doing whatever they need to do to get those results, including reorganizing the department, pulling together their own teams, using procedures or methods of their choosing, going outside the area, or taking on new responsibilities. The focus is on results, rather than doing just the narrowly specified job.[33]

By being less category-conscious and focusing more on people development, these companies have better communication across levels, departments, and business lines. Such companies have more productive people, respond well to change, and have fewer barriers to minority advancement. They invest heavily in education and training and their investment pays off. Over the last 20 years, the integrative companies have been the most financially successful and are well prepared to carry their success into the future.

The corporations that foster equal opportunity are successful in doing so because of their corporate culture and structure. With commitment from the top and accountability for human resource development and equal opportunity throughout the organization, an environment is created in which individuals, regardless of race or sex, can make the greatest contribution that their aspirations and abilities allow. In the successes of their employees and of integrated teams, corporations find that they have the productivity, creativity, and energy to compete and to achieve financial success. Such companies understand that discrimination is a cost to the victim, to the organization, and to society.

A corporation that can fully develop and manage its multicultural work force will find itself to be an organization that can capitalize on the wealth of diverse talents, skills, and insights of its people. By valuing diversity as a critical component of its effectiveness and productivity, a corporation will have the foundation of a corporate culture that will foster equal opportunity throughout its ranks. Clearly, equal opportunity is not only ethical, it is the path to excellence in an age that demands nothing less of corporations. In short, it is good business.

Endnotes

1. George Davis, "The Changing Agenda," in *Ensuring Minority Success in Corporate America,* edited by Donna Thompson and Nancy DiTomaso (New York: Plenum Press, 1988), p. 102.

2. Robert Rankin, "Changing Demographics May Make Affirmative Action Moot in 1990's," *The Philadelphia Inquirer,* July 1, 1990, p. C-1.

3. Ibid.

4. William B. Johnson and Arnold Packer, *Work Force 2000, Work and Workers for the Twenty-first Century* (Indianapolis, Ind.: Hudson Institute, June 1987).

5. *Insights,* a publication of the National Association of Black Hospitality Professionals, Inc., 100, no. 51, September 1989, p. 1.

6. *Foodservice Industry Pocket Factbook,* National Restaurant Association, 1991, pp. 1–6.

7. Richard Martin, "Targeting Minorities," *Nation's Restaurant News,* May 22, 1989, p. F32.

8. Ibid.

9. Charles Bernstein, "Unified Effort Vital to Women's Advancement," *Nation's Restaurant News,* June 18, 1990, p. 29.

10. Ibid.

11. Ibid.

12. Ibid.

13. Equal Employment Opportunity & Affirmative Action, *Proceedings of the National Conference of Minority Hoteliers,* Cornell University, March 3, 19090, p. 7.

14. David R. Claire, "The Corporate Challenge," in *Ensuring Minority Success in Corporate Management,* Thompson and DiTomaso, p. 232.

15. Shelby Steele, "A Negative Vote on Affirmative Action," *The New York Times Magazine,* May 13, 1990, p. 48.

16. Ibid.

17. Ibid., p. 49.

18. Ibid.

19. Ibid., p. 48.

20. Ibid., p. 73.

21. Ibid.

22. Ibid.

23. Donna E. Thompson, Nancy Di Tomaso, and David Blake, "Corporate Perspectives on the Advancement of Minority Managers," in *Ensuring Minority Success in Corporate America*, p. 125.

24. Ibid.

25. Ibid., p. 129.

26. Ibid., p. 132.

27. Ibid.

28. Rosabeth Moss Kanter, "Ensuring Minority Achievement in Corporations," in *Ensuring Minority Success in Corporate America*, Thompson and DiTomaso, p. 333.

29. Ibid., p. 339.

30. Ibid., p. 343.

31. Ibid.

32. Kanter, *The Change Masters* (New York: Simon & Schuster, 1984).

33. Kanter, "Ensuring Minority Achievement . . .," p. 343.

Discussion Topics

1. Affirmative action programs are no longer necessary in corporate America.

2. Employers are willing to hire minorities but have difficulty finding qualified candidates.

3. Few women have made it to the executive levels of the hospitality industry. Discuss the likelihood of this changing over the next 10 years.

4. Most hospitality companies are segmentalist.

Term Paper Topics

1. Select a hospitality industry company and, based on the issues discussed in this article, analyze how it provides for equal opportunity throughout its managerial and executive ranks.

2. Identify hospitality industry companies that have promoted women to their executive ranks. Describe the career ladders of these successful women, the obstacles that they encountered, and the policies that hindered or helped their careers. (Personal interviews will be necessary.)

7

Creating Ethical Corporate Cultures

Robert H. Woods

It is not new for business to be criticized for being socially irresponsible and unethical. As Sherwin noted, "Business has been criticized for its behavior at almost every interface with the rest of society: for being unresponsive to consumers, employees, shareholders, and even the public."[1] However, what is new is the level of criticism currently directed toward business. The public no longer appears content to isolate a few greedy businesspersons as abusive; business as a whole is now being assailed as socially irresponsible and unethical.

While one would assume that public criticism over a long period of time would provide the impetus for change, that may not be the case. Indeed, public opinion of poor business ethics seems to be increasing rather than diminishing. In fact, as a recent poll in *Time* magazine noted, 76% of Americans now see a lack of social responsibility and ethics in business as a major factor contributing to the tumbling moral standards of the United States.[2]

Some authors have suggested that this low opinion of business is deserved. For instance, one noted that unethical business practices have become so widespread that over the last decade approximately two-thirds of the Fortune 500 companies had been involved in varying degrees in some form of illegal activities.[3] In addition, many have suggested that the number of companies actually identified as having been involved in illegal conduct represent only a small portion of those that behave unethically.

Part of the public's association of business with unethical behavior is a result, no doubt, of the headline-making activities of a few individuals (Ivan Boesky, Michael Milken, Gary Hart, Jim Bakker), and there is ample evidence to suggest that such

Robert H. Woods, PhD, CHRE, is an Assistant Professor in the School of Hotel, Restaurant and Institutional Management at Michigan State University. He holds a master's and doctorate from the Cornell University School of Hotel Administration. Previously, he was Director of the Hospitality and Management Program at Appalachian State University. He also has 16 years of ownership and management experience in the restaurant industry. He consults regularly on service and management and human resource issues, and he publishes frequently in leading hospitality management journals. He is completing a text on human resource management in the hospitality industry to be published by the Educational Institute of the American Hotel & Motel Association.

individuals represent only the tip of the iceberg when it comes to unethical behavior in business. Indeed, several authors have recently suggested that unethical behavior by business leaders has become so widespread that it is now considered normative.[4] Such a contention would suggest, of course, that in order to succeed managers must practice unethical behavior to "fit in" in the companies in which they work.

Brennan and Molander confirmed this in their study a few years ago when they found that "honesty in communication" was the greatest ethical challenge that managers faced.[5] Specifically the managers who participated in the Brennan and Molander study reported that they were constantly pressured by normative unwritten "rules" to support incorrect viewpoints, sign false documents, and overlook a superior's wrong-doing—all of which they considered to be unethical practices.[6]

Although the examples cited above represent actions of managers outside the hospitality industry, there is reason for concern in hospitality, as well. For instance, while conducting research on the organizational cultures of five restaurant companies, I found that many of the employees within these companies believed that the managers they worked for were very likely to "say one thing, and do another" in their dealings with both guests and employees.[7] While such behavior might not make the headlines of the popular press, it would, nevertheless, reflect a pattern of unethical behavior. Sadly, instances of such behavior are probably well known to many of us. For instance, consider the ethical ramifications of the following scenario.

As the director of a hospitality program, I was responsible for the placement of approximately 50 student interns annually. One year, we planned to place 22 of the students in Hawaiian hotel properties and had successfully arranged such placements by the end of February. The placements were confirmed again in March and final arrangements made for housing, salaries, and so on. Naturally, the students purchased non-refundable tickets (to save money) at this time and were excited about the summer they planned to spend in Hawaii.

In mid-April, disaster struck. When calling to confirm arrival dates, we were informed by the regional personnel director of a large hotel chain that her property no longer needed the interns.

Apparently, this personnel director had planned to use the interns as replacements for striking employees (rather than as management intern trainees) and, now that the strike was over, had no need for the students. This action displaced six students only two weeks prior to their scheduled departure date.

Although the students were eventually placed in other properties, the scenario raised an interesting ethical dilemma: How should we respond to the regional personnel director? Clearly, this person had not been completely honest with us about her reasons for accepting the interns and, in addition, had not considered her prior agreement with either the university or the students when she canceled the positions. In fact, she had not even felt the need to notify us of her decision.

Our options seemed clear: We could contact the vice president of operations for the company and complain about the regional personnel director's unethical behavior or we could simply let the issue drop. We reasoned that if we called the vice president, our complaint about the regional personnel director might result in rehiring the students. However, such a call would also likely burn our bridges with the regional personnel director. On the other hand, if we did nothing we could preserve the relationship with the regional personnel director (although we now knew that she could not be trusted); but to do so might be perceived as condoning such unethical behavior personally and might indicate to our students that this was acceptable in the real world.

In the end, we decided that since the regional personnel director held an important position her actions likely reflected the accepted normative behavior within the company and that our complaint would fall on deaf ears. Unfortunately, if our assumption was correct and her actions were congruent with normal behavior in the company, this organization has, over time, created an environment in which unethical behavior is accepted and ethical behavior is not a critical cultural prerogative for success within the company.

In this article, we discuss how such a condition could develop within an organization and we make recommendations for managers interested in assessing the level of ethical behavior that exists in their own companies. In the final section, we discuss how managers who find that unethical conditions do exist in their companies can bring about changes in their cultures to increase the level of acceptable ethical behavior.

Culture and Ethics

Before discussing how unethical conditions such as the one described can develop in an organization, or what managers can do to change such conditions, we first must define culture and then illustrate how this phenomenon works. This is an important consideration because, as the example above illustrates, people are often the product of the company for which they work. Indeed, in many cases the personalities of individuals and the company in which they work become inseparable over time. Naturally, then, how the company reacts to problems and what types of actions are condoned within it affect the lives of many of its employees. Therefore, when the top managers of a company behave in an ethical manner in their own dealings, the employees will likely behave that way, as well, because it is seen as acceptable behavior. However, the opposite is also true; when top managers act unethically, middle managers and employees will reflect about the same behavior. In that sense, we can then say that the culture of the organization is, ultimately, responsible for how individuals behave and for what decisions they make.

While "corporate culture" has been defined in many ways, there are some issues on which there appears to be some general agreement:

1. Culture can be found in any fairly stable social unit of any size, as long as it has a reasonable history—one that endures over time. In other words, every perpetuating organization has a culture.

2. Culture is largely taken for granted by most members of an organization; i.e., it is a shared, common frame of reference. This means that the important aspects of each culture are largely tacit understandings.

3. Culture is acquired—it is socially learned and transmitted by members and provides them with the rules for behavior in organizations.

4. Culture governs in social organizations. It is the culture, not specific rules and procedures, that largely determines how members behave in an organization.

Exhibit 1   The Levels of Meaning in Organizational Culture

The Manifest Level
  1.   Symbolic Artifacts
  2.   Language (jargon, sayings, slogans, non-verbal communication)
  3.   Stories (myths, sagas, legends)
  4.   Ritualistic Activities (rites, ceremonies)
  5.   Patterned Conduct (norms, conventions, customs)

The Strategic Beliefs Level
  Strategic Beliefs about:
  1.   Strategic Vision
  2.   Capital-Market Expectations
  3.   Product-Market Expectations
  4.   Internal Approaches to Management

The Deep Meaning Level
  1.   Values
  2.   Assumptions

Source: Robert H. Woods, "More Alike than Different: The Culture of the Restaurant Industry," *Cornell Hotel and Restaurant Administration Quarterly* 30, no. 2, August, pp. 82–98.

5.   Culture denotes an organization's uniqueness and contributes to its identity. Each culture is different and this uniqueness provides a common psychology for the organization's members.

6.   Culture is symbolic because it is manifested in observable language, behavior, and things.

7.   At its core, culture is composed of a pattern of values, strategic beliefs, and assumptions that are typically invisible or taken for granted by cultural members.

8.   Culture *is* changeable, but not easily so.[8]

According to this description, culture is, in effect, the "social glue" that: (1) attracts people to a specific company; (2) holds the organization together; and (3) motivates employees and managers to behave in specific manners (such as the behavior of the regional personnel director described earlier). In that sense, culture is the set of shared values, beliefs, and assumptions that guide decision-making in an organization.

The "levels of meaning" description of culture presented in Exhibit 1 helps define culture. As this model indicates, culture has three important levels: the manifest level, the level of strategic beliefs, and most important, the level of deep meaning.

While the manifest and strategic levels of culture influence the level of deep meaning over time, culture primarily works upward (see Exhibit 2).

The values and assumptions of the level of deep meaning strongly influence organization-specific strategic beliefs, which in turn strongly influence manifestations of the culture. Consider, for example, drawings of planned restaurants adorning the lobby

Exhibit 2   How Culture Works

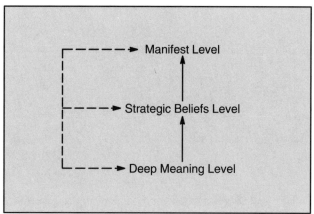

in a corporate office of a restaurant chain. While the drawings may be attractive in the lobby, appearance is likely not the only reason for their presence. Instead, the drawings also likely represent both strategic beliefs (growth and expansion) and deeply held values (professionalism and/or future orientation), which are important beliefs and values in the company.

The decision by the regional personnel director in Hawaii used earlier is another good example of how culture works upward. In this case, the company's norm holds as acceptable decisions such as the one made by the personnel director. However, this norm does not exist in a vacuum. Instead, the reason that it is acceptable is that it likely agrees with specific strategic beliefs (perhaps an internal approach to management which defines relations with employees and other stakeholders as expendable). In addition, it likely agrees with specific values and assumptions (perhaps that profitability takes precedence over stakeholder obligations, etc.).

How Culture Develops

Cultures are not simply created, they evolve over time. Surely, the original values, beliefs, and assumptions that the founder of an organization holds provide the basic building blocks on which a culture develops, but over time there may be substantial deviation from this foundation (see Exhibit 3).

As Exhibit 3 indicates, cultural behaviors become normalized, or accepted, over time. Behaviors that are not congruent with this normalized method of doing things are, of course, considered deviant and undesirable. For example, if a manager or employee were to take actions that were not in agreement with the accepted way of doing things, only three results could occur. The first is that the culture may be altered in the manner depicted above to accept the new behavior. Without support from top management, of course, new behaviors are not likely to be accepted. The second is that the manager or employee who has acted abnormally will be considered a deviant and will no longer fit the needs of the organization. The third potential outcome is that a sense

Exhibit 3   How Culture Develops

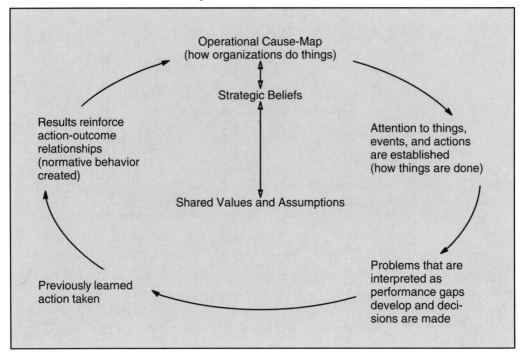

of deceptive communications will result within the organization. When this occurs, management and employees will believe it acceptable to tell the boss only what they think the boss wants to hear, rather than the truth. This, of course, leads to the type of unethical communications described in the Brennan and Molander study discussed earlier.

Consider, for example, the two communication outcomes in Exhibit 4. As Exhibit 4 indicates, creating an environment in which open communications, positive confrontations, and truthfulness are rewarded results in normative behavior that stresses honesty, truthfulness, and candid communication (an ethical environment), while limiting communication, discouraging differing viewpoints, and rewarding only good news results in a defensive, deceptive environment (an unethical environment).

The challenge for managers is to create cultures in which truthful, candid communications are the norm. This challenge is especially important for the leaders or top managers in the company because employees throughout the organization follow their ethical lead in deciding how decisions should be made.

Creating truthful environments is not an easy task, however. In most cases, it is first necessary to assess the current conditions within the organization to anticipate and plan what changes must be made. The remaining pages of this article are devoted to providing a framework that managers should find useful in this task. The framework consists of three issues, each of which is covered separately. The issues are (1) assessing the ethical aspects of the corporate culture, (2) modifying the ethical aspects of the culture, and (3) spreading the news.

Exhibit 4   Communication Outcomes

Organizational Value: Honesty
Action by Superiors

- Limited Communication
- Instills Fear
- Discourages Differing Views
- Avoids Controntations
- Rewards Only "Good News"

- Open Communication
- Instills Confidence
- Encourages Differing Views
- Supports Positive Confrontation
- Rewards Truthfulness

Belief:
Best to agree and not question

Belief:
Disagreement and questioning welcome

Norm:
Defensive, deceptive communication

Norm:
Truthful, candid communication

Source: Adapted from Roy Serpa, "Creating a Candid Corporate Culture," *Journal of Business Ethics* 4, 1985, pp. 425–430.

Assessing the Ethical Aspects of Corporate Culture

Several methods of assessing ethical behavior in organizations have been offered in recent years. Most of these methods fall into three groups, normally referred to as (1) the three-stage model, (2) the critical questions approach, and (3) the balance sheet approach.

The three-stage model consists of (1) developing an understanding of general ethical principles, (2) developing applied ethical principles from the above to real business situations, and (3) identifying cases that provide good examples of the applied principles.

The critical questions approach consists of asking executives to answer broad questions about ethical conduct in their company. Usually these questions are: What are the authorities, rules, and precedents? What are the existing agreements? Is there a conflict with existing principles? Recently, however, we have seen these questions refined to include such specific issues as attitudes toward employee theft, the work ethic, blame shifting, and so on.[9]

The balance sheet approach (which Benjamin Franklin is credited with creating) consists of listing pros and cons for each decision one encounters. Such assessments provide a starting point for discussion, but they do not provide managers with all the information needed because they fail to assess the cultural reasons for behavior in organizations.

Because an individual's behavior likely reflects the beliefs, values, and assumptions about ethics that are dominant within his or her organization, a more thorough approach to ethical assessment considers the influential role of culture in decision-making. We know that culture works upward from the level of deep meaning; this means it is important to assess the deeper levels of meaning of the culture, specifically the beliefs, values, and assumptions of the culture in order to really understand why decisions are made as they are.

While cataloging manifestations (such as the drawings in the restaurant company lobby or the single decision by the regional personnel director described earlier) provides some clues about the culture of the company, attempting to fully describe the culture that is responsible for ethical behavior in this way is not effective. To uncover the real culture in an organization, one must determine the values and assumptions.

Few people talk about the shared values and assumptions of an organization. To do so would amount to conducting regular conversations about such issues as: Why are we in business? What is more important, past, present, or future? Are people within the same company to receive universal treatment (same for all), or are some people to be accorded extra privileges? Each business organization has to come to grips with such issues at some point in time, but not as part of the regular daily dialogue within the company. Organizational members simply "know" these things.

Therefore, acquiring an understanding of an organization's present culture is not a casual endeavor. One cannot simply ask organizational members what is important, nor can generic questionnaires discover such issues. The real values and assumptions are too deeply rooted within the unspoken understanding of organizational members. As a result, cultural assessment involves substantial inquiry. A method used in my study of restaurant cultures, however, did effectively discover shared organizational beliefs, values, and assumptions about ethical behavior. A description of that method of assessment is provided in the following section.

Culture Surfacing

The objective in analyzing the culture of an organization is to bring the deepest values and assumptions to the surface for examination. Hence, the name "culture surfacing."

Careful surfacing of an organization's culture is very time consuming. Four important steps must be completed to carefully surface an organization's culture:

1. Setting the stage properly

2. Processing

3. Interpreting

4. Gaining feedback

Shortcutting these steps generally leads to an inaccurate assessment of the culture, and therefore an unclear picture of the organization's approach to ethics. The four steps are described below.

Setting the Stage

Four important conditions must be met prior to conducting a cultural assessment. The first condition involves proper motivation of the participants. At the very least, a cultural surfacing workshop must be authorized by the ranking manager in the company because this person likely sets the tone for ethical behavior in the organization. Ideally, this manager should also be present throughout the experience. At any rate, the participants should include as many key members of the organization as possible. In many cases, this means the group must include participants from several different groups (operations, marketing, food and beverage, etc.). Key front-line employee representatives should also be included in this session because these people are responsible for "how things are really done" in the organization and their viewpoint should be included in the resulting cultural mission statement.

The second condition concerns location. Cultural surfacing is best accomplished at a "neutral" site, a location where all participants are away from the day-to-day interruptions that are common for hospitality managers. A retreat is a perfect location.

The third condition concerns the amount of time allotted for the experience. In most cases, surfacing culture requires, at the minimum, a full workday (five to eight hours). It is my experience that this can be broken up, if necessary, into two sessions. If attempted in two sessions, the first should be devoted to "processing" the culture while the second is devoted to interpreting and feedback. Finally, the facilitator should either be an outsider trained in conducting such activities or a new member of the organization who has not yet been fully socialized to the existing culture. In other words, the facilitator should be someone who has not yet "gone native" or been influenced strongly by the behaviors of other managers and employees.

Processing the Levels of Meaning

The processing stage should begin with an overview of the levels of meaning approach. In this way, participants are made aware of the importance of surfacing the deeper levels of shared understanding and are exposed to the need to gradually "work into" the most important areas of surfacing. In addition, during this introduction the facilitator should provide participants with some understanding of why culture is important.

After the introductory overview, the assessor or cultural facilitator should begin by providing an outline of the first type of information to be gathered. In using the levels of meaning approach, this first list includes each of the obvious manifestations of culture: (1) artifacts, (2) language, (3) stories, (4) rites, rituals and ceremonies, and (5) norms. I usually start by listing these on large pieces of newsprint and posting them in front of the group.

After providing the outline discussed above and defining each manifestation of culture, I ask participants to note items that they believe should appear on each sheet of newsprint.

The second processing stage, capturing the strategic beliefs that are distinctive to the culture, requires another brief introduction and definition of the issue at hand. I have found it important at this time to remind participants that as we move forward we should continue to concentrate on important issues that drive the company. Specifically, participants should attempt to list issues for each of the four strategic concerns: strategic vision (what the company can be), capital-market expectations (what it takes to please the several stakeholders of the company), product-market expectations (what it takes to compete), and internal approaches to management (how the company should operate). Again, I usually list these items on separate sheets of newsprint and post them at the front of the room.

I have found that processing strategic beliefs can most effectively be initiated by asking the participants to identify the most important objective of the organization. In many cases, this issue will tend to define the "strategic vision" of the company.

Generally, not all participants will identify the same important issue. For instance, at a recent culture surfacing conducted for a restaurant company, various participants believed that "growth," "profitability," "keeping the original concept spirit alive," and "concentrating on improving the existing operations," among other issues, were each the most critical defining mission of the company at present.

After collecting identifying themes for each of the four strategic belief issues, I introduce the final and most difficult topic, that of collecting the shared values and assumptions that provide meaning for members of the organization. Again, I usually introduce our objective by defining values and assumptions and by reiterating the importance of this deep level of meaning. Values, of course, represent the ideals of the organization—i.e., what the organization "should be" as well as the real sins of the organization (how to really upset the apple cart). Values, therefore, represent how members should evaluate one another, objects, actions, and situations.

Assumptions are the premises and precepts upon which thought and action are based. These assumptions typically refer to such items as the distinctive competence of the company (what gives it an edge over competitors), how to direct the business, how to relate to internal and external affairs, how to deploy organizational resources, and "the nature of things."

The process of collecting data that describe the deep level of meaning resembles that followed in the first two stages, except this time the emphasis is on the taken-for-granted organization-specific values and assumptions that actually determine how members perceive, think, and learn. I have found it necessary to break these issues down somewhat to enable participants to come to grips with the important topics in most cases. To facilitate the process, I generally pose questions such as the following:

1. What is the nature of time (past, present, future)?

2. How do you define work (being, doing, observing)?

3. What is the key value in the company (service, food quality, etc.)?

4. Are people considered good or bad (i.e., are managers supposed to direct or control their employees)?

5. What is the role of the customer in the company?

6. How do you define truth (unit level, corporate level, individually, etc.)?

7. Is everyone treated equally (universalism) or are some accorded special privileges (particularism)?

8. Is the environment internally or externally controlled (i.e., does the company determine its own actions or does it respond to the nature of external conditions)?

9. What is the distinctive competence of the firm?

Interpreting the Data

The important objective during the interpreting stage is to gain a group understanding of why each item is included on the lists. I have found that often too much time elapses between the initial listing and completion for all to remember such information. As a result, it is sometimes necessary to go back over why each item is included on the list. To facilitate this understanding, I go back during the interpretation stage and ask participants to clarify why they listed the items on each of the lists. If the culture surfacing is conducted over two sessions, this step can be facilitated by typing the lists and circulating them in advance. In this way, participants have the time to write down their thoughts about each issue and come to the second session prepared—which often facilitates activity and reduces the amount of time spent on interpreting. If completed in one session, it is necessary to go back over each issue as a group.

Initial processing often creates conflicting data. For instance, at one recent culture surfacing of a restaurant company, the initial processing identified differences of opinion about what is most important in the company—food, service, or timeliness. I believe such conflicts illustrate the importance of cultural surfacing, because they highlighted disagreements even among key managers within this company about what really was most important.

Gaining Feedback

The objective during the feedback stage is to rank each of the items on the lists generated earlier. In this sense, the stage is devoted to "agreeing upon" what is most important in the culture. I initiate discussion during this portion of the surfacing by asking each participant to individually rank all items in their order of importance.

After each participant has individually ranked these items, I generally move directly to attempting to reach agreement on the most important issues, the values, and assumptions that determine the most obvious levels of meaning in the culture. Discussion on these issues can become somewhat heated at times because we are dealing with the most basic organizational reasons for existence as well as the reasons why members belong to the company.

It is often impossible to reach a complete consensus of agreement on ranking the values and assumptions that drive the company culture. However, a clear majority of opinion generally can be reached.

After ranking the values and assumptions, I have found that it is relatively easy to rank the strategic beliefs and the symbolic manifestations of the culture in order of their importance because the participants have, usually for the first time, reached an agreement on what is really important within the company culture.

Once these values and assumptions, strategic beliefs, and norms are ranked, the group has a clear understanding of what is considered important within the company. At this point, it is effective to pose ethical questions to the group and to ask each how well the surfaced culture supports the desired ethical environment. Here, one may even wish to employ the critical question approach described earlier.

An alternative to posing the ethical questions at the end of the culture surfacing is to ask participants to create a list of desired ethical conditions prior to surfacing the culture and then review the list at the end to see how well the surfaced culture supports the desired environment identified earlier. In this way, specific problem areas can be identified.

Modifying and Spreading the Culture

While the process described above will provide a complete assessment of the ethical attitudes within an organization's culture, it is only the first step in creating an ethical environment. The assessed culture must also be modified if it is found to include unethical norms, beliefs, values, or assumptions, and then the new culture must be spread throughout the company.

Modifying culture involves two principal steps: (1) introducing congruent new elements and (2) ensuring that past critical cultural elements are maintained. The first step is best completed by a group of managers and employees who draw up a code of ethics for the company culture. The code of ethics created by the International Institute for Quality and Ethics in Service and Tourism (IIQEST) can serve as an excellent guide for this activity. (The IIQEST code is an appendix to Chapter 2.)

Managers can generally facilitate the second step by helping their colleagues and employees think through the cultural implications of changing items that they have surfaced. In this step, it is important for the managers to "futurize" about what the organization will be like when altered.[10] The previous ranking of what was most important helps managers determine what should and should not be saved, of course. By thinking through such issues, the managers can anticipate how changes will likely affect the existing culture. In this sense, managers have to take on the role of company historian to protect the important good aspects of the past. After creating the new vision of what should be in the organization, managers typically also have to mobilize the energy required for these changes (which will undoubtedly include providing the resources that will enable the change to occur).

Spreading the culture requires managers to assume the role of "cultural spokesperson," essentially one of advocacy and education. Spokespersons help other people identify and appreciate the symbolic importance and impact of alterations in the culture as well as ongoing organizational events, persons, things, and actions. This role may be as simple as a manager who has been around for a long time acting as the knowledge source for cultural issues. For instance, a manager of Restaurants Unlimited in Seattle is known throughout the organization as a spokesperson for the culture because he plays this role. Newsletters and other organizational communications often enhance the effectiveness of this role because they spread word quickly. Managers can also fulfill this role by being sensitive to and correcting fictions about culture that are current within the company or by helping other members understand why the culture is so important to the organization.

Whichever method of spreading the culture is chosen, managers who act as cultural spokespersons must be aware that others are listening to what they are saying about ethics in the company. Likewise, others are analyzing the actions of these managers. Because "actions speak louder than words," it is very important that these managers "live out" the desired ethical conditions.

Conclusion

In this article, we have developed a theme that suggests ethical actions are not, in the final analysis, the responsibility of the individual alone. Instead, most actions are the result of managers and employees following the norms of accepted behavior in the companies in which they work. Because of this, hospitality leaders and managers must carefully assess the ethical environment in which they currently operate, and then plan carefully for changing the culture and for spreading the new norms, strategic beliefs, values, and assumptions throughout the organization.

As suggested earlier in this article, there is no quick fix to creating an ethical environment. Managers who rely on mere public announcements, memos, or other manifestations of desired ethical conditions to effect an ethical environment are usually quite disappointed with the results.

Endnotes

1. Douglas S. Sherwin, "The Ethical Roots of the Business System," *Harvard Business Review* 61, November-December, 1983, pp. 183–197.

2. Ezra Bowen, "Ethics: Looking at Its Roots," *Time*, May 25, 1987, p. 26.

3. Saul Gellerman, "Why Good Managers Make Bad Ethical Choices," *Harvard Business Review*, July-August 1988, pp. 85–90.

4. Jeanne M. Logsdon and David R. Palmer, "Issues Management and Ethics," *Journal of Business Ethics* 7, 1988, pp. 191–198.

5. Steven N. Brennan and Earl A. Molander, "Is the Ethics of Business Changing?" *Harvard Business Review*, January-February 1977, pp. 57–71.

6. Ibid.

7. Robert H. Woods, "Restaurant Culture: Congruence and Culture in the Restaurant Industry" (Unpublished PhD diss., School of Hotel Administration, Cornell University, 1989).

8. Craig C. Lundberg and Robert H. Woods, "Modifying Restaurant Culture: Managers as Cultural Spokespersons, Assessors, and Facilitators" (Unpublished manuscript, Cornell University, July 1989); and Lundberg, "Working with Culture," *Journal of Organizational Change Management* 1, no. 2, 1988, p. 39.

9. "Inventory of Ethical Issues in Business," *Ethics: Easier Said than Done* 2, no. 1, p. 49.

10. Lundberg has suggested that during this "futurizing," managers should ask questions such as: (1) how will stakeholder wants be included in the changed organization? (2) what critical future events should we anticipate and what is their potential effect on the changed culture? and (3) how can we set priorities for these future events?

Discussion Topics

1. Could a manager practice ethical behaviors that were not in sync with those of his boss(es) and still survive in the corporate world?

2. If you, as a manager, were aware that your boss was conducting business in an unethical manner, would you blow the whistle even if you knew that it might negatively affect your personal career?

3. Assume that you have recently been placed in charge of organizing in your company a new department tentatively called the Department of Social Responsibility and Ethical Behavior. As the title suggests, the purpose of this department is to ensure that the company practices sound ethics. You have, further, been promised carte blanche support to organize this department. How would you proceed?

4. Is the situation in question #3, above, likely to happen in the hospitality industry? Why or why not?

Term Paper Topics

1. What is the perceived public opinion regarding the ethics of the hospitality industry? Does the public view our industry as ethical?

2. Discuss the continued use of hydrofluorocarbon containers for take-out dishes in fast-food and other food and beverage outlets. This issue has recently received substantial publicity because of the impact on the ozone layer, the greenhouse effect, and the Amazon rain forest. Information should be obtained from both popular press sources (newspapers, magazines) and trade journals.

8

Ethics and the Front Office

Nancy M. Cook

The application of ethics in a property's front office operation can lead to outstanding quality. When ethics is not applied, however, mediocrity, failure, or even lawsuits may result. A brief overview of the functions of the front office will help point out specific areas where ethics can be applied.

Overview

Front office operations are multifaceted: the front desk is the first and last contact a guest usually has with the property. Employees in this department deal with initial inquiries, reservations, requests for special services, and the fair pricing of rooms. The guest does not have the same access to other departments in a hotel like he or she would in another organization. For instance, a client having a billing problem with a typical business is directed to accounting; a customer with a service problem is asked to relay the discrepancy to customer service; etc. In a hotel environment, however, guests vent all their inquiries, anger, frustrations, and special needs to front office employees who are often expected to provide immediate and perfect solutions. Issues related to space and privacy are mediated there. In addition, the corporate image, as reflected in hiring practices, and individual employee ethics are on display at the front desk. Without a doubt, this area of the hotel receives more scrutiny and criticism than any other area. As a result, the issue of right and wrong, legal and illegal should remain in the forefront of every employee's mind.

In this chapter, we will explore the various ways each of the above areas may be handled and the ethical implications inherent in a variety of common situations. Discussion will center on the following:

Nancy M. Cook is Vice President of Operations for Egan Associates, a Boston marketing and advertising consulting firm, and is an instructor in the Department of Hotel and Restaurant Management at Newbury College. A former Front Office Manager of the Boston Ritz-Carlton, she has 14 years of hotel management experience. She has also held positions in finance, housekeeping, and general operations. She holds an AAS in hotel and restaurant management from Newbury College and is a candidate for a master's in education at Cambridge.

- Reservations
- Overbooking, walking, and no-shows
- Disputed charges
- Credit card authorization
- Right to privacy
- Overcharging
- Hiring practices
- Personal ethics

Reservations

The guest's first contact with the hotel—reservations—encompasses several different areas where ethical considerations affect the quality of his or her experience. First impressions are lasting and are generally created through the initial inquiry that a guest has with the property. Therefore, creating a favorable impression about the quality of the establishment can be facilitated by the standards that are set and the training that the employees who work in this area receive.

From management's point of view, the person handling reservations is a key internal salesperson. Thus, from that perspective, the goal is certainly to maximize revenue and sell as many rooms as possible. It is important, however, that the guest be given accurate information by which to make the decision to stay at the property. The description given to the guest by the reservationist should accurately reflect the services available at the property. All advertising and promotional materials should depict an accurate representation of the property. For instance, a guest might ask if there is a swimming pool. The clerk assures the guest that there is, but fails to say that it has been closed for repairs for several weeks. The guest arrives only to be disappointed. How often does a hotel that is undergoing a renovation project offer that information in advance to the guest? Management might argue that if they did, many potential guests would take their business elsewhere. Even when the renovation is not apparent to the guest, failure to mention it is the easiest way for the front desk clerk to deal with the problem. But what about the guest who is awakened at 7:00 a.m. by the sound of jackhammers on the floor above? Too often, the guest must learn the hard way that certain services are limited or unavailable altogether. Again, from a business perspective this could seem like a wise strategy, but the guest is likely to feel cheated and misled.

Assuming a guest has made the decision to stay at your property, it is now the reservationist's job to assist the guest in selecting what he or she feels are the best accommodations. Many properties train their clerks to sell from the top down. In other words, they are instructed to try to sell the most expensive rooms first. The ethical issue arises when the clerk fails to mention the availability of a lower-rate room. For instance, many properties will advertise special promotions such as weekend packages. However, guests frequently fail to inquire directly about the availability of such a special rate, and it is never brought to their attention. It is then possible for guests to arrive at the hotel and learn later that the promotion was available. The "bad will" that this creates potentially damages the reputation of the hotel, at least in the eyes of these guests and anyone else with whom they choose to share this experience.

Another questionable practice involves promoting a special package but then significantly limiting the availability of rooms to be sold at that rate. In other words, the special package rate is the bait that lures the customer in, but, in truth, the rate is often sold out. Should the hotel continue to advertise that special rates offered over a specific period are available when in fact they often are not?

Overbooking, Walking, and No-Shows

When a reservation is made in advance, the guest feels confident that the room and rate are confirmed for his or her visit and that on arrival all requested services will be available. Hotel reservations usually constitute a legally binding contract on the part of both the hotel and the potential guest. The hotel accepts the reservation with the understanding that if it holds a room for the guest as specified in the reservation, the guest will arrive at the appointed time and pay for that room. This contract gives rise to several ethical questions, including overbooking, walking guests, and the handling of no-show reservations.

Overbooking

To begin with, we must define two kinds of reservations: a guaranteed reservation and a non-guaranteed reservation. A guaranteed reservation requires a credit card, advance deposit, or some other commitment by the guest to ensure the hotel will not lose revenue if the guest fails to arrive. A non-guaranteed reservation is held only until a stated cut-off time and will be sold if the guest does not arrive prior to that stated time.

Overbooking occurs when properties sell more reservations for rooms than they actually have rooms available. This practice is very commonplace. In addition, it is one of the biggest ongoing controversies that has attracted the attention of state and federal lawmakers as well as public interest groups.

The pros and cons of overbooking usually give rise to fairly lively discussions. Management maintains that overbooking is not only a sound business practice, but in fact is the only means to guarantee that every room in the hotel will be rented. Managers suggest that if guests did not leave them with empty rooms by neglecting to cancel their reservations when they do not intend to show up, there would be less need to overbook in the first place. On the other hand, a guest has a right to expect that the hotel will honor his or her reservation. In fact, with fluctuations due to cancellations, unexpected departures, and the previous night's no-shows, a hotel that does not have a large number of walk-ins (guests who arrive without prior reservations) will find it difficult to obtain 100% occupancy if it does not overbook.

Overbooking in advance does not necessarily result in the hotel's inability to honor its reservations, but what if it does? Some states are considering legislation to regulate this practice. Florida has already enacted regulations prohibiting overbooking. These regulations specify that the hotel must guarantee space when the guest has made a reservation accompanied by a deposit. If the space is later unavailable, the hotel must make every effort to find alternate accommodations and refund the deposit. In addition, the hotel is liable for a fine of up to $500 for each guest turned away because of overbooking. However, in the absence of any universal laws, regulations, or policies, the controversy continues. It is more than just an organizational issue; most hotel general managers have a sincere desire to accommodate every guest who arrives with a reservation. Their success as managers, however, is usually measured by their ability to maximize occupancy and increase profits. Unfortunately, maximization of their resources very often results in less-than-total guest satisfaction.

Walking a Guest

This leads to another question. How do we handle the guest who has a reservation but cannot be accommodated? The industry term used to refer to this situation is "walking a guest."

Based on the original premise that a reservation is a legally binding contract, failure to honor that reservation is a breach of contract. But what about the ethical question here? Surely, the property has an obligation to secure comparable accommodations for the guest at another property. If the guest has a guaranteed reservation, perhaps the payment of the first night's accommodations elsewhere by the hotel responsible for overbooking is appropriate, or at least, the guest should receive the difference between the contract price and the cost of the alternate accommodations. Furthermore, compensation might also include travel expenses or payment of other expenses that result from the inconvenience. If a guest chooses to sue the property for breach of contract, many courts would award the guest damages that would probably include payment for such expenses. From an ethical point of view, should not the hotel voluntarily assist an inconvenienced guest in every way possible? If a guest does not have a guaranteed reservation, he or she should still be assisted in finding accommodations. Remember, unexpected events can cause a guest much distress and discomfort, not to mention disappointment. In the hospitality industry, our goal is to serve our guests. Every effort should be made by the hotel to ensure that the guests' needs are met.

It is important to note that although we want to believe that all guests are alike and should be treated the same, this is not always true. Very often, front desk clerks will hold rooms for favored guests. It is not uncommon for a hotel to begin walking guests with non-guaranteed reservations much earlier than the stated cut-off time if it appears that the hotel will be unable to accommodate its guaranteed reservations. Equally common is the habit of walking a guest with a guaranteed reservation while there are still rooms available in order to protect a favorite regular guest or a VIP. From an economic point of view, this is probably a good practice, but from an ethical point of view, is it? Is not every guest entitled to equal treatment?

No-Shows

Because the reservation is a contract binding on both parties, the property has a right to expect payment for a room that was held and technically could not be sold to another guest. In industry terms, a guaranteed no-show exists when a property honors the reservation contract but the guest fails to arrive and failed to cancel the reservation. Assuming that the hotel has made clear to the guest the terms by which the room was guaranteed, the billing of no-shows is not in itself the ethical issue. However, what about the hotel whose practice it is to overbook? The operation maintains 100% occupancy, but still bills the guest who failed to arrive. If, in fact, a guest fails to honor his or her part of this agreement, many hotel managers will justify billing based on that fact alone. Of course, the truth is that had the guest arrived after the last room was rented, the hotel would have been unable to accommodate him or her anyway. Is it ethical to bill the guest for a room that was technically not available?

Along the same lines, many hotels require an advance deposit to hold a reservation. If the guest cancels the reservation, especially after the cancellation time, should the hotel retain the deposit even if the room is eventually resold to another guest?

We can be somewhat encouraged by the fact that many properties refund a deposit if a room is resold. However, how many establishments neglect to inform the guest of this fact unless the guest actively pursues the refund? In any event, what documentation does the guest have to prove that a room was or was not sold?

Authorization of Credit Cards

A slightly different but still ethically related concern is authorizing credit card usage.

Most hotels request a credit card for their files to enable guests to establish credit with the hotel. Even if guests intend to pay cash for their stay, they are often asked to produce a credit card anyway. This, in itself, seems to be sound business practice. The ethical issue arises concerning what is done with that credit card left on file.

To ensure the validity of the card, the front desk usually authorizes use of the card for the estimated value of the guest's stay. If the guest did not intend to use the card for payment, this practice needlessly ties up his or her credit for a period of time. If the amount requested at authorization exceeds the actual charges when the guest checks out, few front desk clerks actually call the credit card company and release the hold that the hotel placed on that guest's credit limit. Because many credit card companies limit the amount a cardholder can use, it could very well come as an unwelcome surprise when the guest attempts to use the card somewhere else only to find that he or she is over the credit limit.

Admittedly, taking the time to correct the authorization on every card would require a major effort by the front desk. However, is it not the ethical and responsible way to handle this dilemma? The argument could be made that if the hotel does not put through a charge, or puts through a charge for a lesser amount, the credit will be released after a given period of time anyway. Nevertheless, what happens to the guest whose credit needs cannot be delayed that long?

Disputed Charges

Most persons will agree that when a business owes them a refund that has not been repaid they will expend whatever time and energy is required to collect what is rightfully theirs. Since it is the practice of some properties to charge a token deposit on various items like keys or telephones, one must speculate about what happens to such funds if the guest leaves without requesting the refund or if the front office clerk forgets to remove the charges.

For example, when a key is issued, a deposit is charged to discourage the guest from leaving the property with the key. Sometimes a deposit is charged for using a telephone in the guestroom. In either case, what happens when the guest leaves the hotel but fails to request the return of his or her deposit? Certainly, from a moral point of view the hotel should automatically refund the deposit. But the temptation is certainly there to transfer those funds to a disputed account and wait for the guest to request the refund.

When a guest disputes a charge, quality service demands that the matter be given prompt attention. How often, though, do these inquiries fall on someone's desk to be researched and are then delayed significantly or ignored altogether? Very often, the front desk does not have the information available to resolve the dispute immediately. But a guest should not have to repeatedly contact the hotel to have a billing error corrected. More often than not, many guests will not pursue the matter unless the sum in question was fairly substantial. Failure to rectify these disputes can leave the guest with a negative impression that may result in undesirable publicity for the hotel in the future.

Right to Privacy

Many hotel guests believe their occupancy rights are equivalent to those of someone renting an apartment or permanent dwelling. However, a vast distinction exists between a guest and a tenant. A guest is someone residing temporarily away from home. In other words, a guest has a permanent address elsewhere, while a tenant usually has a contract through a lease and resides at a certain location permanently. Therefore, discussion of a guest's right to privacy when registered at a hotel must cover legal as well as ethical implications:

> Generally speaking, a hotel has an affirmative duty, stemming from a guest's right of privacy and peaceful possession, not to allow unregistered and unauthorized third parties to gain access to its guests' rooms. However, it is understood that the hotel will have access for routine housekeeping and in the case of an emergency such as fire.[1]

When guests register at a hotel, they have a right to assume their privacy will be protected. There are many ways these expectations can be violated if the hotel does not take sufficient time and care to properly train its staff. Quality training ensures that every employee understands the importance of confidentiality when dealing with registered guests.

A number of significant legal issues arise in relation to a guest's room key. The key should be released only to the person or persons whose names appear on the registration card. For instance, if the spouse of a registered guest requests the key to the room when his or her name is not listed on the registration card, the front desk has no right to release the key. Even if the spouse has corroborating identification, it is presumptuous for the clerk to ascertain the present status of the guest's marriage. No third party, not even an unregistered spouse, is entitled to receive the key to a guest's room.

To understand the preceding issue, we should examine the case of *Campbell v. Womack*.[2] Mrs. Campbell had requested the key to her husband's room at a Louisiana motel and was refused. She assumed that she had a right to the key because she had stayed at the property with her husband on several prior occasions. The clerk's failure to release the key resulted in Mrs. Campbell's staying elsewhere where she was then joined by her husband. They eventually sued the motel and its clerk for breach of contract.

The courts were not impressed. Both the trial court and the appellate court held in favor of the motel. The courts said that marriage by itself does not assume consent to release a guest's room key to a spouse:

> A mere guest of the registered occupant of a room at a hotel who shares such a room with its occupant without the knowledge or consent of the hotel management would not be a guest of the hotel as there would be no contractual relations in such case between such third person and the hotel.[3]

Another common situation arises when the friends or relatives of a bride and groom arrive in advance of the wedding couple and request a key to leave champagne or some other gifts in the couple's room. Although playing pranks on a honeymoon couple may be an age-old tradition, the front desk clerk has no right to participate. Regardless of how well-meaning the friends or relatives seem to be, the newlyweds have a right to expect that their privacy will be protected.

Likewise, the information that a guest gives to the hotel on the registration card or in the form of credit identification should be considered privileged information. Confirming this information to any outside third party could be considered a breach of confidentiality. It is not unusual for someone to arrive at a hotel and ask the desk clerk to provide the room number of a registered guest. The visitor should be directed to use the house phones to contact the guest if he or she is registered there. No clerk has the authority to release a guest's name or room number to anyone, regardless of whether the information is given in person or over the telephone.

Moreover, PBX operators and desk clerks must be trained to handle any requests for information carefully. For instance, a caller requesting to be connected to Room 1022 might ask, "Oh, by the way, what's the name of the guest registered in that room?" Regardless of why the caller claims to need that information, the switchboard operator should never release the guest's name. This also applies to any other personal information about the guest to which the employee might have access (such as home address or telephone number). It is not unusual for some guests, especially those who are famous, to prefer that no one knows they are registered at the hotel, except for the people they choose to tell.

Another item that must be handled with great care concerns notifying a guest that there is a problem with his or her credit. Announcing at the front desk with other guests in earshot that the guest's credit card has been denied, or that a personal check cannot be accepted, puts the guest in a very awkward position. Once again, quality training should address how to handle these difficult situations without causing undue embarrassment to the guest.

Ideally, the first step in this situation is to ask the guest to step into an unoccupied office where the problem can be dealt with privately. The guest should always be given the benefit of the doubt and be given an opportunity to explain and rectify the situation before it is assumed he or she is trying to avoid paying the account.

Overcharging

Price gouging, or charging higher-than-normal room rates, is not uncommon during a special event. For example, in one city that hosted the Super Bowl, room rates as high as six times the normal were reportedly charged. This also raises the question of collusion and price-fixing. If rates throughout the city increase significantly during a special event, a question arises whether some discussion on the part of the hotel-keepers precipitated this "coincidence."

One must question not only the morality of this "coincidence," but also its legality. The law clearly states that price-fixing, or the establishment of maximum or minimum prices by two or more manufacturers, wholesalers, or retailers, is prohibited and regarded as a violation *per se*. If we examined a scenario using a 200-room hotel with an average rack rate (room rate) of $75 that was subsequently increased to $150, we find that this hotel receives an additional $15,000 for one night at 100% occupancy (200 rooms x $75). In no way does the guest benefit from additional services at such prices. Is this being dishonest or is it being capitalistic?

Most properties establish rates and instruct their desk clerks to stay within those established rates. However, some properties allow their front desks a certain flexibility in negotiating rates. This sets up a situation in which a clerk is allowed to make judgment calls about how much a customer might be willing to pay. For instance, in the case of a guest wearing a fur coat, it might be assumed that she can afford to pay more. Therefore, she is quoted a much higher rate. But another disturbing situation can also arise. A shabbily dressed guest might be quoted a rate much higher than another guest to discourage his or her staying at the hotel. In this case, the desk clerk decides whether the guest in question is unsuitable for the level of the property's clientele. Do we then, as a business preference, have the right to refuse guests because of their attire? Assuming that a guest is not offensive and does not create any problems for the hotel, "it is a basic duty of the innkeeper to receive the public."[4] The requirement to provide this basic duty dates back to the middle ages and has become common law. In fact, some states consider refusal of guests without proper justification a misdemeanor.

Hiring Practices

This area must be addressed at least briefly in this discussion of ethics in the front office.

As we all know, certain laws prohibit discriminatory hiring practices. But what about unwritten policies that are passed along unofficially? Because of the front desk clerk's high-profile position, a certain level of cleanliness, neatness, and professionalism is expected. However, what about general managers who instruct their front office managers to hire only candidates who are attractive or to avoid hiring minorities? The front office managers are then forced to make an ethical decision to either follow these unwritten "suggestions," even if they do not necessarily agree with them, or risk making their general managers unhappy by their hiring decisions.

Personal Ethics

The area termed personal ethics refers to one's own standards or individual value system.

Front desk clerks, with the high profile that they maintain, are often put in situations that test their own morals. On one hand, as hospitality and service-trained professionals, they are taught to believe that the guests' needs must be met; and most desk clerks go to great lengths to do so. However, what if a guest's request violates a clerk's personal code of ethics? This can be a real dilemma for a clerk who prides himself or herself in going all out for the guest. For instance, the guest might become very friendly with the clerk and then ask the clerk to set up a contact with a drug dealer. Even if the clerk does not use drugs, it is quite possible that he or she knows someone who could supply the items. Should the clerk refuse to help or should he or she make the connection and let the guest do the rest?

In a related situation, what happens to the guest who is looking for an "escort" for the evening. Should the clerk help to arrange something like this? In both of these cases, there would no doubt be a gratuity involved, making the situation very tempting.

We have to look more closely at the issue of gratuities being offered to employees for services not necessarily listed in their job descriptions. For example, a real dilemma occurs when a hotel has no rooms available and a guest comes in without a reservation and offers the clerk $50 to "find" him a room. In many cases, the clerk could register this guest and accept the bribe without anyone learning about it. Of course, this could potentially leave another guest without a room, but the clerk could rationalize that someone may not show up anyway and he or she could certainly use the money. Many times, clerks are offered gifts such as tickets to the theater or a sporting event or some other token gesture in exchange for upgrading the guest to a more expensive room at the same price. Once again, the clerk and the guest seemingly win, but what about the general manager who could perhaps have sold that room at a higher rate?

Another scenario that is not uncommon concerns the guest who stays in one place for several days and becomes very friendly with the staff. The guest asks the female desk clerk for a date, and as much as the clerk might enjoy the guest's company, is it appropriate for employees to date the guests? Many properties have rules that regulate this behavior, but the question in the clerk's mind centers on whether anyone would ever know. Or, the clerk might ask why the property has the right to dictate an employee's social life.

Some desk clerks supplement their income by renting rooms for cash, perhaps at a discount rate, to a guest who will not require a receipt. If the guest does not plan to spend the night, the clerk might clean the room before the guest leaves; otherwise, the room will turn up as one of those mystery discrepancies.

And what about the practice of borrowing things from the hotel. Many employees do not consider it stealing to take supplies home with them. But even using a hotel telephone to make personal calls can be a misuse of the company's funds. Many employees consider taking a couple of towels or some amenities or office supplies as their due. After all, they work very hard at this place. Why not?

Conclusion

I have attempted to describe several opportunities that may require ethical decision-making. In our society, the law determines right and wrong. But most of our laws are an extension of our own moral virtues. The origin of our legal system today dates back to the common laws used in England. Early lawmakers in no way envisioned the variety and complexity of issues that are present in today's society. In an attempt to more correctly address modern issues brought about by societal changes, our legislators have amended and re-amended the very bases upon which laws were constructed. Laws have then become subject to one judge's opinion, with the higher authority (a court) retaining the right to decision-making. If our laws, designed and interpreted by experts in jurisprudence, leave us with much ambiguity in understanding not just the right and wrong of common situations but also the legal and illegal ramifications, how can we expect the average person to safely make decisions that can and will always be considered ethical? This does not attempt to suggest that the individual is unable to distinguish right from wrong. However, many of the ethical issues presented here are not clear-cut and cannot necessarily be dealt with by issuing a new set of policies or regulations. Still, if we in this industry continue to condone unethical behavior, we place the overall reputation of the industry in jeopardy and risk losing the confidence of the very clientele we are attempting to attract.

Perhaps what is needed is an increased emphasis on sensitivity training in handling some of these difficult questions, the implementation of quality assurance programs, and an overall industry-wide watchdog approach to self-regulation.

Endnotes

1. Jack P. Jefferies, *Understanding Hospitality Law*, 2d ed. (East Lansing, Mich.: Educational Institute of the American Hotel & Motel Association, 1990), p. 75.

2. *Campbell v. Womack*, 345 So.2d 96, as contained in Reitzel, Lyden, Roberts, and Severance, *Contemporary Business Law, Principles and Cases*, 4th ed. (New York: McGraw-Hill, 1990), pp. 961–979.

3. Ibid.

4. *Hospitality Law* 3, no. 3, March 1988.

Discussion Topics

1. As a rule, you should not disclose guestroom numbers or phone numbers to third parties. How would you handle an inquiry by someone you know (who together with his or her spouse had stayed at the hotel before) when the spouse is at the hotel and gave specific instructions not to give out information to anyone?

2. You are the front office manager. You are trying to fill a desk clerk's position, and you have narrowed the competition down to four applicants. At this time, the general manager suggests to you that it would be better if you hired a particular person because of his or her appearance. This person is less qualified than the other applicants. What do you do?

3. A regular business traveler whom you know by name has stayed at your property four times in the last two months. When the robe in his room was missing after his last check-out, the front desk was notified to add the charge for the missing robe to his bill per hotel policy. Do you charge this guest? Why?

4. What other ethical situations would you expect to encounter if you were working at the front desk?

Term Paper Topics

1. Interview three or more front office managers about their views on overbooking. Ask them what their policies are as well as what they do when this puts them into a situation where they are forced to walk a guest. How do they handle this? How is the guest compensated? Compare their responses and then offer your own views. It might be helpful to consider the viewpoint of someone who has been walked.

2. In general, should you always adhere to the law, the hotel rules, or your own set of ethical values during the performance of your duties at the front desk?

9

Ethical Concerns in Food and Beverage Management

H. A. Divine

The first focus of this chapter is on ethical decision-making in food and beverage operations. The second is to show the close relationship between the attention given to ethical decisions and the quality of the products and services provided by that organization. It is not the function of this chapter to provide a hard-and-fast list of do's and don'ts, but rather to look at the daily decisions made by employees, managers, and owners and to suggest a way of including an ethical component into this decision-making process.

Food and beverage operations exist in a number of different settings, all with similarities and differences. These settings include hotels, motels, resorts, restaurants of all types, country and city clubs, schools, colleges, health care institutions, business and industry dining, prisons, convenience stores, supermarkets, department stores, and a myriad of other organizational settings for the sale and service of food and beverage. In each of these settings, the sale of food and beverages serves as an important contributor to the achievement of organizational goals. The sale and service of food and beverages is a large business, contributing upwards of 6% of the gross national product, and its importance keeps expanding.

Two characteristics of food and beverage operations that generally come immediately to mind when discussions involve ethical behavior are that this business is still very much a cash business and that the products are both highly perishable and highly portable. These two characteristics provide opportunities for chicanery. Misappropriation, outright theft, and other misuses of cash and products by employees, managers, owners, and vendors are problems confronted by many food and beverage operations. Unfortunately, these also become a single focal point when anyone begins to talk about

H. A. "Andy" Divine, PhD, is Director and Professor of the School of Hotel and Restaurant Management, University of Denver. During 1990–91, he was on leave from Penn State University to do research and consulting work concerning sales and service of alcohol. Dr. Divine worked with community groups primarily in California to develop community standards and industry training programs for servers and managers in outlets selling alcoholic beverages. From 1983 to 1990, Dr. Divine was Director and Professor of the School of Hotel, Restaurant and Institutional Management at The Pennsylvania State University.

ethics in this industry. As important as this unethical behavior (stealing) and its prevention is, it is only one of many ethical issues. Ethical concerns should be pervasive in the decision-making process, not perversely simplistic as would be the case if one dealt only with stealing.

In their book *Strategic Management: Concepts and Experiences,* Rue and Holland seem to capture the essence of the importance that should be attached to the development of a way of incorporating ethical considerations into decisions:

> The question of what is ethical behavior has existed since people began to work together in primitive societies. In those societies what was right and what was wrong became an integral part of tribal customs, practices and mores. Life was simpler and consequently, ethical decisions were simpler. As societies became complex, ethical issues became more complex. Today with rapidly changing technology, increased worldwide communication, and a community that encompasses the entire globe, we can no longer have customs, practices and mores that provide the 'correct' answer to every ethical issue. As managers and employees, we must try to develop within us an ethical discipline that helps guide us and the companies for whom we work to the most ethically "correct" answer possible.[1]

It is only through a commitment to begin thinking through a problem or opportunity with due consideration for the ethical implications that we can become ethical in our actions.

Ethical issues confound the decision processes of management. Rue and Holland suggest a second major consideration in managerial decisions—not only must there be a profit consideration (long and short term), but there must also be ethical considerations of whether the actions proposed to produce the profit are indeed ethically right.

Stress

The hospitality industry may be just now truly confronting the organizational stress that has existed in the production industries for the past two decades. This industry has emerged as an industrial giant in the 1980s, which has caused public attention to be drawn to industry activities. Once thought of only as a collection of small businesses (which is still true for the majority of outlets), the industry is now seemingly perceived as a major economic force. This has forced and will continue to force the industry to be both more publicly accountable and more positively confrontative with emerging public values. Once somewhat immune from public scrutiny, the hospitality industry is now included in the mainstream of public action. Whether this action is directed at the need for public protection in terms of cleaner facilities, proposed labeling laws, truth-in-menu regulations, warning signs relative to alcohol, or provision of non-smoking areas and the like, there is a demand that the hospitality industry be held accountable for what are perceived to be public health issues.

Likewise, there are concerns for the employees who work in the industry, in terms of minimum wage and a plethora of laws and regulations either proposed or in force that would protect the work force. The industry has also become a focal point relative to recycling, regardless of the true contribution to the problem caused by the industry. Too, the concern for discrimination in serving and employing those with physical or other handicaps has resulted in a codification of those concerns into law.

In addition to meeting the strict letter of the law or regulation that codifies right and wrong as viewed by a society at a particular time, there is the need for management to consider the rightness or wrongness of decisions in accordance with a set of values that are internal. How we arrive at those values is critical. Kristol, in a *Wall Street Journal* editorial, spoke of the development of morals, the key to ethical behavior:

> This task, (moral education) in today's America, is performed in the traditional structure of incentives one encounters in real life situations, all of which form the character of one citizenry . . . The home is obviously the key institution for such moral education, since it is there that one learns the rudiments of personal responsibility and moral obligation. School is also very important, since it is here that one learns how to cope with and to internalize impersonal, social discipline. And then there is participation in the activities of one's religious community, where one experiences moral commitment as a bond between generations past and generations present. It is the sum of these crucial experiences that forms one's moral character. It doesn't always work, as we know. But, once again, as we also know, nothing always works.[2]

Many individuals have written about ethics both in general and as they are applied to business situations.

Bases for Ethics

Harry Truman was once reported to have said that all one needs as a guide to ethical behavior is the Ten Commandments and The Sermon on the Mount. While for many in a Judeo-Christian culture this might provide the appropriate bases for deciding right and wrong, there are other bases available.

Sharpin, in his book *Strategic Management,* created a simple model which suggested that individuals have innumerable bases for determining right or wrong: (1) the Bible, Koran, and other "Holy" books; (2) the conscience; (3) the behavior and advice of "significant others"; (4) codes of ethics; and (5) laws.[3]

Sharpin writes, "The strength of the relationship between what an individual or organization believes to be moral and correct and what available sources of guidance suggest is morally correct is Type I Ethics. Type II Ethics is the strength of the relationship between what one believes and the way one acts."[4]

If there is no strong relationship between the way one believes and the way one internalizes whatever bases he or she has to guide that thinking, it is unlikely that there will be any linkage to behavior.

There is a powerful, generally mistaken belief among employees in many organizations in the hospitality industry that they are being "ripped off," taken advantage of, and generally used to produce obscene profits for owners and managers. In general, management has been guilty of myopic perceptions about employees, believing, for example, that employees could not possibly understand cost ratios and overhead cost allocations. With such perceptions, management sees no need to even bother trying to explain the business and profitability of the organization. In the absence of factual data, heresay becomes fact. In that world, it is easy to project that the organization is making huge profits and employees are being abused.

When an individual feels deprived and views the organization as both the cause of the deprivation and as a center of comparatively huge wealth, there appears to be justice in balancing the scales to some degree. The balancing, of course, comes in a myriad of forms, from cheating on guest checks to manipulating the inventory and hundreds of other ways that employees have to sabotage a food or beverage outlet for personal gain.

Cyclical Pattern

When management allows these feelings to fester and the subsequent actions to occur, it becomes a major challenge to reverse the trend. In those instances where management itself exhibits questionable behaviors, the challenge is insurmountable. At the same time that such misappropriations are occurring, there is an inescapable consequence to profitability. When either income is not reported or costs are increased, the result must be one of two things—either profitability must suffer or quality of product or service will decline. Once in this cycle, it becomes extremely difficult to escape.

Exhibit 1 depicts the cyclical pattern that can occur in food and beverage operations when there are feelings of injustice that are felt to justify unethical acts by management and employees. One can enter the cycle at any point, but the unethical behavior seems to come, in most instances, from a feeling of alienation and a need to get even. If an individual feels that his or her rewards are inequitable, he or she has three choices: (1) put up with the inequity by finding a way of psychologically justifying it; (2) leave the job (which does not help if there is a perception that all like jobs provide the same inequities); or (3) increase one's rewards by misappropriating the assets of the organization.

Unfortunately, the third alternative is chosen an alarming number of times. Such actions have predictable negative influences upon profitability since revenues are either decreased or remain the same relative to increases in costs. Also predictable are the actions of most upper management groups—cut costs. This may have negative impacts upon the quality of service and product provided to the guest. As depicted in Exhibit 1, this seems to set in motion another interrelated cycle involving quality, guests, and employers.

As pressures mount, there is a greater feeling of injustice on the part of employees and managers and a greater felt need to get even. As this "flush" cycle gains momentum, it becomes increasingly difficult to stop, reverse, and correct without massive top-level changes.

There are several ethical considerations in addition to the obvious one of stealing, which is against the law and is generally considered unacceptable behavior. Ethical questions abound in terms of reward structure for employees and managers. If upper management is, by word and deed, committed to providing a minimal reward structure in order to maximize short-term profitability, does it not share the ethical culpability for the actions of sub-managers and employees? As management strives to maintain profitability through various cost-cutting programs, often affecting the quality of products and services to the guest, is it also acting in possibly unethical ways? As profit pressures are exerted, how difficult is it to decrease the grade of food product, to utilize frozen product (and not mention the change to the service personnel), to drop the quality of house wines and spirits and maintain a premium price, and other actions that can have a short-term positive effect on the bottom line of profitability? Are there

Exhibit 1   Cyclical Pattern Caused by Feelings of Injustice

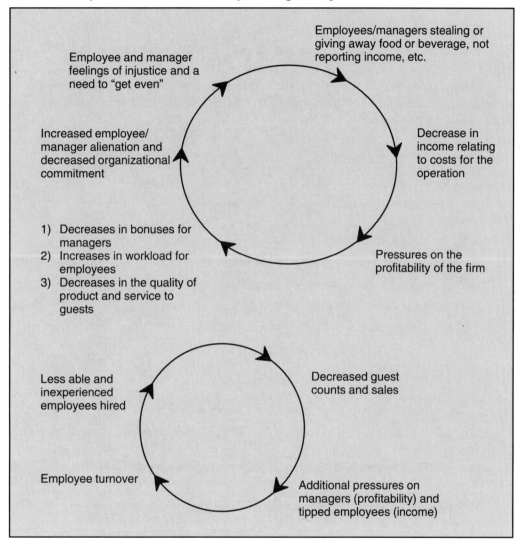

ethical considerations involved when the size of service stations is increased in an effort to save labor dollars?

Beyond the service quality question, there are seemingly questions of reasonable workload and another question of so overloading the service staff as to negatively influence their tip income because they are unable to offer acceptable service. These are often not thought of as ethical concerns but rather as operational expediencies.

Many operational decisions that must be made on a daily basis have relevance to both ethics and quality. In general, there seems to be an inseparability between excellence in ethics and excellence in quality at any given market level. Acting to deceive or mislead a guest or employee would result in an inevitable decline in quality. Such actions may come from managerial decisions—decisions that might have been made without concern for the ethical dimensions of the problem.

Considerations for Decision-Making

Many individuals have written about things that management should consider when making decisions. The following are three different lists of considerations to use as guides in decision-making:

1. Have you defined the problem accurately?

2. How would you define the problem if you stood on the other side of the fence?

3. How did this situation occur in the first place?

4. To whom and to what do you give your loyalty as a person and as a member of the corporation?

5. What is your intention in making this decision?

6. How does this intention compare with the probable results?

7. Whom could your decision injure?

8. Can you discuss the problem with the affected parties before you make your decision?

9. Are you confident that your position will be as valid over a long period of time as it seems now?

10. Could you disclose without qualm your decision or action to your boss, your CEO, the board of directors, your family, society as a whole?

11. What is the symbolic potential of your action if understood? If misunderstood?

12. Under what conditions would you allow exceptions to your stand?[5]

Six questions provide a useful framework for moving beyond concern and confusion to practical and responsible decisions. When a manager is faced with ethical dilemmas, careful attention to these six questions leads to a thoughtful resolution—not the right answer, but an ethically sensitive and well-considered judgment.[6]

1. Why is this bothering me? Is it really an issue? Am I genuinely perplexed, or am I afraid to do what I know is right?

2. Who else matters? Who are the stakeholders who may be affected by my decisions?

3. Is it my problem? Have I caused the problem or has someone else? How far should I go in resolving the issue?

4. What is the ethical concern—legal obligation, fairness, promise keeping, honesty, doing good, avoiding harm?

5. What do others think? Can I learn from those who disagree with my judgment?

6. Am I being true to myself? What kind of person or company would do what I am contemplating? Could I share my decision 'in good conscience' with my family? With colleagues? With public officials?[7]

Also useful are the "Ethics Check" questions:

1. Is it legal? Will I be violating either civil law or company policy?

2. Is it balanced? Is it fair to all concerned in the short term as well as the long term? Does it promote win-win relationships?

3. How will it make me feel about myself? Will it make me proud? Would I feel good if my decision was published in the newspaper? Would I feel good if my family knew about it?[8]

The Dilemma of Serving Alcohol

Food and beverage managers must internalize some of these questions as guides to their decision-making. A current dilemma faced by food and beverage managers and servers presents an ethical challenge. Nearly everyone is aware of the problems of drunk driving and the other societal problems caused by the abuse of alcohol. These problems have been considered serious enough to have caused laws to be written to guide the actions of individuals. Specifically, all states prohibit the sale and service of alcohol to minors and to individuals who are visibly intoxicated. Any server, bartender, or manager who does sell or serve alcohol to either of these classes of individuals could be guilty of breaking the law. As a consequence, there should be no more question of the appropriate action to take in cases of this nature than there would be if confronted with a question of whether to steal or not to steal.

However, there are questions of what constitutes, and how one identifies, a "visibly intoxicated" person, and how far one goes in checking the identification of individuals before serving them an alcoholic beverage. This becomes a managerial decision that certainly has social ramifications and ethical overtones. Most individuals would agree that the establishment has a legal and ethical responsibility to take reasonable care to ensure that these two classes of individuals are not served alcohol. However, if you are a server who makes your living from the tip income given to you by guests who are pleased with your service, you do not want to do anything that might upset the guests. Individuals who have been refused service of alcoholic beverages are generally not pleased. The server is thus placed in an interesting position of knowing or strongly suspecting someone in the party is either underage or visibly intoxicated and should not be served and yet also knowing that not serving will have a negative impact upon their income. At that point, the server may convince himself or herself that the individual really does appear to be sober or of age. After all, it is in the server's best interest economically to do so. However, doing so could be against the law, and both the server and the establishment could be found liable.

In other cases, servers might say that their commitment to not only the letter of the law but the spirit of the law transcends their own economic considerations, and they might intervene. The decisions reached are influenced by the actions and direction provided by management. Is management training servers to identify individuals who are underage or who are intoxicated and showing them how to deal with such situations? And is management then supporting the servers when they act in an appropriate manner?

While there is certainly an individual question of ethical behavior when the server makes a decision to serve or not to serve, there is arguably a larger ethical question of how management supports the server. In both instances (server and management) there is an economic consideration—either individual or corporate. The situation is further compounded by the reality that the sale of alcoholic beverages has seriously declined, which has had a serious economic impact upon organizations that derive substantial income from such sales. The true search for ethical behavior and decisions must occur when there are uncomfortable situations. Everyone can be ethical if there is no cost associated with such action. Blanchard is quoted as saying: "There's a difference between interest and commitment. When you are interested in doing something, you do it only when it's convenient. When you are committed to something, you accept no excuses, only results."[9]

Most managers have at least an interest in being ethical, whether it is in dealing with their employers, social issues, their guests, or any other aspect of their operation. The difficulty is that many managers seem to lack the commitment to take the ethically correct action when the economics of the issue may lead in a different direction.

The strange and often overlooked element is that generally, when implementing a program supportive of a socially responsible position, there are very positive outcomes. Using again the example of serving alcoholic beverages, we know that there are positive returns from improving the quality of service. Certainly, one of the primary elements of judging service quality is the attentiveness of the server. An important component of instituting a good monitoring program to ensure that individuals do not overconsume alcoholic beverages is to encourage server attentiveness to the guest. Thus, the idea of paying attention to the guest and his or her needs, which is essential to providing quality service, is found also to be essential to ensure a safe environment.

Using Ethics in Decision-Making

As operators become ever more mindful that there are ethical elements in many of the decisions they make on a daily basis, they will begin to make these elements part of their decisions. Will this eliminate all unethical behavior from food and beverage operations? Unfortunately, the answer is that it is doubtful. As has been mentioned in this article, the determination of right and wrong is an individualistic one predicated upon one's past that has shaped one's values. As cultures differ, so will individuals' feelings about right and wrong. In certain cultures alcohol itself is unacceptable; therefore, any thought of there being acceptable guidelines for its service is impossible. It is absolutely true that for most of us there is never a right time or way to do a wrong thing. Managers in the hospitality industry must spend more time on determining the long-term ethical impact of their decisions and determining what are the right things to do rather than totally concentrating on doing things right.

The three checklists contained in this chapter are helpful in directing the attention of individuals to considerations that can be taken into account as they make decisions. They have a common core in that they all direct our attention to internal feelings and the long-term and far-reaching effects of the decisions. A food and beverage manager confronting a problem or developing a policy about responsible beverage service is advised to be guided by any of these lists (see the section on "Considerations for Decision-Making"). Each list encourages one to consider the many different audiences affected by the decisions.

Ethical determinations are never really simplistic. However, each individual has a background that has established his or her values. It is up to management to provide the support and direction that allows these basic values to act in positive ways for the individual and the organization. Ethical dealings with people is the most positively powerful role model that top management can provide for middle management and for the employee.

Endnotes

1. Leslie W. Rue and Phyllis G. Holland, *Strategic Management: Concepts and Experiences* (New York: McGraw-Hill, 1989), p. 86.

2. Irving Kristol, "Ethics, Anyone? Or Morals?" *Wall Street Journal,* September 15, 1987.

3. Arthur Sharpin, *Strategic Management* (New York: McGraw-Hill, 1985), p. 24.

4. Ibid.

5. Laura Nash, "Ethics Without the Sermon," *Harvard Business Review,* November–December 1981, p. 81.

6. Michael Rion, *The Responsible Manager: Practical Strategies for Ethical Decision Making* (New York: Harper & Row, 1990), pp. 13–14.

7. Ibid.

8. Kenneth Blanchard and Norman Vincent Peale, *The Power of Ethical Management* (New York: Morrow, 1988), p. 19.

9. Blanchard, promotional matter.

Discussion Topics

1. Elaborate mechanical and accounting controls have virtually eliminated the need for managerial concern for theft and misappropriation of goods and cash.

2. Public health and welfare issues are legal, not ethical, issues.

3. Discuss the ethical vs. legal concerns and the locus of responsibility in the service of alcohol to a visibly intoxicated or underage customer.

4. Discuss the ethical dilemma faced by food and beverage managers in balancing profitability and social responsibility in such issues as truth-in-menu (fresh vs. frozen, substitute brands, point-of-origin products, methods of preparation, etc.).

Term Paper Topics

1. Select a hospitality industry company and, based on issues and guidelines provided in this chapter, analyze how it achieves and maintains ethical standards for behavior in its food and beverage operation.

2. Select a current social issue involving food and beverage operations and unresolved legislation, and prepare a position paper on that issue. The position must

consider the effects of that position on both profitability and ethical/social responsibility concerns. (Examples of possible topics: drunken driving; truth-in-menu; smoking/non-smoking; discrimination in employment based on age, sex, ethnicity, religion, sexual preference, disability, etc.)

10

Ethics and Housekeeping

Kay Weirick

At one time or another, most of us have dusted or run a vacuum cleaner in our home. Despite this universal experience, most of us—except for the professional house-keeper—probably haven't thought about the complexities of cleaning.

Professional housekeepers do more than clean. Their job is a profession that con-sists of intricate tasks, procedures, and management techniques that ensure a hotel's smooth operation.[1] They also know that certain modes of conduct can ensure the job gets done well, in the safest and most cost-efficient way possible.

This chapter examines the choices executive housekeepers and their staff may face on a daily basis—and the ethical implications of those choices.

The Basis of Ethics

Imagine giving someone a key to your home and asking that person to care for your belongings. Obviously, you would want to *trust* that person. You wouldn't want a giant question mark surrounding that person's values, judgment, and dependability. In other words, you would want to say with confidence that the person you hired is *ethical*.

On a very basic level, the relationship between a lodging operation and its housekeeping staff is built on *ethics*. A hotel *trusts* its room attendants and their super-visors to maintain the cleanliness and aesthetics of the property. To do the job, house-keeping staff must continually make choices that affect the well-being of guests and employees. No less than any other profession, housekeeping needs a code of ethics by which to frame these day-to-day choices. It is management's responsibility to clearly communicate that code.

Kay Weirick, REH, is the Director of Housekeeping Services at Bally's Casino Resort in Las Vegas. She graduated from St. Mary's Academy in Amarillo, Texas, and has completed extensive continuing educa-tion programs. She is a Registered Executive Housekeeper, and a National Board Member and Treasurer for the National Executive Housekeepers Association. The author worked in a hospital for ten years as a medical missionary in Bangladesh. She has held executive positions with the Fairmont, Four Seasons, and Registry hotel chains.

Ethics Defined

Making choices is complicated. Ethics help us weigh and evaluate our choices—especially in terms of how the outcome of our choices affect others. As a general definition, we can say that:

> Ethics is a set of moral principles and values that we use to answer questions of right and wrong; it is also the study of the general nature of morals and of the specific moral choices to be made by individuals in their relationships with others.[2]

For housekeeping, we can narrow our definition and say that:

> Ethics is a set of pre-established principles and values that guide the conduct of housekeeping employees in ensuring the comfort, security, safety, privacy, and rights of guests and employees.

Properties promoting a code of ethics must clearly communicate that code—in both written and spoken form. Managers cannot expect people to come to the job with a code of ethics—nor can they expect staff to pick up on implied messages. Some employees come from backgrounds that do not encourage, support, or even provide exposure to the values and conduct traditionally associated with work. Some employees may have limited reading and writing skills; some speak a different language; some come from different countries or cultures. Managers must communicate the property's code of ethics in a manner that is not demeaning, intimidating, or patronizing. In other words, communicating ethics involves ethics—it demands that all employees be treated fairly, equally, and with respect.

People will always be divided on what is ethical and what is not. By clearly communicating a code of ethics, managers can sustain a quality of work that promotes individual pride and the well-being of the whole.

Housekeeping and Ethics

Housekeeping staff clean more than guestrooms; they may also be responsible for cleaning a property's public areas and restrooms, restaurants, and offices. All these areas must be cleaned and maintained on a daily basis. While doing so, housekeeping staff may face concerns that range from sanitation to security to individual rights. Areas which pose ethical questions for housekeeping staff include:

1. Security
2. Safety
3. Privacy
4. Use and disposal of cleaning chemicals
5. Administrative duties
6. Human resources

This chapter will briefly address each area by providing a scenario followed by a general discussion. Each scenario intends to stretch critical thinking by evoking a certain feeling or thought. The scenarios do not draw conclusions about what is right or wrong—nor do they illustrate situations typical of all hospitality operations. Rather, each scenario presents a dilemma that a room attendant or housekeeping manager could encounter on any given workday.

Security

Lodging operations must provide a secure environment for guests and employees. It is unfair, and sometimes even illegal, to expect employees to work effectively when they feel skeptical or uninformed about the property's security.

Security is often confused with *safety*. Security is the broad task of protecting both people and assets—specifically by taking measures to prevent theft, fire, and other emergencies. Safety refers to the actual conditions of the work environment. This section will examine the ethical practices or behaviors associated with housekeeping security—particularly in the areas of key control, detecting and reporting suspicious activities, theft, lost and found, and guestroom cleaning. We will examine safety in the next major section.

Key Control

> *About 10 minutes into your cleaning, you hear frantic knocking on the door. Putting down your cleaning rag, you walk around the corner to see the distressed face of the second man—the one who flagged John down. You realize he has been trying to get by the cart you positioned to block the entrance, but has so far been unsuccessful. "Please ma'am," he says breathlessly. "Can you let me in for a second? Mr. Davis wants me to pick up the notes he forgot for his presentation."*

Like most security issues, key control involves legalities as well as ethics. Registered guests have a right to assume that their security will be protected through careful key control. Managers must communicate key control procedures to every room attendant—both through training and ongoing training. There should be no question in any room attendant's mind about the policies and procedures regarding the use of emergency, master, storeroom, and guestroom keys. Employees should also be perfectly clear about when you can and cannot grant someone access to a guestroom. Even when room attendants recognize a guest, they should still ask to see that guest's room key before allowing him or her to enter a room being cleaned.

The distribution of keys should be noted on a key control log; keys issued to one employee should not be loaned to another. Room attendants must understand that they are responsible for retrieving any keys left in guestrooms or other hotel area. Any keys that come up missing or lost should be reported immediately so that rooms can be rekeyed. Routinely changing guestroom locks can guard against the occasional loss or theft of keys.

Properties should not be shy about adopting new or revised locking systems or technologies. Dead bolts and door chains, for example, can make the easy-to-jimmy lock nearly obsolete. A good key system will help room attendants provide a guest with that extra sense of security.

Suspicious Activities

For the fourth time during your afternoon shift, you've seen a different person going in and out of room 213. You wouldn't think much of it if it hadn't been for the man who tried to take some shampoo from your cart, and the girl in the black boots who tripped on her way to the stairs. To top it all off, there was another man who dropped what looked to be a handful of bills as he knocked on the guestroom door.

Although open to the public, a lodging operation is a private property. Hotels have a responsibility to monitor and, when appropriate, to control the activities of people on the premises.

Housekeeping managers and supervisors are charged with training their staff to spot suspicious activities and unauthorized or unwelcomed people. For example, room attendants should be told how to approach someone they see loitering, or checking or knocking on doors, and how to contact their manager or security in such a situation. Properties, however, cannot demand that employees approach suspicious-looking people. Because of their size, sex, or demeanor, some employees just won't feel comfortable approaching individuals they perceive as threatening.

Security works best when every staff member sees security as part of their job—and knows the level of contribution they can make. Like all areas involving ethics, managers cannot expect their employees to have instinctive judgments. It is up to the property to provide the guidelines.

Theft

You just entered the first guestroom in your section. "First things first," you say to yourself as you go to open the curtains on the morning sun. Reaching the window, you see that an extremely large suitcase rests between you and the drawstring. You know that you'll have to work around the luggage since hotel policy tells you to avoid moving guest belongings. As you look down to watch your step, a shimmer catches your eye. Focusing your gaze, you see four towels in the guest's open suitcase, all neatly folded to display your property's gold-threaded logo.

Hotels walk a fine line when distinguishing theft from souvenir-taking. Housekeeping departments should count on the loss or theft of certain small items from guestrooms—especially those imprinted with the hotel logo. Some properties even consider it a form of marketing when guests take articles such as matches, pens, shampoos, ashtrays, and sewing kits. After all, these items are placed in the room for the guest's convenience and, for the most part, are not reusable.

However, when towels, robes, pictures, furnishings, and fixtures come up missing, a property shoulders significant expenses. Some hotels use plain white towels; some discreetly secure furnishings and fixtures to the wall or floor; some install special locks on windows, storerooms, and exits; some even decorate with less expensive items.[3] For example, a ceramic vase gracing a bureau can be just as tasteful as a vase made of brass or stone. Hotels must weigh the cost of image and taste against the weaknesses of human nature. By making items less distinctive and more difficult to put in a suitcase or edge out a side door, properties could say they are lessening temptations.

Employees, too, might steal. Management must set the standards for reducing employee theft—and must act as a good example. Employees will not take a manager seriously when they see him or her taking home desserts, towels, or office supplies—especially when that same manager asks employees not to steal hotel goods. Managers should lock storerooms, control access to restricted areas, take inventories on a regular basis, and monitor well-lit employee entrances and exits. Managers, too, must assure the protection of employees who report other employees. A manager must uphold the trust that gave an employee the confidence to step forward; very few circumstances require a manager to betray an employee's anonymity. Like all policies, the consequences of stealing hotel property should be clearly spelled out in the employee manual, communicated through training, and equally applied to all employees.

Many hotels see the problem of theft as a strong argument for one more guestroom amenity: the in-room safe. Safes provide both physical and psychological security. Most guests will feel more relaxed leaving their valuables in a safe than in a suitcase—even when a hotel has a reputation for excellent security.

Lost and Found

You're working the lost and found on a busy weekend. Late in the morning, a room attendant brings you an expensive silk blouse that she found in a guestroom bureau. "No telling how long it was there," Pamela says, her fingers lingering on the designer label as you take the blouse from her hands. "It was scrunched real far back so you could barely see it when you opened the drawer."

Three months later, you're sorting through the lost and found items and come upon the blouse. "This really is nice," you say to yourself. "What a great color—and it's just my size." Reviewing the lost and found log, you see that no one has claimed the blouse. You know that hotel policy states that any item unclaimed after 90 days is awarded to the employee who turned it in. You've seen Pamela around since then, but you figure that she's forgotten all about the blouse.

Hotels should set up a system whereby guests are given a certain period of time to claim an item they left behind. Some properties give guests 30 days to claim items that are not considered extremely valuable, and 90 days to claim items such as jewelry, furs, or cameras. Properties owe it to their guests to establish clear procedures for the lost and found. They also owe it to their employees.

In some properties, the security department handles the lost and found function—not housekeeping. Regardless of whose responsibility it is, hotels must be extremely conscientious about keeping accurate records about who turned the item in and when. Some properties award unclaimed items to the person who turned them in, others award cash, some provide special recognition, still others donate items to charity. Basically, it doesn't matter which path a property follows—as long as they follow it consistently. Many room attendants will have a hard time turning in something of value when they feel that the item—if unclaimed—will be awarded to someone else.

Guestroom Cleaning

As you go about cleaning an exceptionally messy guestroom, you can't seem to get your mind off all the bills you have to pay in the next few weeks. Your insur-

ance didn't cover your two trips to the doctor when you had the flu, you got a ticket for speeding, and your credit card went sky high when you charged school clothes for your kids. As you check under the bed, you see a wrinkled T-shirt, beer cans, and candy wrappers. Reaching to collect the cans and trash, you notice that the wads of paper aren't candy wrappers at all but very rumpled $5 and $1 bills.

Employees must have a basic respect for a guest's property. Whether scattered about the room or neatly arranged, a guest's belongings should not be moved or tidied by a room attendant—except when absolutely necessary to complete a basic cleaning task. Room attendants, too, should adhere to a basic rule: what doesn't belong to the hotel in a guestroom, belongs to the guest. Room attendants should never assume they have the right to claim ownership of articles left behind.

In every instance, guest items left behind should be turned in to the lost and found. Room attendants should know they have a critical job in maintaining security in guestroom areas. They must be perfectly clear on what conditions or items they need to report to their supervisor, security, or the front desk. Most employees have the good judgment to report any guns or weapons, controlled substances, foul odor, ill guests, or large amounts of cash or valuables. However, management cannot depend on every employee knowing what is best to do in every situation. It is up to management to communicate and instill these guidelines—and to encourage pride when employees maintain the property's standards.

Safety

Janna has been a member of your staff for less than two weeks. She's fresh out of high school where she was a varsity swimmer and the manager of an intramural basketball team. She tells you that she's strong and energetic and eager to do what she can to do a good job. For you, Janna is a godsend. It's a busy time of year and, unfortunately, you've experienced some turnover. You haven't had the time to provide the intensive training that you know Janna needs, and have depended on your senior staff to help her out on the job.

Looking at your cleaning schedule, you see that a block of rooms is slated for deep cleaning. You know that you must have these rooms ready for the convention arriving at the end of the month. You know, too, that deep cleaning involves moving furniture, using special equipment, and a lot of stamina. Being short-staffed, you see that Janna might be your only hope of getting the rooms ready on time. In the past, you've never assigned deep cleaning to a staff member who hasn't gone through standard training.

Just as a property is obligated to provide a secure environment, it is responsible for ensuring a safe one. On any given day, housekeeping employees may lift heavy objects, climb ladders, operate machinery, and use dangerous cleaning chemicals. All these situations could be harmful to the employee—if the employee is not properly trained in how to do the job safely.

Properties have both a moral and legal responsibility to protect the worker in the workplace. Workers should be able to say—with confidence—that their workplace will not cause them to be sick, hurt, or disabled. The federal government regulates work areas and businesses with respect to safety through the Occupational Safety and Health Act (OSHA). OSHA regulations are quite extensive and mandate safety regulations and practices for many industries—including hospitality.[4]

Basically, managers should prevent the preventable. This means that a property must take every step possible to make working conditions safe. Many workplace accidents are based on sheer carelessness, lack of training in proper procedures, or both. For instance, gloves, goggles, or face shields should be used when jobs require employees to use hazardous or toxic cleaning chemicals. The chemical manufacturer must specify what type of equipment is needed—and the property must ensure specifications are followed.

Dress codes can also protect employees from physical harm. Leather-soled shoes can be slippery on wet surfaces. Long, dangling earrings or necklaces could get hooked around a faucet or other fixture. Employees should know that a certain style of dress or uniform is enforced not to stifle self-expression, but to protect the employee from work-related hazards.

Wet floors and slippery walkways are accidents waiting to happen. So are cluttered floors or cleaning equipment left out and in the way. Simply placing a caution sign in the hallway or training employees in the proper use and storage of equipment could prevent someone from a sprain, strain, or fall. Employees should operate equipment only after receiving the proper training for its use.

Safety precautions also protect guests. Guests do not pay to stay someplace dangerous—they depend on the property to provide comfortable and hazard-free surroundings. No matter how tiny the repair, a property should not sell a guestroom that is in less than tip-top condition. Small rips in the carpet, loose towel bars, tap water that is too hot, sticky windows, or furniture with wobbly legs may seem like minor annoyances, but can actually be treacherous for the unsuspecting. The ethical property puts guest welfare ahead of profit by not selling rooms needing any type of repair—even if that room is the only one standing in the way of 100% occupancy. In other words, guestrooms should be maintained with "zero defect."

Privacy

You're in the middle of stocking your cart for your morning room assignments. While you're arranging your supplies, you hear muffled wailing coming from down the hall. The high pitch bothers you; looking at your watch, you realize the sound has persisted for nearly 15 minutes. As you begin your rounds, the wailing escalates. You stop pushing your cart for a moment and listen. Your suspicions were right: it's a baby. You push your cart a little further, and see that the crying is coming from a room on your list. You approach the room and see a "Do Not Disturb" sign hanging on the knob.

Legally, a hotel owes a guest the rights of privacy and peaceful possession while the guest is in the guestroom. This means that no unregistered and unauthorized third party can gain access to the guest's room. However, a hotel does have access to occupied guestrooms for routine housekeeping and during emergencies.[5]

Different people will have different ideas about what constitutes a breach in privacy and what doesn't. For instance, should a room attendant report an extremely messy room in which guests are staying for a second night? What if hotel property in such a guestroom is broken or damaged? Should a room attendant report or intervene in an argument that he or she overhears? Would casual talk among staff about the comings and goings of a politician or celebrity be improper or just a product of natural curiosity?

Some areas are more cut and dried. For example, room attendants may not snoop in guest belongings, reveal guestroom numbers to others, or discuss guest schedules or itineraries with other guests. Managers, too, should train their staff to recognize situations that can be potentially threatening. Employees should have a sense of when to intervene and when not to; they should know what to do when they see guests arguing or when they encounter a guest who appears ill or confused. In all cases, managers must provide guidance to employees in the proper way to approach delicate situations.

Use and Disposal of Cleaning Chemicals

You've read in the newspapers and in some of your executive housekeeping journals that a particular cleaning chemical is suspected of causing allergic reactions in some people. Several environmental groups also argue that the chemical pollutes lakes, rivers, and streams. Your property uses a cleaner that contains the chemical. So far, no one has come to you with any complaints, nor have you noticed any mysterious rashes or other physical ailments among your cleaning staff. Looking through your purchasing guide, you notice an alternative cleaner that doesn't contain the chemical—and is certified biodegradable. You also notice that the product costs considerably more—almost twice as much as your standard cleaner.

The use of cleaning chemicals is double-edged—it involves both safety and social responsibility. Everyday, housekeeping employees use cleaning chemicals that can be abrasive or harmful to themselves, to the areas or objects they clean, and to the environment. Employees should know that no chemicals are safe to use together. They must know when to use personal protective gear—and be supplied with gear that provides the maximum level of protection. Employees, too, should know which chemicals are safe to use on what surfaces. Unless guidelines are communicated clearly, a property cannot hold the employee responsible. But an employee—if harmed—can point the finger at the property's negligence to convey and enforce the proper use of hazardous materials.

As mentioned in our discussion on safety, various state laws and OSHA regulations require hotel employers to inform workers about the possible risks posed by chemicals they may use to do their jobs. The OSHA regulation also requires that employers provide training in the safe use of chemicals. This regulation is called the Hazard Communication Standard—often referred to as HazComm, or the Right to Know Law.

The responsible use of cleaning chemicals is mandated not only through law, but through social pressure. As we enter the 1990s, more and more industries recognize what it means to do business in a world with limited natural resources. Many people today will reject businesses and industries whose products and services harm people and the environment.

As businesses, hotels must do what they can to lessen the effect they have on the environment. This means that cleaning chemicals must be disposed of according to manufacturer's guidelines—not carelessly splashed down a drain or dumped into a garbage can. Properties, too, must examine the chemicals they use. Managers should weigh and measure the effect of using one chemical over another. The socially responsible property looks to less caustic or damaging alternatives to do the job.

Most guests and employees will appreciate a property that uses recycled or "earth-friendly" products. For instance, hotels that use white instead of colored tissue tell guests and employees that they are concerned about possible dyes that can pollute the water. Recycling paper, glass, and aluminum also shows guests and employees that the property cares about the environment—and can trim waste disposal costs. Taking care of the environment no longer belongs to "fringe" environmental groups; it belongs to everyone—individuals and businesses alike. By its very nature, hospitality has the potential to be among the cleanest industries in the world.

Administrative Duties

Looking at your calendar, you see it's getting close to ordering point for linens. You remember the message at your last staff meeting: cut costs or we'll need to cut staff. Since your last order, you've been approached by a new vendor who can meet your property's specifications at a cheaper price. The vendor also offers you a free case of detergent with your first order. You remember reading an article in the paper which pointed out that the supplier is under investigation for violating worker safety conditions.

Most housekeeping managers will tell you that a property has an obligation to purchase the best cleaning supplies, equipment, furnishings, and linens at the best possible price. Managers must also ensure that the products they buy for housekeeping are compatible. For instance, managers can assume that the floor cleaner and finisher they bought from one supplier will work well together. That might not be the case if a manager buys a cleaner from one vendor and the finisher from another.

Most managers, too, will tell you that they also consider the vendor's services when making a purchasing decision. Some vendors will be honest about the quality of the item in comparison to its price; others will not. Some vendors, too, will go out of their way to provide quick, efficient, and accurate delivery; others may not be so conscientious. The ethical purchaser will consider more than whether a supplier simply meets or undercuts the bid; he or she will examine whether the supplier truly meets the property's specifications—without compromising the quality of the product or the service.

Purchasing is closely related to managing housekeeping's inventories. Managers should establish workable par levels for both recycled and non-recycled inventories—and not deviate from those levels. For instance, it is not fair to ask employees to work harder and faster to maintain an inadequate par level of linens; nor is it good business to make guests wait for cleaned rooms. The drawbacks don't end there. Maintaining substandard inventories means that linens and blankets will be used more frequently—

which essentially lessens their shelf life. In the long run, the housekeeping manager will end up spending more money to replace both tired linens and frustrated staff. Finally, shorting guestrooms on amenities can happen when managers maintain substandard inventories of non-recycled items. It is simply poor business for guests to wonder why their business colleagues received shampoo in their room when they didn't.

Human Resources

You're having your first cup of coffee on the morning after an exhaustive week. You just finished interviewing nearly 15 candidates for the three new room attendant positions. After a great deal of thought and evaluation, you've decided on the three people you feel would best fit the job. You ask your secretary to pull the files on the candidates so you can call each person with a job offer.

Minutes before you're ready to start, you get a call from your friend and colleague in the front office. "Have you filled those housekeeping positions yet?" she asks. You tell her no, and that you've closed on your interviews. "Oh dear," Jean says, "I was hoping you hadn't," and she goes on to tell you how her daughter was just laid off and desperately needs a job to help pay for college. "Cheryl has some experience," she says. "Can't you at least interview her?" She adds that Cheryl worked last summer cleaning cabins at a small upstate resort.

Human resources is another area determined by law as well as social responsibility. On a professional level, housekeeping managers must be well-informed on legislation surrounding the hiring and supervision of staff. Just as important, managers must be in touch with themselves. They must recognize their strengths and weaknesses, and must guard against the preferences and experiences that can shadow the choices they make at work. Managers must deal fairly with all employees—which means that actions and policies should be consistently applied, sometimes regardless of how the manager personally feels.

Housekeeping managers must put aside personal biases when recruiting, selecting, and hiring. They must put them aside during orientation and training. Even though legislation prohibits discrimination in the workplace based on sex, race, age, religion, and physical abilities, managers may still subconsciously favor certain types of people. What this means is that a manager may make human resource decisions based on personality traits or attributes that don't necessarily have anything to do with the job. To outsiders, this can appear as favoritism and—unbeknownst to the manager—can even constitute an illegal or unethical practice.

Like any work force, a housekeeping department comes complete with nuances. Managers must consider the types of workers attracted to housekeeping positions, and the special needs associated with their lifestyles. For example, some properties offer alternative scheduling. Variations include part-time and flexible hours, compressed work schedules, and job sharing. Alternative scheduling can help such workers as parents, students, or retirees better rotate the demands of their personal life with work. Such scheduling options can help attract quality employees and boost the morale of existing staff.

The big question concerning human resources is whether a business has an obligation to employees beyond the paycheck. Some managers feel that the biggest thing they do for employees is to pay them. They feel their responsibilities end with paying people fairly for a full day's work—as well as for overtime. Some managers say you owe your workers more than fair pay—you owe them opportunity for personal growth. They might point out, for instance, that a segment of housekeeping employees come from backgrounds that aren't supportive of education or values traditionally associated with work. With this in mind, is management responsible for informing employees of career opportunities in and outside of hospitality? How understanding should managers be of an employee who has problems keeping a work schedule? Or of the employee with a drinking or drug problem? What about the employee who needs help with a family situation, with finances, or expresses an interest in personal growth? Should a manager provide information on agencies and schools that could meet the person's needs?

One point is clear: managers should be accountable for treating all employees fairly and with respect, and for communicating the expectations of the property. This means that employees are paid fairly regardless of their age, marital status, or sex. It means that all employees are given equal opportunities for promotion. It means that discipline is not used as a threat—but as a tool. But it means, most of all, that managers communicate what the property expects from employees—and what employees may expect from the property in return.

Ethics: The Blending of Two Worlds

In addition to your busy schedule as an executive housekeeper, you manage to work two evenings a month at the homeless shelter. You feel particularly proud that you convinced upper management to donate worn linens and blankets to the shelter. The hotel previously threw out these linens, feeling they were unsuitable to use in the guestrooms. Your hotel has a strict policy about not giving used hotel property to employees. You've always felt that throwing out used items was wasteful, and view top management's willingness to donate to charity as a personal victory.

One morning, a floor supervisor tells you that she caught Melinda, a room attendant, stealing sheets and blankets you earmarked for the shelter. She tells you that Melinda apologized profusely, and seemed to be on the brink of tears. "Melinda was very embarrassed," she tells you. "She literally begged me not to tell you. She promises that it won't happen again." Before you say anything, you remember your interview with Melinda nearly a year ago. She struck you as honest and hardworking. You remember, too, that she appeared financially strapped—some might even say she bordered on being truly needy.

You could say that ethics is so closely tied to an individual's sense of right and wrong that it is impossible to separate personal from business ethics. Each of us brings our own standards and values to the job that are based on our backgrounds. We cannot deny that those standards or values—those personal ethics—determine how we respond to workplace situations, policies, and procedures. In some respects, those ethics might be what attracts us to a particular line of work in the first place.

Our personal ethics shape how we behave in the business world—or at least how we feel toward our actions. For many, it is a matter of degree. As a whole, the hospitality industry is feeling the pressures of a shrinking and changing labor force.

More and more, housekeeping departments fill positions with people of differing ages, social and economic backgrounds, levels of ability, or essentially, people with varying standards and values. Housekeeping managers need to be tolerant of and patient with differences. Most of all, they must communicate and instill the property's ethics in a manner everyone understands.

We can conclude with a statement from an ethics seminar given by Bally's Corporation:

> Throughout the ages, thoughtful writers have described a mature responsible adult as a person who consistently makes ethically correct decisions and has the strength of character to follow through on his or her convictions; is temperate in his or her personal habits and business relationships; and is fair in his or her dealings with others. . .mature responsible adults make exceptional business associates; and exceptional associates make great companies.

I believe that employees want to do the very best they can do. They just need the proper motivation, management's trust, and a product they can feel good about and take pride in. Companies should reward honesty by giving public commendations to those employees who perform acts of integrity. Companies cannot help but profit when employees display integrity and commitment to quality.

Endnotes

1. Housekeeping departments today pose many challenges to managers: technological innovations, growing competition, and increasingly sophisticated clientele. To meet these demands, housekeeping executives must have outstanding supervisory skills, technical expertise, and a commitment to high standards.

Educational opportunities and professional certification is available through the American Hotel & Motel Association under the direction of its Educational Institute. By earning the Certified Hospitality Housekeeping Executive designation, housekeeping executives demonstrate their professional commitment and expertise. For further information, contact the Educational Institute—Certification Department, P.O. Box 1240, East Lansing, MI 48826. Telephone: (517) 353-5500.

The National Executive Housekeepers Association, Inc., also offers a variety of educational opportunities that enable housekeepers to improve their proficiency and gain professional recognition. The Registered Executive Housekeeper (REH) and Certified Executive Housekeeper (CEH) designations result from two programs offered through the association. For further information, write: National Executive Housekeepers Association, Education Specialist, 1001 Eastwind Drive, Suite 301, Westerville, OH 43081. Telephone: (614) 895-7166.

2. Rocco M. Angelo and Andrew M. Vladimir, *Hospitality Today: An Introduction* (East Lansing, Mich.: Educational Institute of the American Hotel & Motel Association, 1991), pp. 389–390.

3. Margaret M. Kappa, Aleta Nitschke, and Patricia B. Schappert, *Managing Housekeeping Operations* (East Lansing, Mich.: Educational Institute of the American Hotel & Motel Association, 1990), pp. 146–147.

4. For a detailed review of OSHA regulations and standards, managers should contact local OSHA or U.S. Department of Labor Offices. Readers may also find a more extensive discussion in Kappa, et al., *Managing Housekeeping Operations*, pp. 141–144.

5. Readers desiring further information on guest privacy should consult Jack P. Jefferies, *Understanding Hospitality Law*, 2d ed. (East Lansing, Mich.: Educational Institute of the American Hotel & Motel Association, 1990), 75–79.

Discussion Topics

1. How "ethical" can we expect housekeeping employees to be? Identify some of the obstacles to ethical behavior.

2. How important is it for employees to speak and understand English? Is there an ethical side to this question that management needs to address?

3. An employee notices towels, washcloths, and ash trays in a guest's luggage. How should the situation be handled?

4. How would you handle a guest who offers money for unauthorized services? How should management respond if they are notified of such a situation?

Term Paper Topics

1. Ethics can be defined as "doing what is right." Do cultural differences change the definition of right? If so, how is it possible to develop a code of ethics for housekeeping where several cultures are often represented?

2. Contrast the concept that a guest is entitled to privacy in his or her room with the fact that housekeeping virtually has total access to that privacy. Can conflict occur between the housekeeping department's code of ethics and the guest's personal code of ethics?

11

Ethics and Hotel Engineering

Alan T. Stutts

A fire at the Dupont Plaza Hotel and Casino in San Juan, Puerto Rico, on the afternoon of December 31, 1986, killed 96 persons and seriously injured another 140. According to the National Fire Protection Association (NFPA), "The Dupont Plaza Hotel and Casino fire was among the worst hotel fires in this country, including the 1980 MGM Grand Hotel fire which killed 85 and the 1946 Winecoff Hotel fire in which 119 were killed. Many of the lessons, unfortunately, repeat themselves."[1]

The NFPA found that engineering—or perhaps a lack of engineering—contributed to the severity of the Dupont Plaza fire and the ensuing loss of life.

The Association report noted a lack of automatic sprinklers in the room where the fire began; the report suggested that properly installed and maintained sprinklers would have controlled the fire. Unfortunately, the NFPA has not recorded multiple-death fires in hotel buildings or other buildings of this occupancy type that are fully sprinklered.

The fire was started by an arsonist in combustible materials that had been stored in one of the hotel's ballroom areas. However, it would appear that not only were the combustible materials stored in an insecure area, they also were stored in a location where a combustible partition and interior finish attached to the walls in the room contributed to the fire's rapid spread.

In addition, the NFPA determined that improperly sealed elevator shafts and utility chases, combined with the heating, ventilation, and air conditioning system, circulated the toxic by-products of the fire throughout the high-rise building.

It was also determined that there was no automatic fire detection system present in the hotel complex that could have alerted occupants to the fire. Once it became

Alan T. Stutts is Associate Dean of the College of Hotel Administration at the University of Nevada, Las Vegas. He received his BS and MPA degrees from the University of Arizona and his doctorate from the University of Illinois. He has done extensive work researching engineering and maintenance operations for the hospitality industry. In conjunction with Dr. Frank Borsenik, he has written numerous articles and also a book, The Management of Maintenance and Engineering Systems for the Hospitality Industry *(3d ed., Wiley, 1991).*

necessary to evacuate the premises, exit doors that were improperly secured trapped persons fleeing the fire.

What is interesting about these findings is that they have been known contributors to serious fires, as noted by the NFPA, since the 1940s.

Eliminating Hazards

Based on the organizational structure of a hotel business, each of the problems identified in the Dupont Plaza fire can be influenced by decisions of a hotel's engineering unit. Thus, the question arises as to how problems like those identified at the Dupont Plaza could occur in the first place. The tragedy therefore provides an example from which to explore (a) the opportunities for ethical decision-making presented to a hotel engineering unit and (b) how decisions might emerge that might not be viewed as ethical by outside observers. Peter Drucker commented that there is no such thing as "business ethics," but there is an ethical side to enterprise.[2]

Questions

Questions for the engineer at the Dupont Plaza might include the following:

- Why were there design errors in this building that could allow smoke from a fire to move throughout the structure?
- Why were combustible interior furnishings permitted?
- Why were combustible materials not stored or secured?
- Although not required, why was an automatic fire sprinkler system not designed into the building?
- Why were exits not inspected for ease of use in an emergency?
- Why was the alarm system not designed to alert guests in a timely manner?

It has been noted that ethics in business is rooted in moral values and moral actions—moral values being basic ideals considered desirable for human interaction, and moral actions being the overt expressions and applications of these underlying values. Believing that the health and safety of the guest should be protected is a moral value; acting on that belief is a legal duty as well. Thus, installing and maintaining automatic fire sprinkler systems directed toward such purposes are legal as well as moral actions. Exhibit 1 lists those legal and moral actions that are examples of a belief in guest health and safety. While there are financial costs associated with moral values, an organization can become high-profit, high-ethic.

Ethics in Engineering

To fully understand how the ethics of a hotel engineering unit might be questioned in light of an incident like the Dupont Plaza tragedy, the relationship between organizational culture and ethics must be explored.

Exhibit 1   Legal and Moral Measures for Guest Health and Safety

---

**Legal and Moral Actions for Hotel
Engineering Units Concerning the Health and Safety of Guests**

Protection From Fire

- Compliance with all required local and state codes.

- Compliance with nationally recognized voluntary standards.

- Evaluation of interior furnishings for their combustion potential, primarily combustion temperature, flame spread, and release of toxic gas.

- Provision of smoke detection devices for each living unit, public area, as well as storage and equipment areas.

- Alarm systems/procedures that acknowledge to the building occupants, management personnel, and fire department officials that an emergency exists and fire detection or suppression devices have been activated.

- Provision of each living unit, public area, as well as a storage area with fire suppression devices.

- Adequately and properly maintained emergency exiting.

- Proper maintenance of fire-detection and suppression equipment.

Protection From Tap Water Scalds

Protection From Electrical Shocks

Protection From Trips and Falls

Protection from Assault and Theft

Protection From Contaminated Indoor Air

Adapted from Alan T. Stutts, *The Travel Safety Handbook* (New York: Van Nostrand Reinhold, 1990).

Organizational Culture and Ethics

Organizational culture can be rooted in a value structure from which moral directives emerge. This defines appropriate moral actions. However, the organizational culture may not encompass moral values—some individuals may condone immoral acts while others fail to consider them. It has been aptly stated that some organizational cultures are neither moral nor immoral, just amoral.[3]

Others observe that the organizational culture is often unseen and unobserved, but it is behind organizational activities that can be seen and observed.[4]

It is generally agreed that an organization's culture comprises shared and accepted assumptions. An assumption is accepted if it is primary in the organization's day-to-day operations and for the most part taken for granted by organizational members. Moral values might be included in the culture, especially if they dictate standards or norms of conduct that guide members in their day-to-day decisions.

In a hotel engineering unit, this might occur on the level of the operating engineer. For example, if an engineer determines that an exit door from the property presents a safety hazard and local fire codes dictate that the door be repaired immediately, a strong moral value of commitment to protecting guest safety and security would result when the engineer repairs the door immediately. On the level of the chief engineer, a strong moral value of protecting guest safety and security would result if he or she encourages installation of state-of-the-art life-saving systems and recommends appropriate technological or structural changes to secure this end.

Organizational culture seemingly emerges as a result of nurturing and development over time. A moral culture is dependent on clearly established moral values, the highest priority being given to moral values, constant maintenance of moral values, and internalized moral values.

Unethical acts in an organization are by and large performed by essentially honest people—people who feel they are under great pressure to achieve. In their desire to win, they compromise themselves.

Moral Values

In defining moral values within an organization, Sathe observed that while codes of conduct and statements by the top brass help establish moral values for doing business, they generally identify very broad clarifications of an organization's expectations, but rarely specify the details that may generate ethical conflicts for organizational members.[5] For example, a moral directive might specify to the engineer that the life safety system should be inspected quarterly. A moral value might hold that any condition on the property that could create a hazardous situation for the guest is wrong. Typically, a moral directive is a specific element of more general moral values. The engineer could adhere to a specific directive and still violate the intent of the value. However, the engineer cannot comply with the value unless the directive is obeyed.

For an organization to be successful in establishing moral values, more than codes and statements are involved. Typically, the consideration of underlying moral values begins with orientation and training. Establishing moral values should be a joint process, shared by employees and managers alike. Imposing targets on people violates their fundamental concept of self-determination.

Ethical issues should become part of the decision-making process (e.g., exceed local code requirements, such as doing a retrofit with keyless locks, installing automatic fire sprinkler systems, etc.). The strategic, economic, and ethical issues must be addressed. Engaging in this type of discussion increases the significance of moral values and ritualizes their inclusion as a part of the decision-making process.

Once moral values are established, they become a high priority in the daily operations of the engineering unit. For example, the sealing and repair of poke-throughs (created by telephone and cable TV installations), which are often hidden from public view, must be done before the turf is mowed in front of the property.

Priority and Consistency

Priority and consistency often present a dilemma for the engineering unit. Once a moral value is clearly established, its priority will be evaluated by organization members, particularly when value conflicts begin to occur. For example, if the chief engineer recommends a retrofit to install automatic fire sprinklers but the property opts instead to expand the existing parking lot to accommodate additional tour buses, the importance of life safety is diminished.

Consistency in applying moral values is critical if they are to be successful. For example, it is absolutely essential that the chief engineer does not hold the engineering unit to a different set of values than he or she demonstrates. It is also critical that a similar perception of value is recognized and practiced by first-line, mid-level, and top management. Some organizations committed to ethical operations have generated ethics hot lines and ethics ombudsmen.

Internalization of Moral Values

When the members of an engineering unit identify with, accept as their own, and are willing to apply the moral values promoted by the organization, the values are internalized. A strong belief that it is in the best interest of the organizational member to do so is essential for this process of internalization to occur. Internalization is reinforced when an organization rewards and disciplines according to the desired ethic. This means that the engineering unit would include ethical behavior as part of the formal performance evaluation for each member in the unit. In some organizations, for compensation purposes, as much as fifty percent of an employee's rating is based on non-financial elements that are not measurable on the bottom line.

Reviewing Actions

There must also be some planned process for constantly reviewing the actions of the people within the engineering unit. As painful as it may be, penalties must be imposed on those who have broken any of the codes of ethical conduct in the company. The unit's disciplinary process must quickly and uniformly impose disciplinary actions on members who violate ethical standards. Any occurrence outside the norm must become widely known as quickly as possible. Typically, the informal communication network is a highly effective medium for spreading news. Punishments must be prompt, certain, and appropriate to the gravity of the case. Unfortunately, the majority of organizations with an ethics committee do not have a panel that sits in judgment of violators.

The problem is not that ethics is irrelevant to an engineering unit, but that ethical issues have usually been left to fend for themselves. Often, the problems associated with day-to-day operations (e.g., budgeting, staffing, etc.) cause the engineer to lose sight of the ethical implications of a decision.

According to Pastin, building a high-ethics, high-profit work unit is a bootstrapping operation.[6] It is started by questioning the accepted answers, asking hard questions about the accepted answers, trying out some new answers, and then asking why once again.[7]

Other Safety Issues

As indicated in Exhibit 1, other questions of safety should also be addressed by the engineering unit. There must be protection from assault and theft, tap water scalds, electrical shock, and contaminated air. While these protections are governed by codes, regulations, and standards, they also require ethical decisions in areas of purchasing and maintenance. They must not be overlooked in the interest of bottom-line success. The engineering unit's day-to-day operation in managing and reviewing sub-contracts and the potential for quality substitutions in construction and renovation also have an implication for an ethical standard of operation.

Ethical and Moral Conduct in the Dupont Plaza Fire

The fire at the Dupont Plaza Hotel represents a classic case for considering the ethical and moral conduct of the office of chief engineer and the engineering department staff. It also represents a classic case for recognizing obstacles that are often faced by the engineering department in its quest to do its job correctly.

The Dupont Plaza Hotel was one of seven properties organized under the same corporate structure. The plaintiffs in the case raised the issue as to whether the time preceding the fire was perhaps one of fiscal restraint. Such a period often means "reduce repair and maintenance costs." Engineering staffing is also a prominent target for several reasons:

- Management often does not know what engineers do with their time.

- Engineers generally command higher wages than other employees.

- Engineers are not always perceived to be directly related to providing guest service and satisfaction.

- It generally takes a period of time before a reduction of maintenance shows up in the hotel's operations, leading managers to believe they can reverse their decisions before they have to pay the price for any reductions. Engineering departments that are understaffed might set aside certain types of work that they feel are not essential.

In the case of the Dupont Plaza, allegations of serious breaches of legal duty were made. The hotel carried fire and casualty insurance in the amount of $1 million, which, in light of the subsequent judgment, was not enough. It is common for hotels the size of the Dupont to carry more than $1 million.

The plaintiffs questioned whether or not the management company took any actions in the period following the fire that might have isolated the Dupont Plaza from the other properties under the management structure. This, obviously, would have restricted the losses to the Dupont Plaza alone.

The case was ultimately settled out of court for $120 million—an amount that seemed to indicate that the Dupont's responsibility went beyond the hotel itself and rested with the overall management company. As a result of the judgment, the company sold some of its properties to meet legal obligations.

During the case, other allegations were made; for example, it was questioned whether the front desk was instructed not to inform other guests in the hotel that there was a fire in one part of the property—the rationale being "not to upset the guests."

Further, it was alleged that during the week preceding the fire management had become aware of arson threats but did not take precautions to prevent or try to prevent arson.

The case took two years to resolve and included more than 135 witnesses (many of them experts) and 150 attorneys. A special series of "courtrooms" was constructed in Puerto Rico to accommodate all the interested parties. Closed-circuit TV linked the rooms together.

Engineering's Responsibility

Unique among the departments of the hotel, engineering has the responsibility for the proper care and maintenance of both equipment and systems that would be life-threatening to guests and employees if not managed properly. For example, boilers and pressure vessels might explode if safeties malfunction or are circumvented. Elevators are, of course, obvious safety hazards if not properly maintained. Cooling towers and/or signs mounted on the hotel rooftop can be very hazardous if not kept in proper working order and if their structural support systems are not checked and maintained. Mortar in the joints of parapet cap stones, lintels, and even fire brick can erode and, if not inspected and corrected, cause debris to fall to the street below.

In terms of systems, there are the obvious alarms and evacuation devices. However, besides the mechanical factor there is the human element. A properly equipped and trained fire brigade, organized and administered by the engineering department, requires fully trained people with proper tools who can rapidly respond to an emergency.

For example, one major international chain has developed a system by which a team of persons is activated on receipt of a floor alarm. An engineer immediately takes a fully equipped fire cart adjacent to a freight elevator, which is automatically called to that floor, and then heads for the scene. A front desk employee (the desk is staffed day and night) grabs a portable rescue kit and heads for the scene as well. The fire department is automatically put on notice. Other employees are activated to assist in evacuation if needed. On arriving at the scene—in less than two minutes—the team uses the fire cart to handle the problem.

In most cases, the emergency is expected to be an in-room fire caused by smoking in bed. The cart contains a master key, pry bar, chain cutters, asbestos blanket and gloves, rope, flashlight, CO_2 extinguisher, and smoke mask. In more than 13 years, the chain's record regarding loss of life in such fires is 100% safe—and that includes more than 50 operating properties. This safety record can be achieved, but it requires motivation, constant training, rigorous standards, and *support from management*. Without the latter, no system will prove fully effective.

When management does not provide verbal and psychological support, or, more commonly, financial support, the engineering department cannot ensure public safety and therefore places the employees and guests in danger. In these cases, the chief engineer has few options. Constant pressure on management is not going to be appreciated or tolerated; neither will whistle-blowing to relevant governmental inspection agencies.

Generally speaking, the chief engineer's only choice is to leave, making the reasons for departure clearly known. He or she can then seek employment where management has a better understanding and appreciation for the relationship of engineering to the health, safety, and welfare of the employees and guests. Giving up a lucrative, relatively secure job to separate oneself from a situation that could endanger others is not always an easy decision, but it is always the ethical and moral decision of choice.

Conclusion

In general, an engineering unit that wishes to create an ethical standard of operation must focus attention on the establishment of moral values. It must give these values a visible and consistent priority and encourage their internalization through supervisory example, reward, and discipline.

Endnotes

1. National Fire Protection Association, *Fire at the Dupont Plaza Hotel and Casino* (Quincy, Mass.: National Fire Protection Association, 1987).

2. Peter E. Drucker, "Ethical Chic," *Forbes*, September 14, 1981, pp. 160–173.

3. Archie B. Carroll, "In Search of the Moral Manager," *Business Horizons,* March-April, 1987, pp. 7–15.

4. Jay M. Shafritz and J. Steven Ott, "The Organization Culture School," in *Classics of Organization Theory* (Chicago: Dorsey, 1987), pp. 373–380.

5. Vijay Sathe, *Culture and Related Corporate Realities* (Homewood, Ill.: Irwin, 1985), p. 11.

6. Mark Pastin, "Lessons from High-Profit, High-Ethics Companies: An Agenda for Managerial Action," in *The Hard Problems of Management: Gaining the Ethics Edge* (San Francisco: Jossey-Bass, 1986), Chapter 11, pp. 218–228.

7. Ibid.

Discussion Topics

1. As chief engineer, you present to your manager information concerning a fire safety hazard that exists in the building, and you are ignored. What actions would you take and why?

2. As chief engineer, you become aware of new technology that will improve the level of life safety in the building. After presenting this information to your manager, you are told to purchase the technology. The manager says the cost will have to come from your personal budget, resulting in layoffs. What would you do and why?

3. Is it ethical for a chief engineer to accept a gift from a vendor with whom the company has done business in the past, but is not planning on doing business with in the next 12 months? Why?

4. If a property's provision of life safety technology exceeds minimum requirements, is it ethical for the property to use this information in its marketing and advertising? Why?

Term Paper Topics

1. Interview five general managers and their chief engineers— two from a small, independently owned property, one from a large corporate property, one from a hospital,

and one from a country club. Contrast their opinions as to whether their respective properties should simply meet or exceed fire codes. Analyze the ethical implications of their opinions.

2. Discuss with five chief engineers the word "ethics." Ask each chief engineer what implications ethics has for his or her job. At the same properties, interview three operating engineers and compare their responses with those of the chief engineer for that property. Evaluate any differences between the chief and the operating engineers and discuss why differences might exist.

12

Ethics and the Question of Security

James V. Papazian

If any one person can have an impact on the ethical considerations within an entity like a hotel, it is the person who is directly in charge of the security department. This is typically the director of security.

Security ultimately affects the profitability of any business, from a department store to a hotel. During the past decade, society has been engulfed in a litigation explosion, a time when courts have consistently decided that severe financial penalties can be imposed on hotels for failing to provide due care to guests as well as employees. Consequently, many institutions, especially those in the hospitality field, have been forced into incorporating a strong and competent security department within the organization.

Harvey Burstein, one of the foremost security experts in the United States, has defined security as the protection and conservation of assets. Ethics is undoubtedly inherent in Burstein's definition because ethics is a means to the end of achieving the desired goals of any hotel security department. Failing to address ethical concerns within any business structure will not maximize the protection given its assets, which can range from merchandise to human lives.

In a sense, both terms, ethics and security, rely on each other. If one or the other element is missing in an operation, the organization can find itself in a precarious situation.

In considering ethical issues inherent in providing security in a hotel, it is imperative that the organization make an effort to hire and retain employees with favorable ethical qualities. If ethics can be defined as a set of moral principles or values (*Webster's Ninth New Collegiate Dictionary*, 1984), then it is clearly evident that the human condition is predicated upon motivational behavior comprising a diversified set of principles and values. What may be morally right for one person may not be right for another. As a result, the work force may include people with different moral standards.

James Papazian is Director of Security for the Flatley Company (Hotel Division), which owns and operates thirteen franchised hotels and resorts in the Northeastern United States. He is a graduate of Saint Anselm College with a BS degree in criminal justice, and he holds an MS in criminal justice and security administration from Northeastern University.

Policies and Procedures

Because of the diversity of people's moral standards, top-level management must provide ethical guidance to assist employees in proper decision-making. In the security department, the director of security has this responsibility. It is apparent, then, that security directors who themselves are unethical will only cause grave harm to their properties. Therefore, it is essential that security managers possess character traits reflecting maximum honesty, truthfulness, and integrity. They must display these traits both on and off the job.

To communicate favorable moral qualities, the organization must develop and implement policies and procedures that can be clearly understood by all employees. Employees must be informed about what is the right thing to do as it applies to each item in their job descriptions. For example, in virtually all hospitality operations, employees are informed that stealing is grounds for immediate dismissal. Regardless of a person's own standards or moral beliefs, he or she should be inclined not to steal because it could result in being caught and subsequently fired.

The existence of clear policies and procedures is important. But it is equally important to ensure that these policies and procedures are distributed and made accessible to employees, and incorporated in employee training programs.

For example, how does a hotel distinguish the legitimacy of action in the removal of property by its employees? A policy and procedure applicable to a clearance system is necessary to differentiate between ethical and unethical intentions. This can normally be found in a package/pass program whereby the employee is required to produce a pass signed by his or her department head prior to exiting with the item in question. Such a system, supplemented by a bag check by security personnel, will provide a policy and procedure of checks and balances.

The existence of policies and procedures is important. But it is equally important that these policies and procedures be properly distributed and made accessible to employees, as well as incorporated in employee training programs.

Adherence to Ethical Standards

A hotel security department can have a significant impact on how employees conform to expected standards of conduct. Because this department is often involved with some controversial activity, security personnel often find themselves under scrutiny by other departments. This in itself can be advantageous, provided the department is a strong and competent component.

It is imperative that all hotel employees be equipped with favorable people skills, especially those working in the security department. Without these skills, the department's objectives of protecting and conserving assets will be difficult to achieve. Above all, the director must have maximum exposure to all employees to the extent that names are familiar and smiles commonly exchanged. A good rapport between security and the other departments will readily achieve the desired objectives.

For example, I found from my own experience as a security director that it was imperative to maintain a favorable rapport between the housekeeping and security departments. Housekeeping is generally the largest department in terms of personnel, and in most cases it is extremely vulnerable to potential unethical employee behavior such as stealing from guestrooms.

As director, I was responsible for ensuring that my staff conducted a thorough investigation into each report of missing or lost property from guestrooms. Our approach was persistent and professional. Investigations included questioning guests as well as employees who had access to the rooms. Not always were allegations of theft resolved, but we did gain the respect of other departments in the hotel because of the way we did our job.

Our approach certainly had a deterrent effect on any employee thinking about stealing from a guest or fellow employee. To have done so would have resulted in an extensive investigation. It must be noted that most allegations of theft are often fraudulent or result from contributory negligence by the guests claiming the loss. Compensation from the hotel is the motivating factor. Therefore, there are occasions when alleged claims of unethical conduct have no merit and are based solely on intentions of being compensated.

Consistent enforcement of a company's code of ethics with its policies and procedures cannot be overemphasized. While management must assist security in this area, enforcement is the primary responsibility of the security department. As previously mentioned, employees represent a diverse group of morals, standards, and values. If these postures are permitted to be expressed without the benefit of controls, they may lead to chaotic and potentially unethical employee behavior.

Security Personnel

Security department personnel must be of the highest moral character if they are to be effective. Any course of action by these staff members that is contrary to the established code of ethics not only displays hypocrisy, but it also justifies similar actions by others. It is not enough that security personnel adhere to policies; they must also maintain higher standards of conduct than non-security personnel. This applies both on and off the job.

I recall a young man I employed as a security officer who was enrolled at the local university on a part-time basis. Now, one common element always present in a hotel environment is the relative ease with which gossip flows. I had this in mind when I received unsubstantiated word from a number of sources that this officer had the tendency to steal jewelry while off duty attending parties. This was obviously an issue of grave concern because security personnel are entrusted with unlimited access to the entire hotel. Prior to my initiating an investigation into these allegations, the young man terminated his employment. Had he not, I was obligated to investigate his alleged conduct to substantiate guilt or innocence in order to determine his employment status.

On another occasion, I had the unfortunate experience of having one of my better officers show up in the lobby in the middle of the night, while off duty, wearing nothing but a scant towel around his waist and conducting himself in a belligerent fashion. Evidently, he had attended a party at a nearby apartment complex and indulged in too many cocktails. After determining all the facts the following morning, I was forced to terminate his employment.

Security must lead by example, and the young man's actions clearly demonstrated unethical behavior. Thus, I had no other recourse. I must emphasize that when it is decided to terminate an individual's employment, the decision must be totally justified. Investigations must be thorough. In order to make ethical decisions, one must develop, as much as possible, foundations based on facts.

But I also had to take into account other ethical considerations with regard to terminating the young man who had too much to drink. Ethically, I felt obligated in some way to help him come to grips with an obvious alcohol problem. However, we should also be aware that there are legal issues to consider when dealing with employees we suspect are having alcohol problems.

Good managers treat their staff members as family. They treat them with respect, dignity, and sincerity. They address employees' concerns with utmost attention, no matter how trivial they seem. The benefits of such a policy are numerous. Managers must assume many roles, not only as supervisors, but also as teachers, friends, and counselors. A manager who forgets that people are his or her most valuable asset is doomed to failure.

Keeping this in mind, let us return to the employee whom I terminated for public drunkenness. He had been employed at the property for almost three years, working full time while attending college. I had heard from another source about his drinking episodes. Although the young man's apparent alcoholism never affected his job performance, I was concerned for his welfare. Thus, I had met with him on several earlier occasions to discuss his problem. During these meetings, he denied having any problems with alcohol. In the end, however, the problem did affect his job performance in a major way and his employment was ultimately terminated.

Several days after firing him, I became concerned about his welfare and his future, so I took him to dinner. At this point, he finally admitted that he had an alcohol problem. It was evident that he was extremely remorseful. He was embarrassed by his actions and sorry for letting me down. It was apparent the young man had finally recognized that his problems were related to alcohol.

This individual had been a valuable member of my department and possessed extraordinary intelligence and people skills. Recognizing this, I took a chance a few months later and referred him to another security director in town. The director hired him and he quickly rose to the top of a staff of 25 persons. He eventually obtained his college degree. He has abstained from alcohol since the towel episode and is successfully employed as one of the top security directors for a large corporation.

Contemporary society has seen a significant increase in drug dependency among people of all ages. Many times, unethical behavior in the workplace, such as embezzlement, can originate from this dependency. When unethical behavior is exposed and termination results, there are occasions when management should be ethically responsible for helping the person involved, either through detoxification or other rehabilitation programs.

Avoidance of Double Standards

All too often, I have seen hotels employ double standards with regard to their employees, especially with line employees and management. For example, numerous properties stipulate that all employees must use the employee entrance when entering or exiting the building. In reality, however, while line employees are required to use this entrance, managers continually use whatever access point is convenient.

Although you may question the ethical significance of this situation, the example is quite valid. Being ethical can be defined as knowing what is right and having the will to carry out that action. The fact that the property's regulations stipulate that the employee entrance is the only one to be used—and that this regulation has been communicated to the employees—satisfies the requirement that the employee knows the right thing to do. The important issue, however, is whether the employee has the will to do what is right. If opportunities to enter and exit elsewhere are minimized by the threat of disciplinary action, the employee can be enticed to adhere to the rules. In most instances, security can be a motivating factor in stimulating acceptable behavior.

Not to be overlooked is the fact that one of the main reasons for using one entrance and exit point is to properly monitor employees as they leave the property. Some hotels have instituted bag searches at this entrance/exit point. Doing so reduces internal theft, an unethical act. Again, this equates with mandating conformance to acceptable standards of conduct.

As previously mentioned, double standards are all too often prevalent in organizations. Many hotels forbid employees from consuming alcohol on the property. Violation of this rule can be grounds for terminating employment. Quite often, however, a manager can be found in the lounge after work enjoying a cocktail. Management may believe that the act itself is harmless, but the prudent executive will recognize the inherent dangers associated with double standards and take action to rectify a potentially dangerous practice.

Training to Enhance Ethics

It is often said that a security director is not only a salesman but also an educator. I am convinced that the director of security is the best teacher for instilling a sense of ethics in the hotel's work force

All new employees must attend some form of orientation prior to performing their duties. This orientation presents an opportune time for the director of security to not only acquaint himself or herself with the new employees, but also to instruct them in such critical areas as fire safety, alcohol service policies, and first aid techniques.

During the orientation, the director must project a genuine concern for the employee's welfare and, at the same time, display a warm and friendly appearance. Establishing this kind of rapport will be beneficial later when the security department seeks the cooperation of these employees in security-related matters. The director should tell the new employees what is expected from them and why certain procedures are necessary.

It should be quite obvious that communication is of utmost importance. You should communicate regulations in a low-key fashion and encourage employees to view you as representing their best interests. Many times, ethical behavior can be encouraged by explaining to employees the repercussions of improper actions such as employee theft. This approach is particularly helpful if the property has a profit-sharing benefit. In this case, it should be pointed out that internal losses can significantly reduce potential earnings.

I ended every orientation I conducted by asking everyone to remain vigilant during their shifts for any suspicious activities and to confidentially contact the security department if they observed anything. Employees were constantly reminded of this during their employment, and as a result many potential problems were avoided because employees cooperated. Security has to be everyone's business.

But training does not end with orientation. In fact, it represents a beginning of what is hoped will be a long relationship between employer and employee. The director of security must continually work with all departments to provide the necessary guidance in promoting ethical behavior. During my own career as a director of security, I attended a majority of departmental meetings to achieve this objective.

For example, I was responsible for teaching the Heimlich Maneuver to all restaurant employees so that their immediate action might one day save someone's life. In fact, this training provided an employee with the knowledge to save a patron's life on two separate occasions. The employee was prepared to act when the occasion demanded it.

Morale within the work force is often an important factor in determining whether employees will adhere to standards and operate in an ethical manner. Poor morale will most likely promote unethical behavior, while high morale will breed high ethical standards that could raise profit margins for the property.

Higher profits can mean higher wages, but we must ask what employees receive besides weekly paychecks. If the answer is nothing, then we are vulnerable to having disgruntled employees on our hands, a situation that can lead to disastrous results.

Training: The Security Officer

We have already pointed out that security officers must maintain a higher standard of ethical qualities than other employees. Therefore, security management must ensure a high level of morale. Specialized training for this group is necessary by virtue of the duties they are expected to perform.

When interviewing potential employees for the security department, I realized that each individual was trying to market himself or herself. On the other hand, I was tasked with selling the job in order to obtain the best possible candidate. I told applicants why their best interests would be served by working for our hotel. I carefully explained that the benefits derived from working for our department encompassed the training standards that were required to be met prior to becoming a security officer. At the conclusion of the interviews, the applicants walked away knowing that if they were hired their employment would undoubtedly lead to self-improvement, something that would result in greater career opportunity in the future.

In my experience, specialized training might include such things as CPR/first aid techniques, crisis intervention procedures, liquor liability, special police officer powers, and criminal and civil law instruction. I have found that training in these areas gives security personnel the sense of purpose that builds a foundation of dedication and commitment toward the hotel. As a result, high ethical standards become a characteristic of the department. Turnover is low, and security personnel gain the respect of other employees in the hotel.

From a practical as well as an ethical perspective, the single most important training a hotel must provide for security personnel is CPR/first aid procedures. Not having security personnel certified in this training is a disservice to both guests and employees. Security personnel usually respond to most requests for emergency medical assistance, and their role should be greater than just calling for an ambulance—especially in a case of cardiac arrest. Having been a security director at a large urban hotel, I have waited as long as 45 minutes for an ambulance to respond.

Due to this unpredictability of medical response, hotels should be prepared to offer first-response medical attention. As noted earlier, the security department is frequently called on to provide this care. If a guest suddenly collapsed in the lobby from a heart attack, security personnel on the scene would be expected to apply CPR techniques. But first they must have been properly trained.

In addition to ensuring that all its security personnel are trained in life-saving techniques, the prudent hoteliers will make certain that key management personnel are also trained. Failure to do so can result in devastating consequences and can determine life or death. Such training can be construed as the highest of all ethical considerations.

The director of security should become involved with various types of training and the certification of other department personnel. Using training as a means of exposing the department to the entire employee population emphasizes the importance of determining the moral quality of a course of action an employee should take in a particular situation.

For example, the director is required to give instruction on liquor liability and crisis intervention to personnel working in liquor outlets as well as at the front desk. Now, consider the case of a young front desk clerk who has completed the mandatory training and who now finds herself confronted by an obviously intoxicated guest intent on getting into his car and driving somewhere. Having been adequately trained, the clerk intercepts the intoxicated guest before he can exit the hotel and uses the skills she learned to persuade him to call a taxi. She may very well have prevented one or more traffic fatalities.

The preceding example illustrates an extreme ethical situation the front desk clerk was forced to respond to. We must examine the repercussions that might have occurred if the guest was permitted to leave the property and drive away. First and most important, there was a strong possibility that the guest or others could have been killed or injured. Second, the hotel and its parent organization could then face a significant financial loss resulting from a civil lawsuit. Third, if loss of life did in fact result, those persons involved with serving the guest alcohol and those who failed to take action could suffer psychological stress. Finally, the hotel could face a harmful public relations situation and risk losing its liquor license.

Businesses, including hotels, tend to compromise on employee training programs because of financial concerns. When a hotel is faced with this situation, the director of security should prepare cost-effective training programs and point out what can happen if management fails to implement these programs.

Most of these training programs involve issues of ethics. Fire training for all employees pertains to what course of action to take during an emergency. Fire safety instruction is mainly predicated on preserving human life in the event of an emergency.

A code of ethics co-exists with criminal and civil law, as well as with the fundamental moral values that society as a whole observes. That being the case, a security director who gives classes to beverage outlets in a hotel on how to spot fraudulent identification associated with underage drinking can satisfy not only the house policy, but the legal requirements as well.

Ethics and the Guest

Anytime an individual registers at a hotel, a relationship exists between the two. Security at the hotel is one important element in its relationship with its guests. Imagine the negative impact on a hotel's reputation if the hotel failed to address such minor problems as noise complaints.

Security plays a key role with ethics as it pertains not only to the hotel's work force, but also to the guests themselves. On one occasion, one of my security officers found a guest who had apparently been drinking excessively to be incoherent and stumbling in a hallway. Confirming the identity and registered guest status of the person, the officer assisted the guest to his room. After having been placed on his bed, the guest immediately passed out. The officer situated the person on his stomach, because allowing him to remain on his back could cause him to aspirate on his own vomit. The man was checked on several occasions throughout the evening because the hotel was concerned for his welfare. The above actions satisfied ethical responsibility by the security department.

What about a situation where a room attendant discovers a gun under a pillow while making a bed? In this actual case, a maid immediately notified security. Security personnel immediately went to the room, but the registered guest was not there. To avoid further disturbance to a possible crime scene, the door was double-locked to prevent accessibility. When the guest returned to his room, security was contacted and I in turn responded to meet the occupant. I explained to him how the gun was found and the applicable state law regarding a permit for firearms. I also explained that under no circumstances were guns permissible on the property (with the exception of those carried by law enforcement agents—this hotel's policy) and that if the weapon were held under permit, the hotel had to retain the gun in a safety deposit box. The man produced a valid license and we consequently stored the weapon for the remainder of his stay.

Security must use discretion at all times. In the preceding example, calling the police initially could have been an option, but without evidence of any crime and keeping in mind the privacy of a guest, the situation was handled in the correct fashion. Failure by the hotel to take action would in itself be construed as unethical.

Guests expect certain ethical standards when they stay at a hotel. For example, they do not expect to smell marijuana as they walk down a hallway nor to be kept awake all night by a loud party. In situations like these, a hotel must have a strong and competent security department.

Minimizing Opportunities for Unethical Behavior

Hotel management is responsible for minimizing the opportunity for unethical behavior. I am often amused when a general manager is bewildered because food and beverage costs are outrageous, yet there are no inventory controls for the storeroom. Being naive to the fact that employees are capable of stealing can devastate bottom-line profit margins.

If we demand ethical behavior on the part of our employees, we must minimize the attractive nuisances that too commonly exist at hotels. If the designated employee parking area is adjacent to the loading dock, do we not have a higher risk of losing assets by means of one's vehicle? Is surveillance equipment used to monitor high-value item areas such as the liquor storeroom? Is a good key control system in place to prevent unauthorized entries? Is lighting sufficient to deter potential acts of theft? Are proper access/egress controls in place to monitor what is being brought in as well as what is taken out? What controls exist to cover after-hours requisitions in the food and beverage storeroom?

While we may demand from our employees behavior that corresponds to the ethical guidelines we dictate, management must implement strategies that prevent employees from committing an unethical act. Doing so not only promotes ethics but also facilitates the realization of profits.

Gaining Assistance for Achieving Ethical Goals

Networking by security departments at different properties is of vital importance and is often the most valuable resource available to the director. Many hotels have similar problems, thus it is extremely beneficial to share information and discuss strategies to rectify problematic situations.

For example, many cities have security director associations that meet on a monthly basis. Guest speakers and open discussions make up most agendas. The knowledge gained from attending can be advantageous and can assist security departments in operational improvements.

One particular city I worked in had a computerized network in which a majority of hotel security departments were on-line with each other to communicate criminal activities that took place at each property. Many hotels are victimized by the same perpetrators, and this system allowed for the necessary precautions to be taken. For example, several credit card frauds were avoided through advance warning.

Insurance companies can be important allies in shaping the ethical composition of a hotel. Due to mutual concerns, many of these companies offer training and services that promote safety as well as security to minimize losses. Such services should be used when available.

Conclusion

Ethics, as applied in a hotel or any other institution, involves human behavior. Human beings are products of their environments, and these environments form individualized values and standards of conduct constituting the ethical and moral makeup of each person.

Coping with these differences in the workplace entails the establishment of a code of ethics that coincides with the rules and regulations of the hotel. Without guidelines of this type, different values and standards of conduct are sure to clash. It is therefore necessary to create a climate in which acceptable standards of conduct are understood by all and consistently enforced.

The security department is challenged with enforcing the rules and regulations of the hotel. Without the benefit of this department, a system of checks and balances is difficult to maintain.

Although not every employee is ethical, it is still possible to motivate people to conduct themselves in an ethical fashion. The security director and his or her staff are responsible for encouraging ethical behavior, which can be facilitated through the establishment of necessary controls. In essence, unethical people can be transformed into ethical employees. A simple locking mechanism supplemented by a strong key control policy will prevent a thief from stealing by not giving him or her the opportunity. Thus, greater profits are realized.

Security plays an important role in educating all employees about the right way to do things, while at the same time providing guidance in the will to act accordingly through enforcement practices.

Discussion Topics

1. While cleaning a guestroom, a room attendant observes a large amount of white powder along with syringes and other drug paraphernalia in open view on the dresser. What course of action should the room attendant and the security department take?

2. As security director, you learn that one of your officers has been involved with a petty theft while off duty. Prior to substantiating the allegations, the officer voluntarily resigns. The officer's job performance has always been exemplary. The following day, the security department in another hotel calls you for a background check subsequent to employing this officer. How should you respond to the inquiry?

3. What obligation does upper management have in providing the resources for building a solid, competent, and ethical security department?

4. A senior-level manager is observed taking an expensive case of champagne from the liquor storeroom during the early morning hours and exiting with the merchandise through an unauthorized back door. You are a security guard. What do you do and why?

Term Paper Topics

1. Taking into consideration the diverse moral makeup employees may represent in a hotel, formulate and implement effective controls that promote favorable ethical qualities and, at the same time, maximize hotel profits. Incorporate fundamental legal concerns into these controls, if applicable.

2. Security departments are regulated by sources of law—i.e., statutes. Identify these sources and highlight points of conflict that may arise when applied to ethical concerns.

13

Hospitality Ethics: A Marketing Perspective

Margaret Shaw

When you think about ethics, issues of morality, justice, fairness, integrity, and social responsibility usually come to mind. When you think about marketing, sales and advertising usually come to mind. In the first case, the assumption is valid: ethics is directly concerned with justice, fairness, and human decency. In the second case, the assumption may not be so valid: advertising and sales are certainly part of marketing but they do not constitute its core.

According to Lewis and Chambers, marketing is "communicating to and giving the target market customers what they want, when they want it, where they want it, at a price they are willing to pay."[1] Obviously, the cornerstone of marketing is the customer, and it is customer satisfaction that drives the marketing decision. But ethical considerations must be part of that decision, too.

Hospitality marketing professionals, like those in any industry, are responsible for delivering to customers what they want, when they want it, where they want it, and at a price they are willing and able to pay. Imbedded here is a social responsibility.

Marketers have a mandate to instill ethical standards for individual and societal concerns as an inherent part of their marketing profession. The *Random House Dictionary* emphasizes this point by its very definition of "ethical": "in accordance with the rules or standards for right conduct or practice, especially the standards of a profession."

The marketing profession is very much aware of its particular responsibility for upholding ethical standards and practices. Laczniak and Murphy explain this point:

> Within the business firm, the functional area most closely related to ethical abuse is marketing. This is because marketing is the function of business charged with communicating [to] and openly satisfying customers. Thus, marketing is closest

Margaret Shaw, PhD, is Associate Professor of Marketing at the University of Guelph, School of Hotel and Food Administration, in Ontario, Canada. She holds BS, MBA, and doctorate degrees from Cornell University. Her industry experience includes eight years in hotel sales and marketing with Hyatt Hotels and Sheraton Corporation in Washington, New York, and Boston. Her publications include the book Convention Sales: A Book of Readings, *which she edited and which was published by the Educational Institute of AH&MA in 1990.*

to the public view and, consequently, is subject to considerable societal analysis and scrutiny.[2]

Marketing professionals must continuously examine their rationales and tactics, and be confident that their decisions are in accordance with the right conduct for ethical marketing professionalism.

Hunt, Wood, and Chonko have noted that "marketing literature has long addressed issues related to ethical values."[3] In fact, such publications as the *Journal of Marketing*, the *Harvard Business Review*, and the *Academy of Management Review* often address various ethical issues as they relate to marketing and marketing management.

In 1985, Laczniak and Murphy published *Marketing Ethics: Guidelines for Managers*. Their book is devoted exclusively to the topic of marketing ethics, and discussions include such subjects as advertising, personal selling, pricing, and multinational marketing. Included at the end of the text are examples of codes of ethics from businesses and organizations like Johnson's Wax, IBM, and the American Advertising Federation.

Yet, it is only recently that the hospitality field has begun to explicitly address the topic of ethics in marketing. Haywood raises pointed questions about hospitality ethics, especially as it relates to marketing. For example, he asks: "Are customers satisfied with the marketing process . . . are there existing mechanisms which can identify and evaluate whether ethical abuses occur in the marketing process?"[4] Perhaps he answers his own question, as he suggests, "The time has come for hoteliers to examine their own standards of ethics, value systems and professionalism."[5]

The purpose of this chapter is to examine ethical considerations for the hospitality marketing professional. Every day, hospitality marketers make decisions about products, prices, distribution, and promotion decisions. These are the marketing tools they use to create guest satisfaction. But are ethical considerations foremost in their minds when they make these decisions? What are, if any, the ethical questions that must be raised? Can we assume that honesty and integrity are an inherent part of our daily decision-making practices? It may very well be that the definition of a quality product is indeed the delivery of a product that is produced in concert with a code of ethics acceptable to the guest, the employee, and the community-at-large constituencies.

Ethical Considerations for Product Decisions

Our core mission in the hospitality industry is to provide our guests with food and lodging accommodations that are clean, comfortable, safe, and secure. Each of these attributes has ethical connotations. For example, how safe? How secure? Locks on guestroom doors are one of the more obvious considerations we offer routinely to our guests. Automatic sprinkler systems, however, are a fire safety item that we do not always find in our lodging establishments.

The American Hotel & Motel Association estimates that fewer than half of the hotels in the United States have sprinkler systems installed in their guestrooms. Some hoteliers installed these systems only after they were forced to do so by state laws. Although it is beyond the jurisdiction of the federal government to force the installation of sprinkler systems, legislation has passed requiring all federal employees traveling on business to stay in hotels with automatic sprinkler systems. Dahl notes that this government segment alone represents an approximately $1.5 billion market.[6]

Do we have to wait for the guest to ask for better protection? Do we have to wait for legislators to force us to action? Or should we take leadership responsibility and provide the best possible fire safety protection without waiting for Congress to tell us to do so whether we like it or not?

The cost of installing a sprinkler system, is, of course, a major concern; but the cost of *not* providing the best possible fire safety protection is of far greater concern. The cost of social responsibility is an investment, not an expense.

Ethical considerations are also inherent in guestroom design. Are the rooms accessible to people with disabilities? Most state laws require that a minimum number of rooms be handicap-accessible, especially in new hotel construction. Federal legislation has recently been passed (Americans with Disabilities Act) ensuring accessibility to public facilities and services. The ethical question is whether we are doing everything we can to incorporate barrier-free guestrooms into the standard guestroom design. Are the guestrooms comfortable and functional for the blind, for a person on crutches, for an individual with the loss of a limb, for the couple with a small child? These guests have a right to safety and comfort, and we have an obligation to provide them as best we can. Indeed, it could be a strong marketing strategy to communicate to the public that state-of-the-art guestrooms are designed with *all* travelers in mind.

Floors for non-smokers are a good example of a product that provides fairness for the growing segment of non-smokers. Hoteliers have an ethical responsibility to provide a service to the non-smoking traveler. But providing such a service also happens to be smart marketing! Creating and keeping a guest is always the goal. Ethical considerations should not be viewed as constraints to the marketer; they should be seen as opportunities for providing greater guest satisfaction.

Ethical Considerations for Pricing Decisions

Pricing is a marketing decision, not a given right for hotel management to charge whatever it takes to earn a profit. The costs of doing business, of course, must be covered to realize a reasonable return on investment. But are the incurred costs reasonable? Has the marketing-minded hotelier asked guests if they want certain costs to be incurred to enhance their satisfaction?

The proliferation of bathroom amenities provides a good example of the reasonable cost concept. Throughout the 1980s and into the 1990s, more and more scented facial soaps, herbal shampoos, beaded bubble bath, body lotion, and braided baskets began to accumulate in hotel bathrooms. Someone has to pay for these items, and it is assumed that these costs are passed on to guests. Interestingly, research shows that 90% of lodging guests in the United States take showers, not baths. Most of the guestroom amenities are probably taken home, where they belong, since the guests have already paid for them. The ethical question centers on whether guests should have to pay for these items in the first place or whether they would rather save $5 on the room rate. The answer is not clear, but the ethical aspect of automatically charging guests for something they really do not want or need must be considered.

The weekend package is another innovation that has strongly emerged in the past decade. The public has responded very positively to this price discount promotion, and for some properties it has become a standard product offering. This is especially true for the downtown metropolitan hotels. The hospitality industry, like other service industries, offers a perishable product and faces fluctuating demand. The weekend package not only boosts weekend occupancies (when the business traveler is absent), it is also a way for non-frequent pleasure travelers to experience the fun of staying at a hotel for a price they can afford. Weekend packages can provide for the needs and wants and "purse-strings" of a local market that normally cannot afford to stay at a first-class hotel.

Most weekend "packagers" are from the local community or surrounding area. This group is largely made up of singles, families, and couples who live within a 50-100 mile radius of the hotel. They cannot afford to pay a $150 corporate rate from their discretionary income for a guestroom at a Sheraton, Marriott, or Hyatt hotel. Because they recognize good price value, they are willing to pay a $59 weekend package rate at these hotels. Weekend packages are not only an example of good marketing but also of ethical pricing.

From a broader ethical perspective, Haywood feels greater community concern should be part of the overall marketing process for tourism organizations. He challenges hospitality management to develop more harmonious relationships among tourism organizations, guests, and the residents of the community. He offers the following suggestions to achieve this goal: "Add value constantly . . . provide top quality as perceived by both tourists and local citizens . . . constantly seek new markets that are appropriate to the organization as well as the community."[7] Indeed, the community itself is an appropriate target market, and the local weekend package market supports the notion of developing and improving harmonious relations with the community-at-large.

Marketers recognize that there are varying elasticities of demand among various target markets. Product perishability, or the short shelf-life of a hotel guestroom, presents opportunities for hotel marketers to develop product lines that address this varying sensitivity to price. Weekend package programs, "kids stay free" programs, and senior citizen programs all address the myriad reasons and needs for the purchase of guestroom accommodations. When primary target markets are absent, it is both legally permissible and ethically astute to offer a perishable product at a reduced price to an interested public.

Price gouging and other unethical guestroom-pricing practices simply do not work, especially in the long run. In the end, the guests determine the price of a room. It is our job as marketing-minded and ethically-minded hoteliers to find out just what guests really want and what price they are willing and able to pay.

Ethical Considerations for Distribution Decisions

Marketing distribution decisions deal with how, where, and by whom a product is sold. In other words, we want to know how to make the product available to consumers—the channels of distribution through which they can purchase the product. In the hospitality industry, commonly used channels include tour brokers, travel agents, and central reservation systems.

Tour brokers and travel agents are intermediaries who sell our products for us. In return, we compensate them by volume discounts (in the case of the tour broker or wholesaler) and through commissions (in the case of the travel agent). An ethical consideration here is the timeliness and reasonable care for the reimbursement of these services rendered.

Travel agent commissions are paid in several ways, depending on the policy of the property. Regardless of the specific policy, travel agents do expect a reasonable rate, which is usually 10% of the retail price. Discrepancies can occur, however, in the timeliness of payments. If the property's policy is to reimburse the agent within a two-week period after the guest's stay, there is an ethical obligation to do so. Although the policy may not be in contractual form, it is simply good marketing management and sound business practice to deliver what you promise. Properties that hold back on payments, whether because of cash flow problems or just poor management in the accounting office, are jeopardizing the reputation of their establishments as well as that of the industry as a whole.

Tour brokers book in large volumes and receive highly discounted rates in return. They also book far in advance. The actual sales of a tour may exceed or fall short of the original tentative booking. Brokers have an obligation to monitor sales of the tour closely and communicate with the hotel on a timely basis if the various tours will indeed fill. Conversely, the hotel is obligated to notify the broker if it has a need or desire to release the tentative room block for other potential business. Although matching needs of brokers and properties was a problem in the 1960s and 1970s, hotel and tour broker relationships have improved significantly in the past decade. Well thought-out and clearly written contracts have encouraged ethical-mindedness in both parties in the highly dynamic tour-market industry.

Central reservation systems (CRS) in the United States are largely owned and operated by hotel companies, and thus they are not considered an intermediary. Nevertheless, the CRS is a critical element of channel-distribution strategies. Prospective hospitality guests often have the option of contacting a property directly to make a reservation or calling a toll-free 800 number. Emerging in the early 1970s, the CRS has been a great success for the hospitality industry. And the advent of computer technology has expanded these programs to include opportunities to book hotel reservations through airlines, car rental companies, and even through one's home computer.

Ethical issues to be raised at this point include concerns about whether the customer is getting similar rate quotes, similar availability status, and similar overall service from both the reservationist at the hotel and the reservation agent at the CRS. Is it possible, and even probable, to get one rate quote from the hotel and a different rate quote from the central reservation system? Unfortunately, the answer is yes. The potential guest has a right to expect similar quotes from each, but this does not occur as often as it should.

In a study conducted by Lewis and Roan, researchers systematically called hotel chain reservation systems and respective hotels in that chain with similar reservation requests.[8] Not only did they find discrepancies in rate quotations for identical reservation inquiries, but they also found differences in how the reservationists handled the particular call.

In the study, the researchers requested a two-person, two-bed room accommodation for a Friday night. The first quote from an 800 number of one hotel company was $145. After further inquiry, the caller finally received a $69 quote—a $76 difference. When the same request was made directly to the hotel, the initial quote was $107—a $38 difference from the initial 800-number quote. The final rate quoted by the hotel ended up at the same $69 weekend-package rate offered by the 800 number. What is happening here? Hotels, indeed, look for price sensitivities or price-resistance, but are these wide and varied discrepancies acceptable practice? In particular, the $38 difference in initial quotes between the CRS and hotel reservationist calls for a closer examination of ethical considerations for pricing practices in the hospitality industry.

A similar study was conducted recently at the University of Massachusetts/Amherst.[9] Six chain hotels from a major business center in New England were selected. Each of the hotels and their respective 800-number listings were called on the same day at the same time inquiring about a one-night transient overnight reservation for the following week. Also, in separate calls, inquiries were made about room accommodations for the following Saturday evening for two persons for one night. The results were similar to those found by Lewis and Roan. For example, for the weekday transient request one hotel quoted a rate of $125, and the 800-number reservationist quoted a rate of $89 for the very same request. In another instance, and with a different hotel company, the hotel quoted a rate of $125 whereas the CRS quoted a rate of $145.

The weekend travel inquiries also proved to be interesting. One hotel company consistently gave the same rates, regardless of who was called. Another hotel company offered an $89 rate from the hotel direct and a $125 rate from the CRS. Adding to the confusion were different rate quotes for the following Saturday, depending on whether the call was made on Tuesday, Thursday, or Saturday. For one hotel in particular, it was found that calling on Thursday always gave one the best rate!

A large part of this problem is due to yield management systems now operating in a number of properties (and discussed elsewhere in this book). Different quotes on Tuesday and Thursday may be understandable. Shifts in supply and demand are to be expected. What is of concern, however, is same-day (and same-time, to be more precise) rate-quote discrepancies for identical requests.

Ethical considerations concern fairness to the guest. Does one have to be an experienced, sophisticated hotel reservation-maker before one can figure out what the best approach is to getting the best rate? Put another way, is the infrequent traveler being discriminated against because of his or her lack of knowledge and expertise on how the hospitality industry works?

Perhaps the growing complexity of central reservation systems and advanced computer technology are partly to blame. Management information systems are growing so fast that temporary miscommunication is inevitable. Nevertheless, issues of care and concern for fairness and justice must be raised, questioned, and answered. It is difficult to explain just why Jill got a $49 rate and Joe a $79 rate for identical inquiries made on the same day at the same time, but from two different sources of the same company. Advanced technology is great, but are codes of ethics built into the black boxes, too? Mismanagement of distribution channels is one matter; ethical practice is another.

Ethical Considerations for Promotion Decisions

Marketing promotion essentially entails communicating to potential guests what you have to offer. The marketing tools used to accomplish this include advertising and personal selling. Because we use these techniques, we have an ethical responsibility about what we say and how we say it to our guests.

Advertising can be very helpful to the consumer who is trying to find out what is available in the marketplace. It can inform potential guests what products or services are available, where they are available, when they are available, and at what price. Consumers have choices and advertising helps them make these choices. This assumes that the advertising is accurate, not misleading, and in good taste.

The American Advertising Federation's Code of Advertising Ethics explicitly addresses these very issues:

> Truth—advertising shall reveal the truth, and shall reveal significant facts, the omission of which would mislead the public. . . . Taste and Decency—advertising shall be free of statements, illustrations, or implications which are offensive to good taste or public decency.[10]

Most advertising fits the AAFC's definition, and hospitality firms and their advertising agencies, for the most part, abide by this code of ethics.

Advertising, unfortunately, can also be misused or abused. For example, a seaside resort hotel may offer "ocean-front rooms" and/or "ocean-view rooms." Is it ethical to offer ocean-front rooms when the ocean front is a good one-half mile away, across the road and down the lane? Is it ethical to offer ocean-view rooms when the view is really a dried-up bay you have to strain your neck to see from the guestroom window? Misleading the guest is not truth in advertising. And worse, that one-time guest will not only fail to return, but will also encourage his or her friends to go elsewhere.

Personal selling in hotel sales is mainly used to book convention business. Meeting planners commonly use direct contact and site inspections to decide where to book their conventions. The experienced meeting planner has a good idea of what a 2,000-square-foot conference room will accommodate, but the inexperienced planner does not. Hotel sales executives sometimes are tempted to exaggerate the number of persons who can actually be seated *comfortably* in function rooms of any size in order to get the sale. If you are selling to an experienced planner, you probably will not get the sale by using this tactic. The sales executive has lost the trust of the potential client. If you are selling to an inexperienced planner you may get the sale, but you will also get an unhappy customer the day the meeting takes place.

Regardless of who the buyer is, this selling approach not only is a questionable business practice, it is also unethical. Poor training may be the reason, but that only shifts the blame and does not resolve the problem. Good business ethics and practice is what really solves the problem.

Ethical considerations can also arise in internal activities in the hotel. The hotel sales executive may feel pressure to reach a given quota of room nights sold and thus inflate total bookings to temporarily reach that goal. The rationale for this usually is "I'll do better next month and deflate those figures." Who is to blame for this kind of practice, which does indeed happen in our industry? The blame falls squarely on management, either because of poor hiring practices or for closing its eyes to questionable ethical conduct within the organization.

The Definition of Marketing Revisited

In his article, "Do the Right Thing," McKay notes the proliferation of books about ethics in the past three years."[11] He aptly points out that "increasingly, society is demanding that business has a broader responsibility than just making a buck."[12] And as Hunt, Wood, and Chonko note, "Ethical values are a managerial issue and not 'just' a societal issue."[13]

In marketing, as in human resources, financial accounting, and other administrative and management areas, doing the right thing is what it is all about. Is it right for the customer? Is it right for the employee? Is it right for the community? These questions must be asked every time a marketing decision is made.

Perhaps the very definition of marketing could be enhanced by explicitly recognizing the existence and importance of ethical standards as part of the profession. This definition of marketing could read something like the following:

> Marketing is delivering to the target market customers what they want, when they want it, where they want it, and at a price they are willing to pay, while upholding professional ethical standards for social responsibility to the community as a whole.

Ethics and marketing are not mutually exclusive. In fact, their synergistic effect creates and keeps a satisfied guest.

Endnotes

1. R. C. Lewis and R. E. Chambers, *Marketing Leadership in Hospitality* (New York: Van Nostrand Reinhold, 1989), p. 9.

2. G. R. Laczniak and P. E. Murphy, eds., *Marketing Ethics: Guidelines for Managers* (Lexington, Mass.: Heath, 1985), p. xiii.

3. S. D. Hunt, V. R. Wood, and L. B. Chonko, "Corporate Ethical Values and Organizational Commitment in Marketing," *Journal of Marketing* 53, July 1980, p. 80.

4. M. K. Haywood, "Ethics, Value Systems and the Professionalism of Hoteliers," *FIU Hospitality Review* 5, no. 1, p. 25.

5. Ibid.

6. J. Dahl, "Congress Passes a Bill Likely to Force Many Hotels to Install Room Sprinklers," *Wall Street Journal*, September 11, 1990, p. A6.

7. M. K. Haywood, "Revising and Implementing the Marketing Concept as It Applies to Tourism," *Tourism Management* 11, no. 3, p. 205.

8. R. C. Lewis and C. Roan, "Selling What You Promote," *The Cornell Hotel and Restaurant Administration Quarterly* 27, no. 1, pp. 13–15.

9. M. L. Molanphy, A. S. Lee, K. Rudoph, and E. P. Hartmann, "Pricing Structure Analysis of Selected Hotels in Springfield Massachusetts" (Unpublished monograph, University of Massachusetts/Amherst, 1990).

10. Laczniak and Murphy, p. 133.

11. P. S. McKay, "Do the Right Thing," *Enroute*, October 1990, p. 53.

12. Ibid.

13. Hunt, Wood, and Chonko, p. 87.

Discussion Topics

1. Ethics in hospitality marketing entails fairness, integrity, and social responsibility to customers. To what degree does the customer have similar obligations? To

what degree is management responsible for guests who behave in an unethical manner?

2. Suggest three ethical opportunities that could enhance a hospitality product for potential guests (such as the no-smoking floors example described in the article). Include in the discussion opportunities for hotels, for restaurants, and for institutional operations such as hospitals and college campuses.

3. Suggest three unethical practices that demean the hospitality product offered to guests. Again, the discussion should include hotels, restaurants, and other hospitality entities.

4. What is price gouging? How is it different from offering low weekend package rates and high mid-week corporate rates for the identical room? In other words, at what point (if any) do large price discrepancies become questionable, unethical marketing practices?

Term Paper Topics

1. Ethics in advertising; i.e., is the hospitality industry doing the right thing? In other words, do fairness, integrity, and social responsibility prevail? Include in the paper specific examples of both good and poor hospitality advertising practice, and substantiate your reasons.

2. Interview three or more hospitality practitioners to determine their views on marketing ethics in the hospitality industry. Compare and contrast the results of the interviews. How similar or different were their responses? Did they each have similar or contrasting perspectives? Was the central focus of each interview similar, or did the topics of discussion vary widely? Based on the interviews, can you draw any conclusions about ethical marketing concerns in the hospitality industry?

14

Ethics and Vendor Relationships

Thomas L. Trace
John F. Lynch
Joseph W. Fischer
Richard C. Hummrich

The hospitality industry is one of the fastest growing in the world. Capital, labor, and material goods are organized to serve a transient customer base. As with any business, items must be purchased. Purchasing is defined as "the acquisition of needed goods and services at optimum cost from competent, reliable sources."[1]

The hospitality industry's goods and services include a wide range of products. The customer is a guest at a hotel, resort, restaurant, or convention center and is traveling for reasons of business or pleasure. As a result, his or her needs are many and purchases must be carefully made to satisfy those needs. Hospitality companies must interact with many companies and individuals as they make these purchases.

Ethics

In any industry, the people and businesses that interact together are naturally forced to address ethical issues. Ethics may be simply defined as the way we act towards one another. Although ethical considerations are based on moral values, the considerations are not the values themselves. In a sense, morality is philosophical and personal, and it is tied to very basic belief systems. On the other hand, ethics is more

The authors are all with ITT Sheraton Corporation. Thomas L. Trace is the President of Hotel Source, the purchasing and supply subsidiary of ITT Sheraton. He holds a bachelor's degree from Notre Dame and a master's from the University of Auburn. A retired Air Force Colonel, he held top-level executive positions with Magnavox, Dialcom, and Telecom Services before joining Hotel Source.

John F. Lynch, Vice President and Director of Purchasing for Hotel Source, is a graduate of Providence College and holds an MBA from Bryant College. His previous positions were with Koala Inns of America Corporation, Canteen Corporation, and the Howard Johnson Company.

Joseph W. Fischer, Director of Headquarters Purchasing, is a graduate of Wayne State University and holds an MBA from Inter-American University. During a distinguished 27-year Air Force career, he held top-level positions with the Army and Air Force Exchange Service, the Department of Defense's worldwide retail organization, ending his service in 1989 as Chief of the Washington office.

Richard C. Hummrich, Director of Operational Supply, is a graduate of the University of New Hampshire and has held executive positions with the Ground Round, Howard Johnson Company, and the S. E. Rykoff Company, specializing in food service equipment and design.

pragmatic, interpersonal, and subject to circumstances. Ethics is the application of moral values to the rough-and-tumble, day-to-day business of living. The Judeo-Christian background of Western societies and their dominance of worldwide trade and manufacturing have given business ethics an orientation that combines elements of both religion and secularism. The basic ideas of honesty, justice, and appropriateness that underlie Western ethics will not be studied in this chapter, but the application of these ideas will be examined in purchasing scenarios.

Purchasing

The definition of purchasing quoted earlier is a very pragmatic definition, addressing the acquisition of goods and services at a good price from a good supplier. For the hospitality industry, goods and services relate to a broad range of finished products required to sustain guest service operations: food, beverage, and tableware items for the catering and restaurant outlet operations; cleaning products, amenities, and towels for housekeeping; and parts, equipment, supplies, and maintenance services for engineering. Optimum cost relates to obtaining the best value (price-quality relationship) for the goods and services being bought. Finding competent and reliable sources is a practical determination.

In the hospitality industry, purchasing is a particularly complex task due to the broad range of products and services needed to sustain operations. This is caused by the vast number of suppliers and is complicated by the highly competitive nature of the marketplace. Ethical issues arise as purchasers and suppliers interact, as sources are selected, and as terms are negotiated. This chapter concentrates on these three areas.

Contributions of Purchasing

It is important to clarify the role of purchasing as it relates to hospitality operations, particularly the contributions that purchasing can make to the quality of hospitality operations. From an historical perspective, it is interesting to note that purchasing has seldom been viewed with regard to bottom-line considerations:

> Until recently, purchasing received minimal emphasis and little recognition for
> its role in helping to attain profit objectives and cost containment goals. Some
> considered purchasing "just picking up the telephone and calling in an order."[2]

This view is now changing. According to Virts, meeting guests' needs in today's extremely competitive hospitality environment means that costs must be effectively controlled:

> Lately, managers have recognized the need to maximize value for the hospitality
> company and its guests. Purchasing should no longer be considered a simple
> matter of ordering needed products; the economic and operational benefits de-
> rived from effective purchasing are too great to disregard the complexities of
> modern purchasing system.[3]

The Need for Upgrading

Profitable hospitality operations in the 1990s will require a continuous upgrading of purchasing policies and practices in order to achieve the value expected by an increasingly sophisticated community of travelers. The ability to sustain or to improve quality standards while controlling costs depends to a large extent on the effectiveness and integrity of the purchasing support function. To clarify this dependency, a discussion of the objectives of the hospitality purchasing functions is helpful.

Objectives of Hospitality Purchasing

There are five objectives of the hospitality purchasing operation:

- To provide the goods and services required to sustain operations

- To maintain inventories at a level that minimizes investment and operational expenses

- To sustain qualitative standards by procuring only those items that meet the standards and specifications established by appropriate operating managers

- To focus on lowering consumption costs

- To maintain the competitive position of the unit or company it supports through the continuous implementation of measurable cost-avoidance and cost-savings programs[4]

The fourth objective means that, in addition to the acquisition cost of a product, other factors such as the product's price-quality relationship, its usable yield, and its impact on labor costs must be taken into consideration to ensure that the best value is attained.

It is important to note that concerning the final objective every purchasing dollar saved has a direct, positive, and immediate impact on the bottom line of the operating unit. Virts succinctly summarizes purchasing's goals:

> The aim of the purchasing system is to obtain the right *product* at the right *price*.
> In addition, the product should be of the proper *quality* and purchased in the
> correct *quantity*. The product should also be purchased at the right time from the
> best *supplier*.[5]

Determining Standards

Management is responsible for determining standards and for establishing specifications; however, purchasing has two major roles in the process. One role is to provide product information to management based on the purchasing office's market knowledge. The other is to assist management in developing specifications that are clear to suppliers and not subject to misinterpretation.

Allocating Resources

Although management is responsible for allocating resources in general and for approving specific purchases, the purchasing office provides the cost data on which management bases its decisions. Buying at the right price does not mean buying at the lowest price, but at a price that is fair to both buyer and seller—an ethical consideration. Quality, service, and price (in that order) are the major considerations when selecting goods from competing suppliers. In hospitality operations even the lowest "as purchased" or unit price may not be the optimum overall price when such matters as transportation, payment terms, yield, preparation, and storage costs are weighed. The ultimate goal is to obtain the best value per dollar spent. "Value may be defined as the lowest end cost at which the function may be accomplished at the time and place and with the quality required."[6]

Determining Quality

Management is also responsible for determining the quality of goods and services necessary to provide a desired level of customer satisfaction. However, purchasing provides the spectrum of products available so that management can make informed choices. Buying a product of the right quality means buying that which is suitable for its intended purpose. For purchasing's purposes, quality means "the totality of features and characteristics of a product or service that bear on its ability to satisfy a given need."[7]

Normally, hospitality products are carefully specified to establish standards at a cost that is within the budget of the hotel. Purchasing must ensure that specifications accurately describe what must be bought. In this regard, one of purchasing's major responsibilities is to ensure that products obtained do not exceed specifications and thus cost more than is necessary.

Purchasing is also responsible for making certain that vendors understand what is required and when it is required. Finally, purchasing must judge whether a supplier is capable of doing what he or she claims they can do. Within the qualitative domain in hospitality operations, functionality also includes safety considerations and warranty provisions.

Establishing Stock Levels

Management within the operating departments normally establishes operating stock levels and necessary backup (safety) stock levels. Buying the right quantity relates most directly to the maintenance of an adequate supply of items to meet operational needs. Purchasing keeps the departments informed of the correct volume or order size to ensure that the best price-volume relationships are taken advantage of and that related discounts can be obtained.

Buying at the right time is closely related to buying the right quantity. In determining when to purchase, considerations must be given to the lead time for order processing, the time and cost of delivery, the status of inventory, and the availability of storage space. Also, buying at the right time has to take into account the variations in pricing that occur in cycles (such as with food products) and with market supply and demand forces. In the process of meeting hospitality needs at the lowest possible cost, bargain hunting is integral to the effort, and good purchasers know when to buy.

Sourcing

Sourcing is the major challenge faced by the purchasing profession. Identifying from whom to buy and negotiating terms are the very heart of the purchasing function. Up to this point, the purchasing office has been working with management to determine requirements as well as to provide information and advice to the requester.

But progression to the sourcing phase clearly shifts responsibility and risk to the purchasing office and its buyers.

Purchasing professionals must consider many factors in order to qualify vendors and to engender competitiveness in the marketplace:

- Local or national vendors
- Relying on a single source or multiple suppliers
- Establishing long-term vendor partnerships or bidding competitively on a continuous basis
- Buying from distributors or manufacturers
- Using minority suppliers

For the hospitality industry, the wide variety of products to be purchased and the multitude of suppliers greatly complicate the process. Although individual hotels or a hotel chain may purchase a large volume of items (if their purchases are viewed as an aggregate), their purchases are really many relatively small purchases repeated over and over again. Thus, local suppliers (or the local distributors of national suppliers) are important elements in the purchasing cycle for the hospitality industry. The buyer's selection of a particular vendor is a complex decision and his or her relationships with individual vendors is anything but simple. Sourcing, selecting, writing the purchasing contract—it is at these points ethical considerations arise. These considerations are examined next.

The Ethical Framework of Purchasing

The general ethical framework that applies to any purchasing operation comes from the basic objective "to provide these materials and services procured outside the company when and where needed and at the least cost for the function or service required."[8]

Implicit in this objective is the basic requirement for buyers to be absolutely loyal to their employers and to the ethical standards those employers set. As an employer's agent to the external business community, the purchaser must represent the employer with the utmost integrity in order to promote and sustain the company's welfare and reputation.

A second requirement is to properly structure relationships with the vendor community. The buyer's conduct should set the ethical tone in these relationships. Every company should publish standards of conduct to clearly define its ethical concerns and to guide its buyers in their purchasing activities.

A closer look at loyalty and the proper structuring of relationships further defines the ethical context in which the hospitality purchaser should operate.

Loyalty

The purchaser's primary responsibility is to the employer he or she represents. There can be no conflict-of-interest; that is, personal benefit cannot be allowed to influence purchasing decisions made on behalf of the employer. (This could be a crime in some jurisdictions.) The conflict-of-interest sanction precludes soliciting and accepting gratuities such as gifts, personal loans, or services from the vendor community with which one deals, even though such gratuities may be legally allowable. Obviously prohibited are such unlawful practices as accepting bribes, kickbacks, and gifts in exchange for special considerations or the falsification of invoices and business expenses. Possibly prohibited are financial interests in companies seeking business with the purchaser's company and serving as an officer or a consultant to such outside companies.

The purchaser is also responsible for protecting proprietary information used in the process of doing business. As in the military where the safeguarding of classified information is among the most serious of responsibilities, the protection of proprietary information is of paramount concern in the commercial world. Finally, a purchaser must document his or her activities and owes the employer accurate records. A buyer is accountable.

Buyer-Seller Relationships

Buyers must treat the vendor community fairly. The Golden Rule applies: deal with sellers in a manner considered "just, proper, fitting and correct if the situation were reversed."[9] This means in the way the buyer would like to be treated if he or she were the seller.

Honesty and courtesy and respect must characterize buyer-seller relationships. Salespersons must be given appointments, met promptly at the appointed time, given a fair hearing, and accorded call-backs on a timely basis. Proprietary information received from a vendor must be safeguarded in the same manner as the buyer's company's proprietary information. Likewise, pricing information (bids and quotes) exchanged between buyer and seller must be kept confidential. Vendors are entitled to fair and open competition without favoritism influencing an award.

Sources asked to bid must be *true* competitors for the award and not merely used to shop for prices or to superficially meet the company's requirement for competitively awarding business. Requests for proposals, purchase orders, and terms and conditions must be clearly understandable. When problems arise, prompt action must be taken to resolve such matters.

An excellent concept is to view buyer and seller as partners who are working together to benefit both companies. A buyer should not expect to acquire goods at a price so low that the vendor's profit is eliminated. A vendor should not offer substandard items or sell goods at such a high price that the buyer will never again purchase from his or her company. Both parties should benefit from the relationship and should look forward to again doing business together. In essence, the ethical foundation for buyer-supplier relationships must be based on mutual trust and a commitment to the long-term benefit of both firms.

Finally, it is the obligation of each person associated with a firm to abide by the firm's code of ethics and to refer any substantive questions about ethical conflicts or misunderstandings to his or her supervisor for resolution. In this regard, most companies hold line management—in the hospitality industry, the purchasing manager or the property general manager—responsible for implementing the company's code.

The Need for Formal Standards

As the purchasing profession has evolved and matured, particularly over the last two decades, the need for a formal set of standards was recognized. The National Association of Purchasing Management (NAPM) has taken the lead in this effort and has published the principles and standards that appear in Exhibit 1. All NAPM members subscribe to these principles. Obviously, while all hospitality purchasers may not be members of NAPM, one can assume that these or similar standards will become accepted throughout the industry as the professionalism of hospitality buyers increases.

What does the hospitality industry purchase? It purchases renovation work, giving new life to aging properties. It purchases furniture, fixtures, and equipment (FF&E), either as individual replacements for worn items or as part of an overall renovation project. It purchases operating supplies for bathrooms and bedrooms, dining rooms and kitchens, public areas and conference centers, building maintenance and grounds, and administrative offices.

In the hospitality industry, property owners normally decide when to build or renovate. They select the design firm and general contractor/project manager. In-house design capability is a major factor that influences the selection of design/project management firms. The owner's conceptual standards and budget establish the degree of flexibility that design firms have in competing for a property's business.

Examples of Unacceptable Practices

Hotel managers must be completely familiar with the owner's standards because comparisons are made between various design submissions, and tradeoffs are sometimes made to stay within budgetary limitations. It would be both illegal and unethical for a design firm to substitute an outside-of-spec item without notifying the owner. An example would be substituting textiles or wall coverings that did not meet the owner's fire safety specifications. A hotel purchaser who is unaware of the fire safety standard or, if aware, fails to ensure that all specifications are met, is not doing his or her job. Obviously, both designer and purchaser are unethical and acting illegally if they mutually agree to deviate from specs without informing the owner. Design and project firms are unethical if they submit pricing, product quality, or delivery commitments that they know are impossible to achieve. Hotel managers are unfair if they constantly modify specifications so that designers and project managers are never able to finalize their bids or to schedule-out the entire project.

Once the owner's representatives have agreed to the particular items that make up a project, a large number of individual suppliers will provide the actual items to the project manager and installers. Rugs, lamps, plumbing fixtures, wall-coverings, and furniture are but a few of the items provided. "Knock-offs" that appear to meet specs, but which do not and which are cheaper to produce, are sometimes provided surreptitiously by unethical suppliers.

Another unacceptable practice occurs when a designer, acting on behalf of the owner, gives specifications to various suppliers but does not provide complete specs to all vendors in order to give a preferred supplier a better chance to win a contract. Sometimes, a designer intentionally works the specifications so that only a single source can meet the requirements. Such unethical actions focus on immediate gain and ignore both the purchaser's and the seller's long-term interests.

Exhibit 1   NAPM Principles and Standards

Principles and Standards of Purchasing Practice

Loyalty To Your Company

Justice To Those With Whom You Deal

Faith in Profession

From these principles are derived the NAPM standards of purchasing practice.

1. Avoid the intent and appearance of unethical or compromising practice in relationships, actions and communications.

2. Demonstrate loyalty to the employer by diligently following the lawful instructions of the employer, using reasonable care and only authority granted.

3. Refrain from any private business or professional activity that would create a conflict between personal interests and the interests of the employer.

4. Refrain from soliciting or accepting money, loans, credits, or prejudicial discounts, and the acceptance of gifts, entertainment, favors, or services from present or potential suppliers which might influence, or appear to influence purchasing decisions.

5. Handle information of a confidential or proprietary nature to employers and/or suppliers with due care and proper consideration of ethical and legal ramifications and governmental regulations.

6. Promote positive supplier relationships through courtesy and impartiality in all phases of the purchasing cycle.

7. Refrain from reciprocal agreements which restrain competition.

8. Know and obey the letter and spirit of laws governing the purchasing function and remain alert to the legal ramifications of purchasing decisions.

9. Encourage that all segments of society have the opportunity to participate by demonstrating support for small, disadvantaged and minority–owned businesses.

10. Discourage purchasing's involvement in employer sponsored programs of personal purchases which are not business related.

11. Enhance the proficiency and stature of the purchasing profession by acquiring and maintaining current technical knowledge and the highest standards of ethical behavior.

Source: Reprinted with permission from the publisher, the National Association of Purchasing Management, "Principles and Standards of Purchasing Practice," *NAPM INSIGHTS* 1, no. 9, September 1990, p. 27.

Many project difficulties can be avoided. The client (hotel) rather than the design firm should conduct the bid and specification review and the final awarding of supplier contracts. The owners, or the project managers they have hired, should make unannounced visits to suppliers to ensure compliance with design specifications during production and to enforce adherence to agreed-on delivery dates. Project management companies hired by property owners often have the experience, product knowledge, and market clout that allow them to negotiate with various vendors to the hotel's advantage. The project management firm's attention to terms and conditions often precludes misunderstandings and unethical behavior.

In the hospitality industry, owners seldom order operational supplies. Property managers and departmental supervisors within the hotel specify requirements and rely on the hotel's buyer to procure the items they need. The array of items is mind-boggling. A diligent buyer can master the variations and specifications for most of the routinely ordered items and can become an effective sourcer and negotiator for such goods and services.

Recurring requirements should foster a buyer-seller partnership between the hotel and the vendor community. The buyer becomes a stakeholder in the seller's business due to his or her need for a consistent source of supply, and the seller becomes a stakeholder in the buyer's business due to his or her need for continuous revenues. As the relationship grows, the proper quality and availability, as a function of price, become clear. The buyer has confidence that the price is appropriate and the seller is assured of continued revenue. Unfortunately, the concept of partnership is not always put into practice.

Industry Practice

Many industries have established standards. The term "industry practice" was originally used in the last century to protect manufacturers, especially textile mills, when overruns occurred. The term now extends to what any particular industry has established as its standards. Unethical businesspersons often deviate from these conventions, misleading their customers into thinking they are purchasing the "standard" item. Examples are commonplace. In the bed-linen industry, standards exist and set parameters for the grading of sheets. For instance, percale is commonly assumed to mean a thread count of 180, signifying 90 threads per inch in one direction and 90 more in a perpendicular direction. However, sheets labeled percale—with thread counts as low as 160—can be found in the marketplace; these sheets are cheaper to produce. Most buyers are not able to distinguish between the 180- and 160-count sheets by sight or touch. It is unethical for the vendor not to inform the buyer of the deviation and to take advantage of his or her assumption that percale is 180 count.

The terry industry has established standard sizes. The size of a "hotel bath towel" is 27 by 50 inches. Deviations in towel sizing are designated as "upgraded luxury hotel" if the size is larger and as "inn quality" if the size is smaller. Not all vendors make customers aware that their sizes differ from accepted sizes. Needless to say, these sizes can change after laundering, which is the salvation of the unethical seller. Unethical suppliers can use standard size confusion to their advantage. This is also demonstrated with specifying the size of soap. During the development of sizing standards, a numbering system was developed to define the size of bars of soap. For instance, a number 2.25 bar actually weighs two ounces. The subterfuge occurs when the seller supplies a number 2.25 bar when a buyer specifies a 2.25-ounce bar. The smaller bar passed off as a larger one increases the seller's profit margin. If caught, the seller can blame it on an honest mistake. Those sellers whose products deviate from industry standards and who fail to inform their customers like to view themselves as sharp businesspersons. Such sales often violate laws and they certainly raise ethical concerns.

"Let the buyer beware" is not a concept that fosters buyer-seller partnerships and long-term benefits to both parties.

Misrepresentations by the seller of operational supplies are illegal. Manufacturing mills have quality standards for terry products, table linens, and bed linens. These standards of quality are designated first quality, second quality, third quality, and run-of-the-mill. It has not been unknown for unscrupulous sellers to mix cheaper, lower-quality goods in a shipment when a buyer has specified first quality.

Food and beverage suppliers also can engage in deceitful practices. The best silver-plated flatware and holloware are termed hotelplate. This signifies a nickel base piece with a specific thickness of silver applied. However, various cheaper base metals can be substituted, including stainless steel, which does not bond well with silver. Of course, the thickness of the silver can vary. The unethical seller can easily misrepresent these products.

Buyers can also deal unfairly when purchasing operating supplies. Under the guise of reducing the price, buyers will sometimes knowingly overestimate the usage of an item that a seller is asked to supply. The logic here is that the more one buys, the lower the price. So the buyer inflates his or her usage figures to get an acceptable price. When the order is placed, the buyer then asks for the lower figure. This leaves the vendor with less profit margin than the quantity ordered would dictate. Another widely practiced behavior is for the buyer to not pay the seller within the terms of the invoice. This delay obviously affects the seller's cash flow and profits.

Conclusion

Purchasing in the hospitality industry faces the same ethical considerations as other industries. Hotels are widely dispersed, make a large number of relatively small purchases on a recurring basis, and are served by a widely divergent community of suppliers. Although management is responsible for funding, determining standards, establishing quality criteria, and setting inventory levels, buyers assist in all these functions. Purchasing's primary function is sourcing goods and services and negotiating terms. Ethical issues arise as buyers interface with suppliers. A sense of loyalty to one's firm will assist the buyer in avoiding conflicts of interest. Approaching sellers as partners having mutual interests will assist the buyer when attempting to properly structure relationships with the vendor community.

The examples of ethical failures highlight the disloyalty, self-interest, and deceit that sometimes enters buyer-seller transactions. Ethical issues in purchasing are generally straightforward: Is what is being done honest, fair, appropriate, and to the long-term advantage of both parties? An affirmative answer indicates that the purchaser is properly focusing his or her efforts.

Endnotes

1. Eberhard E. Schering, *Purchasing Management* (Englewood Cliffs, N.J.: Prentice Hall, 1989), p. 4.

2. William P. Virts, CPA, *Purchasing for Hospitality Operations* (East Lansing, Mich.: The Educational Institute of the American Hotel & Motel Association, 1987), p. 3.

3. Ibid.

4. John Stefanelli, *Purchasing Selection and Procurement for the Hospitality Industry*, 2d ed. (New York: Wiley, 1985), pp. 44–46.

5. Virts, p. 6.

6. Paul V. Farrell, ed., *Aljian's Purchasing Handbook*, 4th ed. (New York: McGraw-Hill, 1982), p. 8-4.

7. Ibid., p. 9-4.

8. Ibid., p. 2-2.

9. Ibid., p. 7-2.

Discussion Topics

1. Training employees in ethics is a corporate responsibility. List the pros and cons of this argument.

2. Precluding employees from accepting all gifts is unrealistic in today's business world. Acceptance does not necessarily indicate a conflict of interest. Are these valid statements?

3. The Golden Rule applies to buyer-seller relationships. Explain why this is or is not true.

4. A hotel buyer insists that a local printer hold the printing firm's monthly awards luncheon in the hotel's conference room if the buyer awards the printer an exclusive printing contract. Is such a business tradeoff appropriate?

Term Paper Topics

1. Examine buyer-seller interactions in a segment of the hospitality industry. Survey several hotels, motels, or resort properties and identify the suppliers with whom they have had the longest relationships. Determine the factors they have contributed to these continuing relationships from both the buyer's and seller's perspectives.

2. Buying firms and their suppliers sometimes both buy from and sell to each other. When a firm gives preference in its buying to those suppliers who are also buying customers of the firm, the practice is termed "reciprocity." This practice is controversial. It may be viewed as the promotion of sales via purchasing power. The Federal Trade Commission (FTC) and the National Association of Purchasing Management (NAPM) have both addressed the issue of reciprocity. Examine the legal and ethical aspects of reciprocal buying.

15

Ethics and the Accounting Function

Peter D. Keim

If ever there were an area of business where a lack of ethical behavior could cause disruption to the organization, the accounting function must surely rate among the most susceptible. Put in its simplest terms, the role of the accounting function is to "keep score." Although businesspeople like to measure all sorts of activities, the dollars taken in and paid out are among the most intensely watched measurements in any business entity. The opportunities and pressures for distorting these measurements for the benefit of one constituent or another are almost endless. The results of distortion, from both a legal and a practical perspective, can be disastrous.

Quality and Ethics in Accounting: Bridging the Gap

As the fundamental act of measuring business activity, accounting is quantitative in nature. However, the role of the accountant includes other responsibilities as well. The quality of the accountant's work must be assessed by considering not only the preparation of various documents but also the timeliness of their completion, their accuracy, their consistency in both format and presentation with those of prior periods, and the disclosure of underlying information about company policies, major transactions, and similar issues. Compliance with standards established by the company—or imposed on it by outside authorities such as the IRS, the SEC, and the FASB—must also be considered.

In addition, there are certain ethical issues that must be considered in evaluating the quality of an accountant's work. Since the accountant is specifically trained for the preparation of accounting reports, it is only natural that the accountant be involved in their interpretation, which can take many forms. One of the key decisions that must be

Peter D. Keim is President of the Keim Company, Inc., of Durham, New Hampshire. The Keim Company provides management consulting services specializing in financial and economic analysis for hotels. Mr. Keim received his bachelor's degree from Cornell University and his MBA from Drexel University. He is a charter member of the International Society of Hospitality Consultants and, prior to joining the faculty of the Hotel Administration Program at the University of New Hampshire in 1987, he worked for twelve years as a Senior Principal with Laventhol & Horwath managing the Management Advisory Services practice throughout New England.

made by an accountant in interpreting reports is to identify his or her constituency. As we will see, the accountant's clients in a hospitality enterprise are numerous, and each has a hidden agenda. The interpretations of accounting information can be as diverse as the accountant's constituency. It is therefore important that the accountant provide an interpretation that is unambiguous to as much of the constituency as possible.

Compliance with legal requirements is another area of qualitative analysis. This task also has specific ethical implications, because noncompliance with the law is unacceptable. If an accountant is asked to report transactions in a manner that violates legal requirements and he or she acquiesces, it is an abrogation of personal responsibility and standards, notwithstanding that such reporting might be a directive from above. An example might be taking an overly aggressive position in preparing a tax return by deducting certain expenditures that may not be properly deductible in the hope that they will not be detected by the IRS. Another example might involve claiming that a certain transaction was done in compliance with particular statutes when interpretation of the statutes may be quite unclear. The ethics of these situations are clear. The quality of the accountant's work, moreover, is quite suspect, since ethical responsibilities were ignored in favor of expediency, perhaps. The tax returns may be done neatly, on time, in good form, and otherwise fully in compliance with expectations, except for their errors of commission.

Quality is defined as compliance with established standards. It seems to be clear that established standards should include not just performance and compliance criteria, but also ethical criteria. Ethical criteria include basic honesty, full disclosure as required by regulatory agencies, putting forth a total effort, trustworthiness, avoiding real or apparent conflicts of interest, discretion in both behavior and disclosure to others of confidential information, and similar moral issues.

Just how one can measure compliance with these criteria raises additional ethical considerations, since few of us can claim moral perfection in our actions. An open, sincere dialogue seems to be the most effective way to establish a positive environment for such evaluation, since a one-sided critique would tend to place the evaluator in a glass house, so to speak.

The Impact of Ethics on Accounting

In considering the impact of ethics or morality on the process of accounting in business, it is important to understand the responsibility of the accountant. In the hospitality industry, the accountant prepares a variety of products, including journals, ledgers, the daily report, operating budgets and forecasts, payroll checks and records, tax returns, financial statements, inventory records, and other financial documents and analyses. The principal consumers of these products are management, employees, owners, investors, lenders, vendors, and local, state, and federal government officials. These consumers are the accountant's clients, and the ethical pressures brought to bear upon the accountant in fulfilling the sometimes conflicting needs of these clients can be tremendous.

The accountant's position can be likened to that of a division manager in a large organization. The amount of influence that can be brought to bear on the accountant's performance can be substantial. Since most policy originates at the top of any organization, it is necessary to understand the relationships that the accountant holds within the organization and the corporate culture or general operating philosophy that prevails. In her essay "Ethics Without the Sermon," Laura L. Nash gives some insight along these lines:

> In deciding the ethics of a situation, it is important to distinguish the symptoms from the disease. Great profit pressures with no sensitivity to the cycles in a particular industry, for example, may force division managers to be ruthless with employees, to short-weight customers, or even to fiddle with cash flow reports in order to meet headquarters' performance criteria.[1]

The ethics of the organization tend to prevail.

It is important to understand the various roles the accountant plays from time to time as well as the diverse sources from which accounting information is derived.

The accountant's roles include auditor, bookkeeper, consultant, systems analyst, cost accountant, tax expert, financial analyst, controller, clerk, and a variety of others. Each of these roles requires the accountant to approach his or her responsibilities from a different perspective and to use different skills and techniques. Needless to say, the pressures can be significant, and the temptation to shortcut the process or otherwise do less than a complete job in the interest of saving time can be real.

In like fashion, diversity is the keynote in describing the myriad ways in which accounting information is gathered. Many different sources of transactions exist in a hospitality enterprise, including restaurants, lounges, health clubs, concessionaires, the paymaster, the front desk, accounts payable, accounts receivable, and other areas. Information can be transmitted electronically, by word of mouth, on pre-printed forms, checks, invoices, time cards, and on other similar source documents. Thus, one can easily see just how complex the accounting function can be in any business enterprise.

It should not be surprising that ethical pressures can be as diverse as accounting itself. One only has to consider the so-called hidden agendas of the many different clients of the accountant to see that this is so. Among other objectives, owners typically expect maximum returns on investment, minimal exposure of liquid assets, and rapid turnover of receivables. Vendors look for prompt payments, the use of minimal discounts, and adequate evidence of liquidity for the purposes of granting credit. Lenders are interested in debt service coverage, the relationship between debt and equity invested, both short- and long-term profitability, overall credit-worthiness of the borrower, and other concerns. Local and state government officials look for evidence of compliance with licensing statutes (e.g., the mix of food and beverage sales) and prompt tax payments. Employees expect paychecks every week, accurate W-2 forms in January, and prompt processing of health insurance claims. Guests insist on accurate food and beverage checks and guest accounts and responsible handling of advance deposits. Other clients expect similar items, all of which involve the accountant from time to time.

With all of these tasks to perform, the accountant must have some frame of reference against which to measure his or her own performance. Shakespeare said it best:

> This above all,—to thine own self be true;
> And it must follow, as the night the day,
> Thou canst not then be false to any man.[2]

In a multi-role environment such as the accountant has, identification of "thine own self" is not just difficult but nearly impossible. How does one handle the murky swamp of decision-making when faced with a variety of clients, all with different ex-pectations? It would seem that the conflicts of loyalty preclude effectiveness unless there are strict guidelines or standards for compliance. How does one resolve the con-flict between the "corporate brain" and the one supposedly raised at home and in church by a loving family and a thoughtful community? This clearly raises the issue of the relationship between business behavior and ethical principles, which has frequently been one of conflict.

What are some of the ethical conflicts that face the accountant? It is difficult to say just which one is the most frequently encountered or the most flagrant in its abuse. Judging ethical behavior by degrees of wrongness does not seem to be an appropriate way of resolving ethical conflicts. This sort of approach tends to lead the practitioner down the "act-utilitarian" road of ethical thinking.

Act-utilitarianism as an ethical approach provides justification for actions if the damage done is minimal or is commonly expected anyway. This is "the end justifies the means" kind of thinking. Act-utilitarianism places the accountant in the position of defending one constituent's position or viewpoint against all others' viewpoints, be-cause, under this theory of ethics, an act is right or wrong depending on the desirabil-ity or undesirability of its consequences from the perspective of the perpetrator of the act. For someone with as many constituents (clients) as an accountant, this is far too narrow a point of view.

Examples of the kinds of ethical conflicts commonly encountered by accountants in the hospitality industry include the following:

- The general manager of a hotel wants to show as high an occupancy percent-age and average rate per occupied room as possible. Therefore, the GM di-rects the accountant to exclude out-of-order guestrooms from the inventory of rooms available and include complimentary rooms and staff rooms sold in rooms revenue at full retail value.

- The owner of a restaurant directs the accountant to take all discounts offered by vendors, even if the discount cutoff date has passed, in the hope that the vendors will not catch the error.

- A vendor offers the purchasing agent of a large food service unit a kickback if the purchasing agent will direct a larger proportion of the business's pur-chases to the vendor.

- A food and beverage director whose compensation is partially contingent on departmental profitability overstates month-end inventories deliberately to reduce the cost of food and beverages sold, thereby increasing apparent prof-itability.

- An employee punches a friend's time card as well as his or her own in order to increase the friend's earnings for the week.

- The manager of an operation instructs the accountant to delay the implemen-tation of raises granted to employees for two weeks, pending approval by the owner, who had already instructed the manager to grant the raises.

- A management company president, whose incentive compensation is based on a percentage of income before fixed charges, directs that all repair and maintenance items costing more than $500 be capitalized as capital improvements.

- The owner of a hotel decides to add a $.75 "access fee" to each guest's account every time a guest places any telephone call outside the hotel, whether the call is completed or not.

- The chef decides to substitute one-pound lobsters for the usual one-and-a-half-pound lobsters without adjusting the menu price accordingly.

- The owners, in an effort to improve the appearance of their balance sheet in connection with applications for short-term borrowing and vendor credit, decide to liquidate some certificates of deposit and pay down their trade accounts payable. They do this knowing that cash flow from operations in the next two months will permit them to re-establish the CDs and still keep the vendors' accounts on a 45-day pay basis.

All the preceding examples are common situations in the hospitality industry that involve ethical considerations. All are practices that typically could be discovered by the accountant acting in an internal audit, or fraud detection, capacity. Some of these practices are blatantly illegal. Others just constitute sharp or ethically questionable business practice.

Identifying these or other ethically questionable practices imposes yet additional ethical dilemmas on the accountant. The so-called corporate brain may recognize the usefulness of the practices, while the personal ethical standards of the accountant may cause him or her to react negatively. The rationalization of the acceptance of these and other ethically questionable practices because "everybody does it" is nothing more than abrogating one's conscience for a surrogate in the form of systemic constraints.

Engaging in "whistle-blowing," on the other hand, may have its own serious set of adverse consequences. Employees following directions from management or owners that force the performance of unethical acts are assuming for themselves the mantle of illegitimacy. Granted, it may be difficult or nearly impossible for an employee to stand up to his or her boss and say, "I won't do that because it's wrong!" and still expect to remain employed. The real dilemma comes when the act being required is of such small consequence—e.g., excluding out-of-order rooms from the available rooms inventory—that no one is really hurt by the act. The question arises whether acquiescence to this act will open the responsible party or parties to further, more serious breaches of ethical principles in the future. A prostitute is a prostitute, whether the fee is $2 or $1,000.

The Marriage of Theory and Practice

Great creativity often comes from stormy relationships. It may be safe to say that the relationship between the theory of ethical behavior and the practical application of ethics in real life could be a potential hurricane.

Most students of ethics—including philosophers, scientists, religious leaders, and others—tend to separate theory and practice, if only for the simplicity thereby gained in analyzing ethical situations. The theoretical side of ethics tends to be concentrated in the home, church, and child-rearing environments as well as in the world of academia. However, the responsibility for practical applications in business falls to corporate or other business leadership. It may be said with some accuracy that, when entering the world of business, one unlearns some of the ethical principles by which our personal lives are conducted in favor of other principles by which certain aspects of business are conducted. This is the crux of the conflict between one's corporate brain and one's heart.

This separation of theory and practice has made it less likely for corporate leadership to be influenced by academic criticism. However, business in the 1990s seems to be awakening to the need for more ethical behavior in the face of numerous incidents and practices: the many Wall Street scandals and the blatantly unethical, amoral actions of the officers and directors of many savings and loans institutions during the 1980s; more widely publicized prosecution for tax fraud (e.g., Leona Helmsley); and the recent wholesale investment in American real estate by offshore capital. Additionally, the binge for material things that characterized the emergence of the so-called yuppie generation in the 1980s could be a result of the decreasing influence of ethical theory on the reality of day-to-day life.

On the other hand, there seems to be increasing awareness in everyday life of the need for more attention to ethical principles. In academia, more and more business schools are adding courses in practical ethical applications to their curricula. Religious leaders are focusing more on ethics in their sermons and writings. The media are raising the issue of ethics when reporting on many business scandals and questionable corporate practices.

It certainly seems that, in order to foster a more highly developed awareness of ethics as the underpinnings of business, corporate leadership must act more symbolically on behalf of the organization. Nash observed the following:

> The Greek root of our word **"symbol"** means both signal and contract. A business decision—whether it is the use of an expense account or a corporate donation—has a symbolic value in signaling what is acceptable behavior within the corporate culture and in making a tacit contract with employees and the community about the rules of the game. How the symbol is actually perceived (or misperceived) is as important as how you intend it to be perceived.[3]

The key point here is that corporate leadership must not only make decisions that are in the best interest of the larger community—i.e., its employees, customers, and the world at large—but also make sure that the results of these decisions are consistent with ethical behavior. To do otherwise is the height of hypocrisy and represents abandonment of principle.

Another quote from Nash further highlights the relationship between action and intent:

> The goodness of intent pales somewhat before results that perpetrate great injury or simply do little good. Common sense demands that the 'responsible' corporation try to align the two more closely, to identify the probable consequences and also the limitations of knowledge that might lead to more harm than good. Two things to remember in comparing intention and results are that knowledge of the future is always inadequate and that overconfidence often precedes a disastrous mistake.[4]

The idea of creativity arising from the stormy relationship between theory and practice was identified earlier. There can be little question that creativity is certainly necessary if many traditional business decisions are undermined by theoretical, ethical considerations. In order for the business to continue, some decision must be made with respect to any ethical dilemma, and in order to achieve the corporation's goals of profitability for investors, security for management and employees alike, and service to the community in which it exists, management must be creative in finding the right blend of behaviors to satisfy all constituents. True corporate or executive responsibility includes not only operating from one's own code of morals but also creating an environment of moral codes within which others can operate comfortably.

So, too, must the accountant attempt to satisfy all of his or her clients. The conflicts of loyalty must be solved with creativity in decision-making, not necessarily creative accounting. Creativity in decision-making implies that some flexibility must be present. If an accountant is so narrowly constricted in the ways and means of performing his or her duties or in making reasonable decisions that there is only one way to do any particular task, then creativity cannot exist. However, granting the accountant enough "wiggle room" in which to make decisions—such as how best to organize information for presentation to management or the owners, considering each constituent's particular needs and capabilities—tends not only to maximize the accountant's effectiveness, but also to ensure comprehension and reduce or eliminate misinterpretation of the information by those to whom it is presented.

Creativity in accounting, on the other hand, while certainly within the bounds of legality (e.g., accrual basis vs. cash basis, or tax basis vs. financial statement basis reporting) can lead to misinterpretation of results unless it is clearly explained. Creative accounting can lead to trouble and unethical behavior when there is inadequate training or guidance for the accountant or when there is intent to deceive. In these circumstances, clearly wrong decisions can be made, either unwittingly or deliberately. For example, an accountant could easily distort the results of operations by overstating profits through capitalization of normal repair expenses or using LIFO (last-in, first-out) basis inventory valuation during inflationary periods, which would artificially increase period-ending inventory values and reduce the cost of sales. Additional examples of creative and illegal accounting include check kiting, lapping of receivables, and other fraudulent yet relatively easily hidden accounting practices.

One critical question that raises ethical considerations is whether an agency relationship exists between the accountant and the owners of the business or between the accountant and management. The flip side of this is the nature of the relationship between the accountant and the remainder of his or her clients. Is it a "quasi public-servant" relationship, indicating accountability to a broad constituency? Or is it just the insider in management representing management's viewpoint in a way that appears to be acceptable to the majority—act-utilitarianism at its finest?

If in fact a legal agency relationship exists between the accountant and either ownership or management, the nature of the relationship of the accountant with all other constituents is clear. The accountant has a clear fiduciary relationship with his or her principal, and all others are secondary. There should be little or no conflict of loyalty. The accountant's actions in handling ethical dilemmas would tend to be resolved in the best interest of the principal, in accordance with the fiduciary responsibility.

Under these circumstances, we hold that full and complete disclosure of the nature of the relationship is required so that all third parties are on notice and can make their own decisions accordingly. Such decisions could include retaining their own professionals to interpret information provided by the accountant in a clear agency relationship. Failure to make this disclosure places both the accountant-agent and his or her principal in violation of generally accepted ethical standards.

Among a number of owners and executives in the hospitality industry there remains the perception that this agency relationship still exists, if only in their minds. This agency takes the form more of an acknowledgement of authority, not of accountability. Enforcement of this belief in the mind of the accountant is sometimes accomplished through subtle, and occasionally not so subtle, forms of intimidation. This intimidation itself is blatantly unethical in the view of the larger community. The fear of losing employment frequently prevents the accountant, or anyone else caught in a similar situation, from taking effective action against his or her boss, regardless of the personal ethical standards of the accountant.

How can such a situation be resolved? What good is accomplished if the accountant resigns his or her position to protest blatantly unethical behavior and then is unable to secure new employment? What assurance is there that new employment, if found, will be any different? These are not easily answered questions. Many other factors must be considered. Resignation in the face of future unemployment serves no interest other than personal satisfaction of resolving an ethical dilemma. If the action forces the accountant to draw unemployment or go on public welfare, then society-at-large pays a price, in addition to the indignity suffered by the accountant.

On the other hand, if the accountant remains in the position—believing that doing so is in either his or her or the company's best interest—the accountant is placed in the uncomfortable position of having sold out to a lower standard. Equally important is the position of the employer company. The company may be judged guilty of extracting loyalty from employees against all others without consideration of common morality, the law or society itself.

As in most arenas, the best defense is a good offense. The ideal situation occurs when, during the hiring phase of employment, the accountant has the opportunity to qualify the company on its ethical principles. If these principles are not compatible with the individual's, the choice is clear. This is the occasion to lay out expectations and gain an understanding of the rules of the game. It should be incumbent on all who seek employment to investigate the ethical norms of the prospective employer in order to satisfy oneself about the acceptability of the employment offered. If such satisfaction is gained, then, should an event occur that violates what was represented, there are grounds for resolution of the conflict through discussion, negotiation, and reasonable settlement.

Employers are in a stronger position than employees. An employee's failing to live up to established standards in the ethical arena generally results in termination of employment. The employer who does not conduct background investigations of prospective employees should be prepared to live with the results if the employees turn out to be dishonest. At least, if the employer was misled during such investigations, there is recourse in termination, hopefully before too much damage is done.

When we look at accounting from the non-accountant's perspective, several issues arise. Most are related to the perceived orientation of accounting as a technical medium of conveying information. Certainly, accounting can be viewed as a language, the language of measuring business activity. It has its own terminology, its own conventions, and its own standards. An individual must devote considerable time and effort to gain expertise in accounting. Becoming a Certified Public Accountant (CPA) requires dedication and perseverance beyond mere academic pursuit.

The complexity of current tax codes and other regulations affecting accounting makes it almost impossible for the layman to function effectively in business without the advice of professional accountants. Herein lies the potential for substantial ethical conflict, since the relationship between top management or owners of a business and the accountants depends on accurate communication and no small amount of understanding.

Management's and ownership's desires for liquidity, return on investment, and cash flow heavily influence business decisions. Modern American corporate management tends to focus on short-term profitability, to the detriment of long-term planning and growth strategies. This forms part of the rationale for some hotel general managers' insistence on maximizing occupancy and average rate statistics, even if it means artful juggling of the records. The collective corporate brain of American business and industry typically takes courses of action—including making financial reporting decisions—that maximize profits at the expense of long-term survival. The stories of lengthy discussions between top management and the accountants over how to report specific transactions are legion. The number of accountants who have been fired for their refusal to accommodate top management's desires for reporting or not reporting certain information grows annually. Virtually all such occurrences are the result of either deliberate concealment of management actions, misinterpretations of accounting data, or misunderstanding the meaning of certain financial disclosure requirements.

Yet, herein lie some of the ways in which ethical conflicts can be resolved. The accounting profession has diligently developed and adopted a comprehensive set of accounting principles and standards, as well as a professional code of ethics. These guidelines are under continuous review by the Financial Accounting Standards Board (FASB) of the American Institute of Certified Public Accountants (AICPA). In addition, the Securities Exchange Commission (SEC) has adopted numerous rules and regulations governing the reporting of financial information for publicly held companies. The Internal Revenue Service (IRS), as we all know, has a complex set of rules and regulations for recording and reporting financial transactions. With all of these guidelines, standards, rules, and regulations, one would think that there is little room for interpretation. Certainly, much interpretive freedom has been eliminated, thus reducing the opportunities for outright fraud and deceit. However, since the business environment is not static but evolutionary, new situations arise almost constantly that require interpretation and decision-making. It is within these areas that the greatest room for ethical distortion may take place, and it is incumbent on those responsible for making and reporting the decisions to use the existing framework of standards and regulations as guidelines for remaining within normally accepted ethical bounds.

Endnotes

1. Laura L. Nash, "Ethics Without the Sermon," *Executive Success: Making It in Management* (New York: Wiley, 1983), p. 498.

2. William Shakespeare, *Hamlet*, Act I, Scene III.

3. Nash, p. 505.

4. Nash, p. 501.

Discussion Topics

1. "Window dressing," or selling marketable securities to raise cash to pay off trade creditors in order to improve the balance sheet's current ratio, hurts no one. In fact, it satisfies the creditors, and makes the operation's balance sheet look better to lenders.

2. Internal auditors' roles as "internal police" give them the absolute right to identify fraud where detected and any other absence of compliance with company policy or the law. However, where such disclosure would jeopardize their employment, they are entitled to remain silent.

3. Minor infractions of company policy regarding expense reimbursement don't really hurt anyone, and the individuals who get away with it by improperly coding personal expenses as company expenses don't deserve the same treatment as those who commit outright fraud.

4. Quoting from the text of this chapter, ". . . when entering the world of business, one unlearns some of the ethical principles by which our personal lives are conducted in favor of other principles by which certain aspects of business are conducted." Identify and discuss several such principles on each side; i.e., personal principles unlearned and business principles learned that represent ethical conflicts.

Term Paper Topics

1. Identify and describe several standard accounting and/or financial management practices in the service industries that represent "surrogates for conscience" or a justification for actions taken that are in apparent conflict with accepted ethical principles. Illustrate how these actions violate ethical standards and discuss how management and owners alike can enforce compliance with ethical standards while at the same time achieving their mutual goals.

2. Identify two hospitality industry companies that have become recognized for creative management and decision-making and explore how their accounting and financial reporting systems have evolved along with management systems. Discuss any ethical conflicts that may have arisen as a result and how management has resolved or should resolve these conflicts.

16

Ethics and Hotel Information Technology: A Business or Moral Issue?

Richard G. Moore
Roy Alvarez

Most hospitality industry workers would say they behave ethically on the job. And most guests would probably agree that they behave ethically while staying at hotels. Owners and stockholders of hotel companies would undoubtedly say the same about their behavior as owners. Unfortunately, this may not be the case. It is this chapter's thesis that certain forces not only cause all of us to qualify our ethical behavior, but, for those of us in the hospitality industry, to use hotel information technology (IT) in unethical ways.

Definitions

We begin our discussion with key definitions. Ethics concerns the moral principles and values that guide the conduct of the members of a group, institution, or other association of stakeholders who share common interests or circumstances.

Western thought has accepted as its ethics the concepts of personal freedom and emancipation as well as the principle of the Golden Rule. Ethics in the hotel industry involves volition, the free will of actors who are engaged as providers and users of the hotel industry's services and products. Are the ethical principles practiced in our industry based on a different set of moral principles and values than those we accept as being reflective of a democratic society?

Turning to another aspect of this essay, we must ask if ethics also concerns information technology (IT)? Is the use of computer and communications technology an issue when discussing the ethics of our industry's stakeholders? The answers to these questions are not simple. For one thing, technology is inanimate. It is value-free.

Richard G. Moore is Associate Professor of Information Systems at the Cornell University School of Hotel Administration. He holds a bachelor's degree, a master's degree in engineering, and an MBA from Cornell. He is the author of several published articles and travels throughout the world as a leading consultant in computer technology for the hospitality industry.

Roy Alvarez is a lecturer in information technology at Cornell, and is pursuing his doctorate. He holds a master's degree in instructional design from Auburn and an MPS from Cornell. He is the author of several published articles.

Therefore, how can one discuss its ethics? On the other hand, when technology is used as a tool to enhance or detract from ethical behavior, is it not reasonable to consider its impact on ethics?

The key idea of this chapter deals with the role IT plays in the ethics of the hotel industry and how this role has been institutionalized to undermine individual ethical behavior. Furthermore, we will explore the consequences this use of IT has had on the many stakeholder groups in our industry.

This discussion is organized in four parts. Part I provides symptoms and consequences of unethical IT use. Part II provides historical backgrounds on the evolution of IT and the evolution of the hotel industry and how these circumstances have given rise to these symptoms and consequences. Part III describes current industry characteristics and how they affect this issue. Part IV focuses on important considerations that would encourage industry players to use IT as a tool to enhance ethical behavior and consequently derive benefits from doing so.

Part I: Symptoms and Examples of Unethical Behavior

The following examples are symptomatic of a pattern of IT-related unethical behavior in the hotel industry. Most examples describe an event or set of circumstances in which institutional decisions regarding technology have been made to benefit the ultimate success of a company. These decisions often come at the expense of the individual or at a cost of encouraging the individual to act unethically.

Maid Dial-In Systems

Maid dial-in systems (MDSs) are computer systems that integrate the in-room telephone with the front desk computer system to enhance the communication between the housekeeping staff and the front desk staff about the actual availability of a guestroom and the automated availability status of that room in the computer system. The systems work as follows: When a housekeeper enters a room, he or she dials a special code into a touchtone phone that is sent to the front desk computer. The codes communicate different room statuses, such as occupied and ready or vacant and ready. (Many hotels also have inspectors from the rooms department confirm certain statuses.) The initial value of these systems is to reduce mistakes in assigning rooms to guests. For example, they help eliminate assigning new guests to already occupied rooms or to rooms not yet ready. A second benefit of these systems is the ability to register guests more quickly into rooms. Sounds great, but . . .

In addition to the enhanced communications described previously, we should consider what else has happened with the introduction of MDSs. First, the earlier systems presented a new technology to an element of the work force that was not prepared for it. Nor had this work force been exposed to similar technologies in other aspects of their work or personal lives. For example, the Motorola Maid Aid system developed in the early 1970s required a housekeeper to carry an acoustic coupler that attached to a telephone. It had a series of buttons to push, lights to decipher, and cards to insert that often frustrated and confused a staff that included non-English-speaking, modestly educated, and technophobic personnel. (One light on the device was labeled "Call Home." What would you expect one to do when that light was on?) As an early technology, MDSs were difficult to use and quite unreliable, and they increased the frustration of management as well.

Despite the less-than-ideal introduction of MDSs, there remained a commitment to this technology. Newer systems have been developed with a higher level of technical responsiveness, and they have become easier to use. For example, newer systems do not use an acoustic coupler. They use the standard touch-tone phone found in most hotel rooms. This latter point is significant, but many would argue that there is still a high degree of frustration and anxiety caused by newer systems. Adding to this frustration and anxiety is a new capability of the MDS that may generate unethical use by management.

The new systems can now track time and location attributes of a housekeeper's work. These features may have been designed to enhance the original goals of the MDS: to better serve guests through enhanced communication between housekeeping and front desk departments. However, the decision to introduce these newer versions of MDS has tempted management to behave in unethical ways. In particular, these systems have encouraged some to use them as personnel monitoring systems rather than communication systems. "Big Brotherism" is a term we associate with unreasonable control one exerts over another. MDSs are sometimes used to control employees because of the quantifiable measures they offer. This is another example of how a well-intentioned technology decision, which may be beneficial in the larger arena of positives and negatives, has in fact allowed the individual to suffer. ("Where were you those missing 15 minutes?" "Why did that room take you 10 minutes longer to clean?" "Why can't you be as productive as my star housekeeper?") This occasional negative attitude may be easily rationalized as acceptable because in balance the systems really work.

Vendor Systems

Unethical behavior surrounding IT can involve vendor systems and vendor response to the marketing and support of their systems. We are not insinuating that all vendors' actions or attitudes are unethical; however, in the attempt to develop products that have wide market appeal, they slip into unethical behavior in spite of their intentions.

For example, most IT is designed for a performance range that is fuzzy at its extremes. By fuzzy, we mean that the systems may or may not work without any apparent significant or harmful degradation in performance. It is sometimes difficult to anticipate the quality of performance until it is too late. The over-cautious vendor or vendor salesperson will not encourage a sale at these extremes. Others may not proactively admit the potential final cost to the purchaser to make a system perform satisfactorily in the fuzzy domain. To explain how this might happen consider the following two scenarios.

First, a system that has never been successfully installed with the maximum number of peripheral devices the hardware manufacturer claims a computer can theoretically support is sold with a configuration near or at that theoretical limit. (The front desk system that has never been installed with more than 10 terminals is sold and installed with 20 terminals.) The added burden on the computer's processor causes the system's performance to slow to a crawl. Everyone feels the consequences. Vendor personnel must face the aggravation and anger of the hotel's management team. They in turn must face the aggravation and anger of their front desk clerks and others who work with the system. Clerks, cashiers, reservationists, and management must face the aggravation and anger of the guest who may now have to wait in long slow lines to check in or out.

Second, a vendor may be tempted to oversell a system on the basis of its software capability. For example, a customer may ask the vendor if a front desk system can pre-block a specific room when making a reservation for a guest. The vendor may say yes without asking exactly what the customer expects or means by pre-blocking. Without getting clarification, the vendor may understand pre-blocking to mean a notation on a comment line that notifies hotel personnel not to sell a particular room. This certainly has the potential to achieve the desired outcome the customer wishes. However, for the customer to accomplish pre-blocking successfully, hotel personnel would have to become incredibly clairvoyant because they are not going to have a clue how to manage pre-blocking in this system any other way.

What the customer really wanted was a system that would take a pre-blocked room out of the system's automated inventory. A reservationist or front desk clerk would not be required to actively prevent a room from being sold or given to another guest, a task that is absolutely unreasonable. Few vendors do not understand this system requirement.

Vendors may rationalize that the risks they take with customers are justified. The short-term health of their companies and their ultimate ability to serve their wider customer base may be based on the vendors' abilities to generate revenue; and revenue for vendors comes primarily from sales.

Even vendors who avoid the risks of selling systems at the fuzzy edge may face a completely different set of ethical questions associated with supporting their existing installed base of systems. Vendor companies that grow quickly from sales sometimes do not grow as quickly in the support area. They may not have the opportunities or resources to build the needed infrastructure necessary to support a growing and in many cases widely dispersed customer base.

Again, fast growth in revenue may allow the vendor to satisfy the needs of most customers, but it does not justify the sometimes disastrous consequences a few customers may suffer on the vendor's account.

Minibars

Minibars are now commonly found in hotel rooms and allow guests self-service to beverages and snacks. Some brands of minibars are highly automated. They can record electronically the specific products and the times they were dispensed and then automatically add the correct charges to guests' computerized bills. Other types of minibars are not automated and require a physical accounting for billing purposes.

Comparing the results of these two technologies, we find a reverse effect occurring: the less-automated environment encourages a higher level of unethical behavior than the computerized one. Why is this the case?

The problem is a temporal one. With computerized minibars linked automatically to a hotel's computerized front desk system, it is virtually impossible for guests to leave their rooms to check out without having use of the minibars noted on their bills by the time they reach the front desk. However, in the non-automated minibar environments, front desk clerks must ask guests who are checking out if they have taken anything from the minibars.

The temptation for guests to respond unethically is heightened in the latter set of circumstances. They may be tempted to deny any charges in order to save a few dollars. Additional ethical issues come into play when one considers other burdens incurred by guests when hotel management decides to choose the less automated minibar technology. First, the hotel has shifted a task to the guests—having to account for their purchases. Although this procedure saves the hotel labor costs, it costs the guests because they have to perform that accounting. Second, because a hotel employee must take a physical inventory, it is possible that subsequent guests may be charged for items consumed by the previous guests. This may happen whether or not the previous guests acted ethically at check-out.

We should consider possible motives for management's choosing minibar technology.

First, there is a desire to provide guests with a higher level of service; after all, the guests have the convenience of easy self-service to beverages or snacks without having to call room service or leaving the room.

Second, the hotel benefits because minibars are viewed as revenue generators. Increased revenue generally means higher employment, better products, more satisfied investors, and more satisfied guests. The decision appears to be a good one for both business reasons and ethical ones if one believes that a decision that benefits most at the expense of a few is a reasonable position to take.

Part II: Background

Ethical behavior in the hotel industry is problematic; the preceding examples illustrate this. Why is it that so many reasonably good and well-intentioned individuals are able to exhibit such questionable ethics when they act as a group? This question can be answered with two propositions.

The first is that widely accepted beliefs about progress and its positive contribution to the human condition may in fact place limits on our ability to behave ethically in the cultures, business or otherwise, in which we find ourselves.

The second is that the particular progress of information technology and the progress of the hotel industry seem to reinforce proposition one. Let us look more closely at these ideas.

Progress

Most people accept the ideal of progress without giving it much thought. However, a closer look may help us better understand the ethical behavior we find in our industry.

Van Doren offers a widely used definition of progress: progress is "irreversible, ameliorative change."[1] Consequently, there are two conditions that must be met for progress to happen. First, there must be change, a before-and-after difference. Second, the ameliorative quality of the change must be judged by a value standard. If we consider these two conditions when discussing progress in social affairs, it may be said that progress occurs when a change leads to enduring improvements in the human condition.[2]

Improvements in the human condition are the consequences of utilitarian forms of rationality designed to increase wealth. We only need to consider how increases in overall wealth have reduced hunger, the toil of labor, disease, etc., and most of us can see we are the better for it. But are we all better off just occasionally, or better off all the time? With all our wealth, why do people live in cardboard boxes, or suffer from malnutrition? Why is ozone burning a hole in the atmosphere, and why are our lakes dying from acid rain?

Writing about the relationship of ethics and progress, Olafson offers a criticism for this accepted view of progress.[3] He argues that the goal of maximizing wealth as a means of improving the human condition is ethically bankrupt because its rational approach is void of moral considerations; it is a goal that has created a "managerial and manipulative character" that institutionalizes values rather than guaranteeing them on an individual basis.

> [T]he great effort to liberate man from the terrors and sufferings of his condition within nature will have resulted in subjecting him to a new form of control through a managerial, technical form of rationality that is essentially empty of any sense of moral personality, either in its bearers or in its clients.[4]

We, too, have become more critical of the consequences of "progress" as we face up to problems of pollution, overcrowding, and so forth. We are beginning to realize the ethical tradeoffs we make every time another wilderness is destroyed to produce more wealth, and we have endeavored to place limits on this progress. But what of the progress in information technology and the hotel industry? Have these brought with them consequences we may also criticize?

History of Technology

Technology is generally considered to be the application of scientific knowledge, and its exploitation has transformed society from one dependent on agriculture and limited commerce to one dependent on science-based engineering, global markets, and information. Many believe that information technology in particular has done much to enhance individual self-determination and capabilities; there is wide acceptance of a person-machine symbiosis.

Not everyone, however, is so sanguine about information technology. Many see it as counterproductive to the ideals associated with the human condition. Ideals often cited as being threatened include political freedom, fairness and equality, expression of individual differences, the spontaneity and opportunity of human contact, creativity, personal initiative, and equal access to information. Contrary to these ideals, information technology has been accused of eroding human progress by encouraging the de-skilling of work, a cementing of organizational rigidity, an increase in stress and alienation, and the loss of human contact and privacy.[5]

These two diametrically opposed views of information technology and the human condition can be understood by looking at the way in which we may choose to apply it.

From a societal perspective, Moshowitz has argued that technology may be used to coordinate social diversity and individualism as well as to control it.[6] He cautions that in the interest of the community, the uses of information technology to control diversity may dominate so that the coordination of diversity does not become unmanageable.

Moshowitz is afraid this tendency to control will undermine individual initiative to be creative and free. This belief supports Olafson's view of the emergence of managerial and technical control mechanisms in our institutions, including business corporations.

Fromm, arguing from a social-psychological perspective, draws similar conclusions.[7] Humans are much less controlled by instincts than are animals, giving us the freedom to choose actions that may be unique from those chosen by others. But this freedom condemns us to choose, and significant choice is filled with risk and anxiety because we generally lack the knowledge to avoid serious errors of judgment.

Fromm claims that we exhibit a socially conditioned tendency rooted in our human makeup to avoid serious and consequential choices. Instead, we seek safe havens to avoid real freedom, and this in turn has encouraged highly structured and controlled human environments.

Dependence on authority and conformance to the anonymous rules and structures of an automated society are and will continue to be examples of these safe havens. This not only supports Olafson's view but goes further in suggesting that as individuals we may actually condone the managerial and technical controls he claims are morally bankrupt.

Do we find this tendency to control through managerial and technical devices a characteristic of the hospitality industry? If so, have we come to accept this form of social control as valid within the context of progress and accepted ethical behavior? If we are to answer these questions, we must review the progress of our western hospitality institutions.

History of the Hospitality Industry

It can easily be argued that progress in the hospitality industry has clearly meant the maximization of wealth. Furthermore, this progress has been achieved through mechanisms of social control found in managerial and technical rationalism. Has this always been the case? We must look at the evolution of this social control in our industry.[8]

Social control for the purpose of maximizing wealth has evolved from paternalistic traditions found in early family-run operations to the current bureaucratic practices we find in today's large hospitality organizations. Have our ethics gone from bad to worse?

Western hospitality management traditions were rooted in the family-run country inns and guest houses and were highly supported by paternalistic attitudes and class distinctions. Because these businesses were quite small, they had flat structures compared to today's standards, and they were highly authoritarian. The owners were in control and protected the interests of their workers as long as the latter supported the interests of the family, much as a parent protects the interests of a child. Workers accepted this arrangement because there was little room for advancement or job mobility. A tradition of class distinction and a family's identification with a particular trade reinforced this acquiescence to being controlled by an inn's owner.

It was not only the employee who was controlled by this set of circumstances. While the economic interests of the owner were paramount, it became his responsibility to care for his workers as pseudo-family members. If both parties abided by this understanding, loyal service for security was the trade.

Social or rational control has increased in many respects with the growth of hospitality institutions. These larger companies have produced more vertical structures and job specialization to deal with the complexity of these institutions. They have also placed owners and workers at a greater distance from each other, given the logistical constraints associated with large bureaucracies.

At the same time, the industry has seen a rise in competition that forces companies to become even more efficient in maximizing returns on investments to increase wealth. Consequently, explicit rules of behavior have replaced tradition; a law-like system of bureaucratic controls, based on power and rational systems, has come to treat employees and guests as technical objects to be efficiently integrated into an organization's business systems.

When individuals are considered a part of a well-oiled machine, a consensus or value deficit results. It becomes easier for all involved to rationalize unethical choices because the institution has depersonalized their environment. In these institutions, we are no longer held accountable for our ethical standards. We are expected to sacrifice moral principle for the aim of progress, the maximization of wealth!

Part III: Current Industry Characteristics

The preceding view of progress has been with us for a long time, and the harmful impact it has on our ethical behavior does not seem to be dissipating.

As long as we institutionalize our decisions and distance our personal ethics from these decisions in order to fit the cultures of our business organizations, we can expect to continue to use IT in ways described previously. However, some may not believe we are following the same path. Some may believe circumstances in our society or in our industry are changing. Let us look at some of our industry's current characteristics to judge whether or not maximizing wealth will continue to be the banner of those who would be part of our business.

The industry is becoming ever more competitive and global. We believe that pressures to operate more efficiently will continue to drive decisions. It is also recognized that the labor pool will decrease substantially, with a significant shift from skilled jobs to low-paying, low-skilled positions in the service industries. This labor force will also continue to have certain characteristics that will make impersonal decisions for increasing wealth easier. Line employees will continue to have major asset responsibility at the source of business transactions (cashiers, clerks, etc.). Line employees will continue to come from highly culturally and economically diverse backgrounds. Our industry will continue to suffer from high turnover. Management will likely continue to work very long hours and burnout will remain an issue for us.

This competition for customers and the necessity for finding profitable substitutes for traditional sources of labor will guarantee a continued reliance on the progress of IT. The dilemma we all face is that every time we cut payroll, de-skill a job, or reduce morale, we damage our product—service for the guest. As this happens, our guests will find it more difficult to pay the increasing room rates and restaurant bills that hotels will have to charge to remain competitive.

Part IV: What Is to Be Done?

A champion is needed to promote the issues surrounding a more responsible and ethical use of IT. By champion, we do not mean a single person, but an interest group or stakeholder group from the milieu of our industry. Several possibilities exist. Consider the guest.

The Guest

The guest is certainly a key player in the unethical behaviors caused by IT, both as an initiator of these behaviors and as a target for the unethical behavior of others. Can we expect the guest to champion this cause? Do we want the guest to take the initiative with this cause? We should consider these questions together.

First, the guest can passively become a champion by choosing to spend his or her resources in other ways. An economic boycott of this nature would be difficult to coordinate and is not likely to arise from a grass-roots movement. A guest may encourage a more ethical use of IT through legislative action. For example, if the systems for yield management continue to allow for unethical overbooking situations, a consumer-led movement to legislate against this practice, if successful, would significantly damage the revenue potential of the industry. In both cases, if the industry pushes the guest to demand more, the industry has lost. It would be too late at this point for any changes to be relatively painless. It would create reactive measures that might be difficult to manage and control, rather than proactive measures designed in the industry's strategic planning mechanisms.

The Trade Unions

A second champion group could be the trade union. We offer this possibility because workers in the hotel industry are among those most negatively affected by unethical IT use. They suffer from many of the adverse consequences of introducing IT into the workplace discussed earlier in this article.

If we consider the impact of MDSs as technology that encourages the worker to champion ethical IT use, we encounter the same thing we saw with the guest. On the one hand, if a management mentality of "big brotherism" defined the way the systems were used, workers might be more willing to defend themselves from this control mechanism by turning to trade unions or government protection. On the other hand, workers may simply choose to respond in an unethical way themselves and sabotage the system by providing inaccurate and incomplete data when doing their work.

If we consider the history of trade union negotiations in our industry as they have related to the introduction of IT, we find that the most common concern is economic. It has been typical for union negotiators to focus on wage increases as the cost to management for introducing technology. There has been little concern for issues associated with trade union members' quality of work life as affected by new IT. This is expected. Historically, American trade unions have focused on "bread and butter" issues, at the expense of others. Furthermore, there is a preconceived notion of union management, distrust, and conflict. A move by labor to champion ethical IT use would likely cause a knee-jerk, confrontational reaction by management and owners. Finally, this approach might exempt other stakeholder groups from having to alter their behavior significantly since the focus of any change would be on labor itself.

Government

An alternative to labor's dependence on the trade-union movement is to seek the protection of government; however, past responses to protect workers have been limited to health and equal opportunity issues. Our legislatures would find adjudicating changes in IT use legally and politically difficult to do. This clearly is an unlikely and undesirable way to champion ethics.

The Vendor

The vendor is another potential champion of ethical IT use. This is possible because a majority of the industry's IT is vendor-developed and supported. One could argue that they most easily could make the changes in their systems or the way they support them to raise the level of ethical use of these systems. Why not build in a mechanism to prevent overbooking? Why not turn down a sale?

The vendor may be in the most difficult position to champion the changes we suggest. First, as a segment in our industry, vendors have historically been the stakeholder group with the most significant mortality rate. Their "Boot Hill" of IT reads like the Who's Who of computer companies. Economic survival is always of paramount importance to this group, to the point where short-term decisions, although not conducive to long-term success, may be driven by short-term mortality.

Furthermore, vendor survival is a matter of building systems that have broad appeal, so that the high development costs can be recovered across a large number of sales and installations. Appealing to such a wide customer base requires the vendor to develop safe systems: those that meet basic requirements of reliability and functionality. They can only sell what the customer base is willing to buy; it is a demand-driven market. For vendors to champion more ethical IT systems and use, the vendors would have to place their survival at risk—a risk that may be impossible to consider. While we can expect the vendor to play a key role if we are to become more IT ethical, we cannot expect the vendor to be leading the charge.

The Stockholder

A fourth possible champion is the stockholder. There are two problems that make this unlikely.

First, most stockholders are too far removed from operations to be able to judge and respond to the circumstances described earlier in the article.

Second, stockholders are often viewed as having aims that are in conflict with the long-term health of a company. This is due to the nature of financial markets. The psyche of most stockholders is not one of ownership; therefore, their view of success will be affected by their profit motives.

It is interesting to note that Japanese companies, which have a reputation for making decisions that are designed to ensure long-term success rather than short-term profits, generally do not have stockholder interests represented on their boards of directors. They want these boards to make decisions on long-term profit goals, and not on short-term profit pressure.

Earlier we said, "Our guests will find it more and more difficult to pay the increasing room rates and restaurant bills hotels will have to charge to remain competitive." This statement is worth returning to because it speaks to the ultimate success factor of our industry—guest satisfaction. And directly, through exposure to guest-contact IT, or indirectly, through behavior of guest-contact employees who use IT, the guest will measure service as it is adversely affected by unethical uses of IT.

Management or Owners

We do not think any of the stakeholder groups discussed previously offer much hope of improving the ethical uses of IT; this leaves us one last possibility—enlightened management or owners, the former in companies publicly traded and the latter in companies privately held.

What do we mean by enlightened? We mean a management and owner philosophy that recognizes the importance of ethical behavior for the long-term health not only of our industry but also of our society. This includes a strong focus on the human resource, and the participation or consideration of those who work in our hotel companies in the design and evaluation of IT. The goals of this participation include consensus building and conflict avoidance.[9] If IT is to be ethically used, then the various players involved must agree to the ethical standards of its use.

Second, enlightened management and owners will recognize the importance of working with vendors to develop, install, and support systems. Our industry must set higher expectations for the common tasks these systems are required to achieve, and it cannot be accomplished in a demand-driven arena without this cooperative dedication.

Finally, enlightened management and owners must establish a more honest relationship with guests. IT cannot be used to maximize company success at the expense of guests. This approach will continue to frustrate and anger consumers who are being asked to pay dramatically escalating prices. Alienation is not the way to build consumer confidence and ensure the reasonable repeat business our industry depends on.

Conclusion

Can this happen? Perhaps increasing competition will cause some to turn to this approach as a competitive strategy for positioning themselves in a shrinking labor pool and more cynical consumer base. Perhaps new levels of IT knowledge and understanding of IT issues by top management and owners will make the ethical question clearer, and consequently cause them to more clearly respond to these issues. Perhaps globalization of the industry will bring in new philosophies that will raise the expected level of ethical behavior in all aspects of the business. But, perhaps all these circumstances will encourage a further entrenchment of unethical use of IT! Unfortunately, the hotel industry is a microcosm of our larger society, and we see no evidence that things will change for the better.

Endnotes

1. C. van Doren, *The Idea of Progress* (New York: Praeger, 1967), p. 7.

2. Roy Alvarez and Heinz Klein, "Information Systems Development for Human Progress," in *Systems Development for Human Progress,* eds. H. K. Klein and K. Kumar (Amsterdam: North-Holland, 1989).

3. Frederick A. Olafson, "The Idea of Progress: An Ethical Appraisal," in *Progress and Its Discontents,* eds. Gabriel A. Almond, Marvin Chodorow, and Roy Harvey Pearce (Berkeley: University of California Press, 1982), p. 533.

4. Ibid.

5. Alvarez and Klein.

6. A. Moshowitz, *The Conquest of Will: Information Processing in Human Affairs* (Reading, Mass.: Addison-Wesley, 1976).

7. E. Fromm, *Escape from Freedom* (New York: Avon Books, 1967).

8. H. Klein and Roy Alvarez, "Information Systems in the Hotel Industry: Part of a Problem or Part of a Solution?" in *Computers and Democracy,* eds. Gro Bjerknes, Pelle Ehn, and Morten Kyng (Avebury, England, 1987).

9. Ibid.

Discussion Topics

1. A mailing list company has approached a hotel's general manager and offered to buy the hotel's guest history data for $1 per guest. It assures the general manager that the hotel's anonymity will be protected. The sale of the 25,000 records on file looks very tempting, especially since everyone's bonus can be positively impacted if the data is sold. What are the options? What should the general manager do?

2. The general manager of a 500-room hotel is faced with a dilemma: the sales department wants another secretary to handle some of its administrative work on the hotel's automated sales system. The general manager can afford to do this by eliminating the system trainer position. What are the ethical tradeoffs the general manager must consider in doing this?

3. An employee in the sales department quit and went to work for a competing hotel. The employee found that dialing in to his former employer's computer system was still possible because his former password had not been deleted. When he mentioned this to his current sales manager, the manager insisted that he use their competitor's data to their own advantage. The employee indicates that he does not think this is the ethical thing to do. His manager then gives him an ultimatum: either he does it, or he will be fired!

    The first issue is what accountability the former employer has in this episode. Second, what are the employee's options? What should he do? What would you likely do? What would others do?

4. A guest checks into a hotel, and the clerk verifies her credit card as having sufficient credit to cover the cost of the room for the entire stay. In fact, the clerk initiates a transaction that reduces the credit amount of the credit card account for the entire amount of the expected room charge even though the guest has not spent a night yet. That evening, the guest goes out to eat and attempts to use the same credit card to pay the bill. The restaurant's cashier runs a credit check on

the account and finds it has insufficient credit to pay the restaurant bill. This has happened because of the hotel clerk's previous action.

Is the hotel justified in automatically reducing the guest's credit limit, even though she had not yet incurred the full expense? Would this situation be different if the guest gave the clerk a credit card she had no intention of using to settle the final hotel bill? What obligation does the hotel have in informing guests that their credit will be drawn down in this circumstance?

Term Paper Topics

1. You work for a small hotel that is in the process of selecting and installing a new computerized property management system. Your employer has asked you to view the process of selecting, installing, training, and operating the new system from an ethics perspective. Specifically, the general manager has told you he believes that by setting high ethical standards, all of the hotel constituents (vendor, employees, customers, management and owners) will win. Produce a report that would identify keys for each step in the process. In your report show, where appropriate for each constituent group, high ethical standards that should be expected from them with regard to the new system.

2. With the advent of large guest history systems, hotels are beginning to capture and use massive amounts of data and information about each of their frequent guests. This ranges from family names and birth dates to personal preferences regarding newspapers, flowers, and type of wake-up call.

   Research the capabilities of these guest history systems. You should identify the kinds of data and information they use, and provide some illustrations for how hoteliers and staff expect to use these resources.

   Once you have collected this material, analyze what you find in terms of the following questions. What do you think about the ethics regarding the collection, use, and safeguarding of this information? Is the kind of data and information collected and used conducive to ethical or unethical behavior? Are those you questioned likely to use these resources ethically or unethically? How does one balance the opposing views of the professional who may say, "The more we know about you, the better guest service we can provide," with that of the guest who may ask, "How do I know what they will do with the information?"

17

An Overview of Ethics and the Law

John E. H. Sherry

> The task of management is fundamentally ethical, having to do with the creation of values that enhance and contribute to the development of human civilization. There is no task that can be more important nor more challenging.
>
> —*Professor Rogene A. Buchholz*

Business ethics, then, has to do with the authenticity and integrity of the enterprise. To be ethical is to follow the business and cultural goals of the corporation, its owners, its employees, and its customers.

> Those who cannot serve the corporate vision are not authentic business people and, therefore, are not ethical in the business sense.
>
> —*Bowen H. McCoy*
> *Managing Director and President, Morgan Stanley & Co. and*
> *Morgan Stanley Realty, Inc., respectively*

> One of the basic tenets of ethics is the principle of cooperation and sharing. And one of the most precise measurements of the maturity of an individual or of a society is a concern for those who come after us. It is our ethical obligation to do our best to enable those who follow us in life's relay to have as good a chance to win as we had when the baton was passed along to us.
>
> —*Ivan Hill*
> *Founder, Ethics Resource Center*

John E. H. Sherry is Professor of Law at the Cornell University School of Hotel Administration. He holds a bachelor's degree in economics from Yale University, an LLM from New York University, and a JD from Columbia University. He is the author of four books: The Laws of Innkeepers *(1981),* Business Law *(1984, with others),* Legal Aspects of Food Service Management *(1984), and* Supplement to The Laws of Innkeepers *(1985). He has been admitted to the New York and Ohio State Bars, and is admitted to practice before the U.S. Supreme Court. Recognized as a world expert in hospitality law, he is a past president of the International Forum of Travel and Tourism Associates in Jerusalem, and past U.S. Diplomatic Representative to the 1980 UNIDROIT Draft Convention on the Hotelkeeper's Contract in Rome.*

Definition and Function of Business Ethics

The role of ethics in business management has grown significantly in the last decade, aided in part by the lapses of Ivan Boesky on Wall Street and the savings and loan scandal nationwide. Other examples involving individual companies have also received extensive media attention. This chapter is intended to initiate a process of ethical management rather than to pass moral judgment on past instances of managerial wrongdoing. It will also underscore the limits of law as a method of social control and the need to practice ethical management as a positive attribute of business leadership.

Before embarking on our quest for a process by which to incorporate ethics into management, we must define what we mean by business ethics. Is it wishful thinking or a trap for the naive and unwary manager? Does ethics have any role to play in the brutal and unforgiving game of business? If so, when, where, and how?

Business ethics may be defined as a method by which managers at all levels establish moral standards in organizations that produce goods and services to support society. This itself raises a question: Whose moral standards? Those of the manager or those of the organization? And, equally important, if these are independent of the other, which standard governs when they conflict?

First, we must recognize that managers are moral agents and reflect the moral postures of their respective organizations. Second, we must also recognize that businesses, including hospitality enterprises, are morally responsible to a broad spectrum of *stakeholders*, both within and outside the organization. Internal stakeholders include employees and shareholders. External stakeholders include customers, suppliers, the government, and society. Third, we have to acknowledge that this notion of moral agency is not universal. The traditional school of management policy argues that ethics has no place in business and that the sole determinant of successful management must be profit, subject to legal constraints.[1]

The Function and Limits of Law in Management

This analysis assumes that moral agency as a management precept is the better approach, rather than sporadic attempts by government to regulate by law the morality of the marketplace on an industry-wide basis. In other words, every time a crisis in business morality occurs and is brought to public attention, pressure builds to regulate the problem by appropriate government agency action. This solution assumes that law or the legal process is the only method of confronting immoral business behavior, and that therefore anything legally permissible is necessarily morally acceptable.

There are a number of difficulties with this solution. First, law is reactive: it only responds to problems after the fact. Second, law is uniformly negative: it generally condemns wrongs rather than requires conferral of benefits. For example, our civil rights laws are activated only by violations, i.e., a refusal to admit to places of public accommodation or employ certain classes of individuals. These laws do not compel or encourage admission of protected classes of persons. Likewise, whereas our federal constitution forbids the states from denying equal protection of the laws to any person, it does not compel the states to pass laws benefiting such persons. Third, government laws and regulations are often incomprehensible, costly to administer, and contradictory among regulatory agencies.

Law, whether public or private, does not fully resolve the problem of enhancing ethical business behavior. Law, however, does clearly establish minimum standards of conduct that serve as a foundation for moral development.

How is law manifested in business practice? It is expected that business managers must obey the law, but this means anticipating the legal aspects of their jobs as well as responding to actual legal requirements.

Prevention or Minimization of Legal Consequences

Enlightened business management requires prevention of legal consequences, or at least minimization when prevention is not possible (e.g., an unanticipated fire that damages a hotel or restaurant). In this case, a properly implemented crisis management plan may save guest lives and property or at least minimize increased liability for loss or damage to such invitees. The issue here is not only the individual one of business cost or damage control, important as that may be, but the collective one of affirmatively aiding a larger constituency, such as innocent bystanders caught in the path of danger.

This raises a fundamental dilemma. If ethics in business practice means treating all stakeholders fairly and responsibly, not because the law commands so but because our own sense of business self-respect and integrity encourages such action, does business self-interest to the exclusion of all other concerns make this goal impossible to fulfill?

Economic and Other Interests

The answer lies in recognizing that economic self-interest is not the sole responsibility of management, just as obeying the law is not the sole means by which moral leadership is asserted and maintained. All interests, business and human welfare, must become elements in the process of management. Economic considerations, although dominant, must be balanced against other values in determining the best course of action to take.

The Integration of Ethics Into Management

But how and where is this formidable balancing task to be accomplished?

Institutional Concern

First, it is essential to understand that ethical management must be an institutional concern of high priority to the board of directors of any organization. The board must raise ethical issues and evaluate the ethical implications of its decisions and actions together with other business policies. The ethical character as well as the business acumen of directors must also be evaluated for purposes of their election and retention. If directors are morally deficient, needless to say, the organization may be subject to moral manipulation. Of course, it is easier to eliminate a morally questionable director who transgresses a law or management policy than to predetermine the ethical character of a director as such. However, this does not excuse shareholders from initially evaluating such character traits. Likewise, a board must not shirk responsibility to discipline and/or remove officers who violate the standards of conduct of the organization.

A Business Code

Why should there be such a business code at all? Essentially, a business code does make clear the organization's ethical policies and provides a means of educating as well as measuring compliance by all concerned. Why the need for a code of ethics for each company rather than an industry-wide code? Apart from the specter of anti-trust prohibitions, the varying needs and policies of individual hospitality entities make agreement on an all-embracing code more meaningful than "be good" and "don't be bad" unlikely.

What can be done at the operational as well as the strategic management level? Rogene Buchholz states the case for involvement:

> Management at all levels, but particularly top management, must recognize the most important role they play in institutionalizing ethical responsibility through-out the organization. Managers have many avenues available to them to shape the corporate culture including the setting of objectives for individuals and sub-units in the corporation, developing and implementing the reward structure for other individuals in the organization, modifying organizational structures for the accomplishment of ethical goals, and developing measures of ethical perfor-mance. Managers not only have responsibility for efficient and effective use of the material and human resources the corporation has available but must also be concerned to create a responsible institution that cares about the ethical and moral impact of its actions and will take corrective action when ethical issues arise that need to be considered.[2]

Meeting the Needs of Constituencies

If this is the process by which business management must enhance its ethical practice, how does this responsibility relate to the hospitality industry? Other than the obvious general applicability of what has been reviewed previously, we have a unique responsibility as a service industry. The way we treat our employees, shareholders, customers, vendors, and, to a lesser degree, our community becomes critical. We are labor- and customer-interface intensive, not product-intensive. Therefore, we need to tailor our ethical policies and practices to meet the needs of our constituencies on a continuing, face-to-face basis. Because of the high degree of competition within our industry, our ethical posture is as important as our marketing and other management skills. Any perceived unethical reputation, whether justified or not, will be reflected much more quickly in our industry by customers who may refuse to deal with us as well as by unionized employees who may file grievances. This is due to the higher de-gree of personal interaction at all levels in a service-oriented environment. Because of the wide choice of competing businesses in the first instance, such reactions can be dev-astating and very hard to overcome.

Standards of Ethical Conduct

Rather than attempt to construct a model of ethical behavior suitable for every business need, we should develop standards of moral leadership consisting of critical questions for management. Laura Nash[3] has done so in the following action plan for implementation by managers, to which Frederick Sturdivant and Heidi Vernon-Wortzel have added cogent comments:

- **Have you defined the problem accurately?**

  Make sure that you have a clear understanding of the problem. The more facts you collect and the more precise your use of those facts, the less emotional your approach will be.

- **How would you define the problem if you stood on the other side of the fence?**

  This question demands that you look at the issue from the perspective of those who may question your ethics or those who are most likely to be adversely affected by your decision. Are you being objective?

- **How did this situation occur?**

  Look into the history of the situation and make certain you are dealing with the real problem and not just a symptom. You will gain perspective and contribute to your understanding of the views of others if you examine the problem historically.

- **To whom and what do you give your loyalties as a person and as a member of the corporation?**

  Nash points out that "every executive faces conflicts of loyalty. The most familiar occasions pit private conscience and sense of duty against corporate policy. Equally frequent are situations in which one's close colleagues demand participation (tacit or implicit) in an operation or decision that runs counter to company policy."[4] Managers must ask to whom or what they owe the greater loyalty. One executive made his stand dramatically clear to subordinates. His predecessor as head of a large division of a major corporation had been jailed for price fixing. The new division head invited his four immediate subordinates to take a ride with him his first day in the new job. He drove them to a vantage point where they could see a nearby federal prison. He told the four that if they ever felt any sense of misguided loyalty to the "good of the corporation" that might cause them to consider committing an illegal act, they should return to this spot to consider the decision.

- **What is your intention in making this decision?**

  Ask yourself the simple question, "Why am I really doing this?" If you are not comfortable with your answer, do not make the decision.

- **How does this intention compare with likely results?**

  Sometimes, regardless of the goodness of the intent, the results are likely to be harmful. Therefore, it is important to think through the likely outcome.

- **Whom could your decision or action injure?**

  Even though a product may have a legitimate use, managers should reconsider whether to produce and distribute it if the product is likely to fall into the wrong hands and result in harm, managers should reconsider whether to produce and distribute the product. This issue is particularly difficult. Drain cleaner in the hands of a child could be lethal, but a "childproof cap" could prevent injury. Installing code-approved but highly flammable furnishings in guestrooms is economically justified but is likely to increase the life-threatening consequences of a hotel fire. Is it ethical to install these furnishings even if it is legal to do so?

- **Can you discuss the problem with affected stakeholders before you make a decision?**

  If you are planning to close a property, should you talk with affected workers and the community beforehand to help assess the consequences? If you are changing benefits packages, should you hold meetings to discuss the changes?

- **Are you confident your position will hold up in the long run?**

  Can you sustain the commitment you have made? Can you foresee conditions that are likely to make you change your mind? Will today's good decision be tomorrow's bad decision?

- **Could you disclose without misgivings your decision or action to your boss, your CEO, the board of directors, your family, or society as a whole?**

  Arjay Miller, former president of Ford Motor Company and later dean of Stanford Business School, used to suggest the following public opinion test: "Ask yourself, 'Would I feel comfortable in reporting my action on TV?'" Decisions that seem very private and confidential often end up receiving full public disclosure.

- **What is the symbolic potential of your action if it is misunderstood?**

  The essence of this question is the issue of sincerity and others' perception of your action. Politicians campaigning for office engage in many symbolic acts to attract various voter groups. For example, in the 1988 presidential campaign the Democratic candidate, Michael Dukakis, rode in a tank to appeal to the so-called "hawk" element of the electorate. George Bush, eager to attract the conservationist groups, appeared in a variety of photo opportunities in park lands. These symbolic acts sometimes backfire, as they did in this campaign, and create more resentment than goodwill. Managers face the same problem. A CEO may hire a minority member to "sit near the door." But without making a real commitment to the effort, employees are likely to greet the effort with cynicism.

- **Under what conditions would you allow exceptions to your stand?**

  Professor Nash asks, "What conflicting principles, circumstances, or time constraints provide a morally acceptable basis for making an exception to one's normal institutional ethos? For example, you learn that a highly productive, loyal office manager 'borrowed' $250 and subsequently repaid that amount to a petty cash fund. The company has a very strict policy against personal use of company funds. The employee manual states quite clearly that 'such action will lead without exception to immediate termination.'"[5] What would you do? The money was borrowed to pay emergency medical bills. Would you feel differently if the money had been used to pay gambling debts? What if the employee had been with the company only 18 months instead of 12 years?[6]

A Value-Oriented Strategy

The important consideration in the preceding strategy is the longer-term value of the process, not the short-term benefit of the result. Obviously, managers are human and the frailties of humanity are legion. It is equally true that pious pronouncements of good intentions without subsequent action are irrelevant at best, and cynical at worst.

Must management rely solely on blind faith or heavenly intervention to produce results? If not, what alternative should be employed? A better path is that of "informed fairness," fairness based on analysis and a full understanding of each situation that confronts the manager. This means the commitment of time, resources, and energy to the task of addressing social values as well as economic efficiency.

To detractors who would argue that economic survival of the fittest negates social responsibility, the answer should and must be that the environment of hospitality management encompasses all values, not one to the exclusion of the other. Equally important is the fact that economic survival of the fittest means moral as well as economic fitness. John Casey has translated this concept into practice by observing, "The vocation of a leader in a company is more than making a living. It is making a life."[7]

Ultimately, the hospitality manager, like any other moral agent, is fallible, but fallibility is a virtue in the resolution of ethical problems. Casey explains:

> Leadership is a process; a moving picture, not a snapshot. Being a value-oriented manager does not promote the manager into an ethical leader. For that we need layers of insight and spontaneous flights of constructive imagination. But by anticipating consequences, leaders afford themselves the opportunity to exercise moral leadership. . . . Without our overdoing it to the point of Hamlet-like wavering, the knowledge that our judgments as human judgments, are flawed can help us protect those who would be hurt by our errors. And, that sense will have added something for everyone.[8]

Because Casey comes from a service background, his observations have special validity. Like him, we operate on the front line of human interaction. We deal directly with each other and internal as well as external stakeholders to a much greater degree than those who make or grow products. Growers and manufacturers operate through a multiplicity of intermediaries, many of whom are not involved in the ultimate delivery of the product. Therefore, their ethical responsibilities, though equally important, are more diffused, with differing responses emanating from differing sets of problems. Our challenge is more direct. Therefore, Casey speaks to our strengths as well as our inherent weaknesses. His credo is one of hope mixed with reality, a vision not of utopia but of a sensitivity to moral values. He lauds courage and persistence to employ not only our rationality but our humanity in the pursuit of human welfare.

Conclusion

There is no question that we uniquely possess the means to pursue this daunting endeavor. All that is required of each of us is to recognize its importance, be presented with a meaningful and workable set of organizational standards, work for managers at every level who are given the time, resources, and rewards to meet the standards, and expect accountability by those few who are either unwilling or unable to do so. As Kenneth Goodpaster has said, "The competitive and strategic rationality that has for so long been the hallmark of managerial competence must be joined to a more disinterested community-centered rationality."[9]

How well we succeed in the endeavor may well determine how society judges the quality of our profession in the years ahead. The industry is emerging into the twenty-first century as a leading component of the national economy, and much will be expected in all aspects of our performance. Quality in the economic sense must include quality in moral leadership in order that the industry does its share to meet the challenges that confront its constituents.

Endnotes

1. Milton Friedman, "The Social Responsibility of Business Is to Increase Profits," in *Business Ethics, Readings and Cases in Corporate Morality*, edited by W. Michael Hoffman and Jennifer M. Moore (New York: McGraw-Hill, 1984), pp. 126–131.

2. Kenneth E. Goodpaster, "The Concept of Corporate Responsibility," in *Just Business: New Introductory Essay in Business Ethics*, edited by Tom Regan (New York: Random House, 1984), pp. 320–321. Amplified in Rogene Buchholz, *Fundamental Concepts and Problems in Business Ethics*, (Englewood Cliffs, N.J.: Prentice Hall, 1989), pp. 123–125.

3. Laura L. Nash, "Ethics Without the Sermon," *Harvard Business Review* 59, 1981, pp. 79–90.

4. Ibid.

5. Ibid.

6. Frederick D. Sturdivant and Heidi Vernon-Wortzel, *Business and Society* (Homewood, Ill.: Irwin, 1990), pp. 123–125.

7. John L. Casey, "Teaching Ethics," in *Business in the Contemporary World* 2, no. 4 (Waltham, Mass.: Bentley College, 1990), p. 18.

8. Ibid.

9. Goodpaster as amplified in Buchholz, p. 147.

Discussion Topics

1. Discuss the dilemma created when a hotel executive's duty to promote business income conflicts with his or her duty to halt dram shop violations on the premises.

2. How would a restaurant manager cope with sexual harassment of employees by VIP customers?

3. Currently there are few women executives in higher-level hospitality positions. Will this scarcity of women in executive roles remain constant or change within the next ten years?

4. Analyze the ethical implications of convention overbooking in light of the argument that it is economically necessary as a competitive strategy.

Term Paper Topics

1. Describe the ethical implications of the employment-at-will doctrine in relation to whistle-blowing by middle and upper hospitality managers.

2. Describe the pros and cons of using ethics to support voluntary affirmative action programs as a tool to attract and retain minority hospitality work staff.

18

Ethics and Labor Relations

Harold Morgan

In the hospitality industry there is an adage that is often repeated: People are our most valuable asset. If they are not committed to serving our customers' needs, we will fail. In our industry, the issue of ethical and fair treatment of employees and its corresponding impact on the experiences of our guests is crucial.

It should come as no surprise to any manager or management student that the last few years have seen a significant increase in legislation and court decisions affecting the workplace. Managing has never been an easy task, and the smorgasbord of outside influences waiting to get you has made it even more difficult. This has increasingly put a strain on the ability of managers to use independent judgment when making decisions that affect employees. More important, I believe that laws and regulations have made managers shy away from determining the ethics and fairness of situations. As a result, managers tend to focus on laws and court cases rather than on making the right decision.

As difficult as it is to manage ethically in today's environment, the difficulty can increase when a union and a collective bargaining agreement are present.

In this chapter, I will discuss some of the tensions involved in this increasingly difficult situation and provide some guidelines for solutions.

The "Art" of Management, or So You Want to Be a Hotel Manager

Consider the following scenario:

- You are the graduate of a well-respected institution of higher education.

- You have taken a full battery of courses, including yield management, food chemistry, engineering, MIS, hospitality, hotel accounting, etc.

Harold Morgan is Vice President of Human Resources for Bally's Health and Tennis Corporation. Previously, he was Director of Employee and Labor Relations for Hyatt Hotels Corporation. He received his bachelor of science degree from the Cornell University School of Industrial and Labor Relations.

- You have worked during your summer and winter breaks in hospitality related jobs.

- You have interviewed with all the top hospitality companies.

- You have received two solid job offers with top firms.

- You are on your way to becoming an assistant front office manager in an 800-room major convention hotel in the Sun Belt.

Now, how will you be spending the next 40 years of your work life? Yield management? Feasibility studies? Forget it!

In fact, the majority of your time will be taken up with something you will affectionately call "people problems." The truth is that people problems are not problems at all—people (human resources) issues are the material of management. Every day on the job you will be forced to deal with human resource issues. More important, you will be forced to deal with the ethics of your decisions.

Another fact of life you will soon discover is that most people problems will fall into one category—employees not behaving the way *you want them to*. I am sure that some social scientists would diagram this in the following way:

behavior ≠ expectations

The problem is that most managers will view these behavioral problems as an *employee* problem. This is wrong. In most cases, people problems are the direct result of one thing—poor communication.

If we take this thought one step further, we could say that, in reality, all of management is communication. Every function that you carry out as a manager would somehow be defined with the word "communication" in it. For example, training has recently become a buzzword in our industry. What is the definition of training? The communication of expected behavior.

OK, so management equals communication. What does this have to do with ethics and product quality? Everything. If, as managers, we do not learn to master the fundamentals of communicating with our employees, we do not have a prayer of achieving a level of management that can be described as ethical. If we do not get close to this ethical ideal, we will never provide a quality product.

The correlation between these two issues is that close. To summarize, people problems are *not* "people problems." By definition, if management is communication, then people problems are, in many instances, communication problems on the part of management.

Great! So now what am I supposed to do?

How do you even begin to manage ethically? For years, managers have wrestled with this question. There is no easy answer. More important, you can never achieve Nirvana when it comes to managing. Instead, you will always reach higher levels of competence in balancing the issues of any specific situation. The best starting point for determining the answer to this question is to ask another question: "What is the most important management skill?"

Here are a few hints:

- You never took a specific course in it.

- You never really think about it.

- Very few managers are good at it.

- You will immediately believe you are good at it.

- Your employees will always criticize you for it.

What is it? Listening.

Listening

The biggest reason managers fail is not because they lack the technical skills to do a job. They fail because of personality problems or for not being able to get along with managers and employees.

What is the best defense against such reasons for failure? Listening.

What is the best way to begin the process of communicating? How can you become a better manager and also bring some ethical standards to your workplace and your organization? By listening.

Only by knowing your environment and the concerns of the people in that environment can you manage well. The starting point is listening.

Once managers begin to understand this concept, they can begin the job of managing well and, more important, managing ethically.

Making Ethical Labor Relations Decisions

Now that I have pontificated long enough, it is time to address what my editor wants—ethics and labor relations. The immediate problem with this discussion is that some people might say that having the word "ethics" in the same sentence as labor relations is a contradiction in terms! The typical image of labor relations people (both management and union) is not entirely positive. Images of smoke-filled rooms and employees' jobs being decided by poker games are not to be taken lightly.

Do not follow in the footsteps of those before you in dealing with this area. The only way to make correct ethical labor relations decisions is to make informed decisions based on the law, your union contract, the goals of your organization, and, most important, ethics.

It is important to digress here briefly. I can personally admit that it is easy to fall into the game of making deals, trading decisions, and just trying to get by. The difficult course is to make rational decisions and to take tough stands when you are right. In the long run, your employees and the union may not like these decisions, but they will always respect you for the stands you have taken.

A Personal Example

Perhaps one of the best examples of this was my first major blunder as a personnel director.

I was the personnel director of a 400-room hotel in a very strong union city. The hotel had two restaurants: a specialty Italian restaurant and a 24-hour, full-

service restaurant. A server named Amanda had been working a four-day-a-week schedule for a long time in the full-service restaurant, even though the hotel's union contract had no requirement that management continue this practice. (Let's assume in this case that past practice for a single employee's work schedule is not an issue.) Amanda had never been a particularly good employee; her tenure and four-day-a-week schedule were the result of one "minor" condition: She was related to a high-level union official. One day, the controller mentioned that the hotel could save a great deal of money by having all employees (including Amanda) work a five-day-a-week schedule. He had calculated that the hotel had 35 additional employees who could be laid off. The hotel would save money in benefit costs since, by contract, full-time benefit payments were paid to any employee who works three days a week or more.

The controller was right. The hotel could save a significant amount of money. (For purposes of this example, we also need to assume that there is no ethical dilemma in laying off 35 employees, although it really is an ethical problem. However, we can assume that the job market is excellent for experienced hotel workers and they will easily find other jobs.)

The contract stated that if we changed schedules we must rebid the schedule based on seniority. We did this and everybody seemed happy until our business agent told me that the high-level union official was furious because his relative now had to work a five-day-a-week schedule and she was hounding him to get her back on four days. The agent asked me to do something to help him out because of the pressure that he was subjected to from the official. He also suggested that we rebid a single four-day-a-week schedule. He assured me that Amanda would be the only server to bid on the schedule. He also assured me that no grievances would be filed and everything would work out fine.

What should I have told him?

Suppose I did the wrong thing and complied with his suggestion. Why was this the wrong decision and what better solutions do you have?

In examining this example, please keep in mind the following questions:

- What is a contract and what are the parties' obligations when they sign a contract?

- What obligations do you have, ethically, to a work force, regardless of a contract?

- What obligations do you have to your organization from a legal perspective, regardless of a contract?

Morgan's Laws

First Law

There are many possible solutions to the problem described above, including the easiest—make her work five days. However, I will tell you that my solution violated Morgan's first law of labor relations: "Never knowingly violate a contract (even if someone asks you—including the union)."

Second and Third Laws

My solution also violated the second and third laws: "Never owe the union a favor" and "Always make professional, logical decisions that consider the ethics of a particular situation and their impact of the decision on the work force."

These laws will help guide you in making ethical decisions when the immediate solution may not be apparent.

Let's consider a few more examples.

You are the human resources director of an 800-room major convention hotel in a city with a long history of powerful labor unions. The physical structure of this building is enormous. There are many alcoves, stairwells, and back hallways (nooks and crannies) where your employees can disappear. Your convention services manager tells you that he is having problems with a few of his convention services attendants. They disappear for long periods of time and he cannot find them. He suspects that they are smoking marijuana when they are gone because they come back to work glassy-eyed and smelling of pot.

He suggests that the next time they appear ready to leave, he will follow them to find their hiding spot. After that, it will be a simple matter of catching them in the act.

He does this and discovers a back staircase that leads to a small storage closet. He tells you that he was able to see them smoking marijuana through a crack in the door. The next time this happens, the manager catches the employees and brings them to the human resources office.

A union shop steward is brought in and the manager explains that he is going to recommend the employees' jobs be terminated for non-performance of duties, leaving the work area without authorization, and possession of a controlled substance. The shop steward asks to see the marijuana, but you find that the manager does not have any of the evidence. We are now in a classic situation of a manager's word against a employee's word.

At the same time, you begin to wonder how the manager was able to see the employees through a crack in the door. You decide to examine the back stairwell yourself.

You discover that it is virtually impossible to see anything through the crack in the door.

The manager's allegations might not hold up in an arbitration case. Obviously, your case is not good. It is important, however, to take another look at the initial situation. What mistakes were made in the beginning of the case and how could you have better handled it? What precautions could you have taken prior to catching the employees? How could you have resolved the problem by communicating with the employees before they were caught?

Fourth and Fifth Laws

This case is proof for Morgan's fourth law: "Always go to where the incident occurred." Why? Because of Morgan's fifth law: "Never forget that the decisions you make as a manager may impact someone's livelihood."

Our business has a nasty reputation for being a high-turnover, "revolving-door" industry. Most of our managers are very accustomed to having large changes in the work force. I believe this has a subconscious impact on most managers. They forget that when job termination occurs we are not just adding to our turnover percentage. We are taking away someone's livelihood—their ability to care for their family and keep them clothed and fed and keep a roof over their heads. Never forget this.

In the beginning of this chapter, I discussed the need to make ethical decisions in order to create an environment in which employees will take care of our customers. The preceding example illustrates this point. Management's ability to make a fair and well-investigated decision in a termination case is the ultimate ethical decision.

Another excellent example of this point is management's use of spotters' or shoppers' reports. For the uninitiated, spotter services are companies that are hired to secretly evaluate a business to determine how well services are being provided. One of the more common uses of these services is to evaluate the honesty of employees. The area that always receives a great deal of scrutiny is the bar/lounge operation.

There is no question that bars and lounges pose a unique challenge for management. They are difficult areas to fully control, and the temptations on the part of employees can be great. Let's consider an example that includes the use of spotters' reports.

You are the director of food and beverage operations in a hotel with a large food and beverage operation ($20 million a year). Unknown to you, your general manager and controller have hired a company to review your operation. Your general manager shows you the report and tells you that, overall, it is excellent. But she does ask you to carefully investigate the section of the report concerning your high-volume lounge. She feels there may be some serious problems and employees may be stealing.

What is your course of action for investigating the situation and what is your game plan for solving the problem, if one exists?

Your initial response should be that you need more facts.

The report specifically says that a particular bartender is not ringing up drinks and is pocketing the money. The report also alleges that he may be involved in this wrongdoing with a cocktail server because he does not ring up all the drinks that she in particular serves.

What are you going to do?

Ninety-nine percent of the food and beverage directors in the world will attempt to fire these employees. They will either get additional facts or they will set up the employees in another situation to get additional evidence.

Please understand there is nothing wrong with this choice of action. In fact, when there is a good-faith doubt about an employee's honesty, management certainly has a right to think in terms of termination. (It is OK. This is an ethical decision!)

However, I would like to raise an additional train of thought. What steps has management taken to develop systems to *prevent* employees from being dishonest? I am not saying that management has an obligation to out-think every possible dishonest act. However, how about implementing certain basic controls? Does not management have an ethical obligation to prevent dishonest acts in the first place? Do we not have an obligation to our company, owners, and stockholders to run the business in a professional way with proper economic safeguards?

The sad truth is that there are very few businesses in this industry that have accomplished this. Very few hospitality companies have the necessary checks and balances in place to conduct their operations professionally and to simultaneously discourage employees from dishonest acts. I believe this is unethical for our companies and our employees.

In the preceding example, the food and beverage director will ultimately find that there are few checks and balances to substantiate the general manager's case. Everything will turn out to be circumstantial evidence.

How can you make an ethical decision about an employee's livelihood if you are not providing a work environment where you can make informed judgments that will ultimately lead to ethical decisions?

You cannot.

Sixth Law

Hence, Morgan's sixth law: "Always look to yourself (management) first. Evaluate whether management is part of the problem or part of the solution."

Seventh Law

We have spent a great deal of time discussing how to evaluate situations, what to look for, and how to proceed. We have avoided, however, two very important commandments in making ethical labor relations decisions. The first one is quite simple: "Investigate. Investigate. Investigate." (The seventh law.) What we have really been saying is that you must fully investigate a situation in order to make ethical decisions.

Eighth Law

The eighth law is related to the seventh, and it is important that you learn how it is derived.

You are a regional vice president for the western division of a nationwide restaurant chain. All terminations of employees with five or more years of service must be approved in advance by you or a member of your staff. You receive a phone call from one of your restaurant managers who requests permission to terminate a six-year employee for excessive absenteeism. He tells you the case is well-documented and that the union will not be able to challenge the discharge. The employee is currently on suspension awaiting your decision.

How will you proceed? What should your decision be?

It is always difficult when you are not directly involved in a situation to make these kinds of decisions. However, as a non-involved party you also have the unique ability to make a fair judgment without any personal biases. In all likelihood, you do not know the employee and you will not have any preconceived ideas.

Therefore, what do you do?

Regardless of your faith in the manager, I recommend that you never take anyone's word for how well a case is documented. By the way, this is the eighth law: "Document. Document. Document." However, only management or a representative of management should be involved in the preparation and custody of such documentation. Always review the documentation yourself. And make certain you review the entire file. You will be amazed how little documentation is contained in most files. You will also be astounded at the number of contradictions.

For instance, let's assume that this employee does seem to have a problem with attendance. What does the last formal evaluation say about the employee's overall performance? (I am making a big assumption that there ever was a documented formal evaluation!) What is your decision if the last evaluation of this employee (six months ago) is excellent in all areas and does not indicate an absenteeism problem? What is your decision if this employee has never had a documented evaluation? How is an arbitrator going to rule in this situation? Why am I asking so many questions?

Ninth Law

I ask these questions because if you are going to make ethical decisions, you must always ask an endless amount of questions (remember law five). Even after you make what you believe to be an ethical decision, you should continue to ask questions. (By the way, law nine is: "Ask. Ask. Ask.")

When we discuss asking questions, we usually find another terrible mistake on the part of most managers. This is the tenth law.

You are the rooms division manager at a 350-room hotel. It is your day off (this is truly a hypothetical situation). Your front office manager calls you at home and tells you the following story:

A front office employee disappeared from his work station without authorization for 20 minutes. When he arrived back at his work station, he was suspended pending investigation. He is now on his way back to the hotel. Your front office manager asks whether or not she has your authorization to discharge the employee.

What is the first question you must ask your front office manager?

Tenth Law

Morgan's tenth law is: "Get the employee's side of the story." What did the employee say?

Think about it. This manager was considering terminating an employee (taking away his livelihood) and had not asked the employee why he or she left the work station. What if the employee left because there were no bell attendants on the floor and the employee decided to help a guest get to his room?

Quite obviously, this would be a good decision on the part of the employee.

As we enter a very competitive time for all hospitality companies, we increasingly hear the phrase "employee empowerment." If we really want to empower our employees, should we not first consider their ethical treatment before worrying about empowerment?

Exhibit 1   Morgan's Ten Laws

1. Never knowingly violate a contract.
2. Never owe the union a favor.
3. Always make professional, logical decisions that consider the ethics of a particular situation and their impact on the work force.
4. Always go to where the incident occurred.
5. Your decisions may impact someone's livelihood.
6. Always look to yourself (management) first. Evaluate whether management is part of the problem or part of the solution.
7. Investigate. Investigate. Investigate.
8. Document. Document. Document.
9. Ask. Ask. Ask.
10. Get the employee's side of the story.

Summary

Let's take time to summarize where we have been and where we are going. It is absolutely essential for the future of our business that we manage our employees in an ethical manner. This must take priority over all considerations. In no way is this to minimize other factors (with all due respects to my company's general counsel). However, better decisions will flow from viewing decisions from an ethical viewpoint rather than viewing them in regard to what a particular contract says or the way in which a law is interpreted.

At this point, it is beneficial to apply the ten laws (see Exhibit 1) I have described to the following case study.

Final exam time!

You are the human resources director of a 650-room hotel with a predominantly minority work force. There is a union contract, and the relationship between management and the union has not been good for a number of years. Both the union and management are doing their best to hurt each other in every way possible. You are doing your best to ensure that employees are not being hurt in the cross fire between management and the union.

Jenny, a 13-year housekeeper, is caught during a routine check leaving the hotel with nine packages of saltine crackers. These crackers are available to employees in the employee cafeteria. When stopped, she becomes extremely agitated and runs away from the security officer. She returns to the employee entrance without the crackers and leaves the building.

Your security officer submits to you the required incident report and it is waiting on your desk the next morning when you arrive at work. You check and discover that today is the employee's normally scheduled day off.

What is your first step, and how will you proceed in this case?

You have thoroughly investigated the case. You find that Jenny's file is excellent and contains no other documented problems. Your director of housekeeping tells you Jenny does excellent work and she would hate to lose her. However, she adds that despite Jenny's record, she would hate to create a precedent that would never allow management to terminate an employee for theft.

You have also interviewed your security guard. All the facts check out, and there were other management witnesses to verify his report.

What should you do next?

You now call the employee in and ask her to explain her side of the story. She arrives in your office with a shop steward. They explain that Jenny is a diabetic and needs to continuously eat small amounts of food to keep her blood sugar at its proper level. She usually carries a few crackers that she gets from the employee cafeteria so that she can eat something during the day.

Let's assume for a minute that you believe her. You verify with her doctor that the employee is diabetic and that she needs to eat small amounts of food during the day. The doctor even tells you that she specifically asked a number of months ago if the saltine crackers in the employee cafeteria were good for her condition.

What is the next step? The employee's story is true and management's story is true.

The employee inadvertently was leaving the hotel with some food from the employee cafeteria. She did not act maliciously, but there is no question that the incident happened.

Later that afternoon, your general manager talks with you and insists that theft is theft. Even though there are a great number of mitigating factors in this case, the GM does not want to give employees the idea that theft of any amount is permissible. A past practice of allowing such thefts by employees could be used against the hotel.

I have no intention of giving you the answer to this puzzle now. However, there is a series of decisions and actions you can take that will result in a truly ethical decision and also avoid the list of potential problems that your general manager has given you. What is your decision? You can find the answer at the end of this chapter.

Before I leave you with a list of additional problems, I would like to offer a little bit of wisdom instead of more laws.

These types of decisions will be the most difficult that you will ever deal with in any business environment. Never lose sight of this fact. If a decision regarding an employee seems easy or cut and dried, you have probably missed something. Return to "Go" and collect 200 minutes to reconsider. Also, never forget that the easy decision is usually wrong. It takes intestinal fortitude to even begin examining the ethics of your decisions. However, if you are going to be a great manager, you must make this commitment.

Many companies may laugh at this article. They will tell you there are too many other problems that you must deal with in order to be successful. Do not listen to them. Push the system until it gives. Do not let yourself become part of the problem.

Solution to Problem

There is a solution to this dilemma that can meet the needs of all sides. The solution is to discipline the employee for her actions (a written warning would suffice), but also sign an agreement with the union stipulating that the decision is non-binding and non-precedent-setting in future discipline cases.

This solution also satisfies the ethical issues involved in this case. Is it ethical to terminate a housekeeper with 12 excellent years of service because of one error? I think not. However, there is a justified concern that making an ethical decision in this case could hurt the hotel in making judgments in other cases that might involve more serious theft issues.

There is one last thought to ponder. What would you do if the union refuses to sign a document that makes the case non-precedent-setting? What choices do you now have?

Discussion Topics

1. Your general manager is new to a union hotel. Your previous general manager was very friendly with the top union officials. In fact, he was so friendly that he attended their weekly poker games. They have asked the new general manager to continue the tradition. They tell him that these games help foster a good relationship between management and the union. Your general manager has come to you, the human resources director, for guidance. What is your counsel, and what is the basis for your decision?

2. Your general manager is new to a union hotel. This hotel does not have a good relationship with the current union. The GM tells you that he is under strict instructions from the corporate office to improve the relationship with the union. He holds a meeting with you (the human resources director) and the secretary-treasurer of the union. At the meeting, he explains to the union official that he wants to improve the relationship and develop a better working rapport with the union.

   The secretary-treasurer is delighted. He invites the general manager to a small get-together at his house with other union officials. He says this would help to develop this new relationship by meeting with some of "the guys." The general manager does not ask your advice and tells the secretary-treasurer that he will attend. Everyone shakes hands and the meeting ends. Do you have any counsel for your general manager or is his decision acceptable to you?

3. You are the general manager of a major downtown convention hotel. Your hotel wants to expand the number of guestrooms. The city council is not willing to grant the permits necessary to begin construction. Your hotel has a contract with a very strong and politically connected union, and you are certain the union can significantly influence the opinion of the city council. You have an excellent relationship with the union. Do you enlist its help?

4. You are the owner/manager of a small independent restaurant in a major city. You have an excellent relationship with your current union. The president of the union asks you to hire her son as a waiter. She shows you his résumé and it

appears that he has extensive restaurant experience and would probably be qualified for the job. What do you tell the mother?

Term Paper Topics

1. You are the senior vice president of human resources/administration for a national restaurant chain. Your firm has numerous collective bargaining agreements with the national union. Most of your employees under contract are part of a multi-employer health and welfare/pension trust. The other trustees of the plan have asked you to become a trustee. What is your decision and why? Issues to ponder or agonize over:

   a. What constitutes a multi-employer plan? Under what legal rules do these plans operate?

   b. What legal responsibilities would you have as a trustee of the plan?

   c. In a typical collective bargaining situation, what are your legal and ethical responsibilities to your company?

   d. What are the legal and ethical conflicts that may arise if you are representing your company from a collective bargaining standpoint and your trust fund from a fiduciary standpoint?

   e. Relate the concept of trustees of multi-employer plans to the concept of corporate boards of directors.

   f. Knowing what you now know about multi-employer plans and trustees, would you change the rules? What changes would you make?

2. Identify a local service business that is very labor-intensive and has a significant problem with tardiness and absenteeism. (This should not be difficult!) Interview the human resources director to determine what steps have been taken to mitigate the problem. For instance, are doctors' notes required? Are employees being sent to company doctors for second opinions? Is there a tracking system for keeping lists on all incidents of tardiness and absenteeism?

   Research the concept of no-fault point systems. Design your own plan. What are the elements of your program? What ethical dilemmas were involved in designing your system? Are there any exceptions to what are considered "no fault" incidents? Are there any better and more ethical ways to solve the problems of tardiness and absenteeism?

19

Ethics in Competition Based on Management by Values

Gerald E. Goll

This chapter is not a litany of ideas or a series of examples of ethical and unethical competition. Rather, it explores a single methodology for evaluating whether competitive practices are, indeed, ethical or unethical with a specific contrast to whether they are legal or illegal, lawful or unlawful, and on what basis the distinction may be made. It is assumed that the readers of this entire volume have a plethora of their own examples of both ethical and unethical behavior. This chapter presents a model for evaluating those examples.

Discussions of ethical behavior in business too often take the narrow approach of merely focusing on individuals taking bribes or making payoffs. The mass media have a field day exploiting investigations of unethical behaviors of elected officials as well as lawyers, the profession from which so many elected officials come. Laws are being passed that purportedly will ensure ethical behavior—or at least reduce the incidents of unethical behavior. Such laws will miss the point just as have most of the contemporary "in" discussions of ethics because they attack the symptoms rather than come to grips with the problem.

A Legal-Ethical Dichotomy

Management in American society may very well be facing a legal-ethical dichotomy. Many behaviors that are viewed collectively to be legal may be considered individually as being unethical, while certain ethical behaviors are not condoned because they are, in fact, illegal.

The hodgepodge of room rates in a typical hotel is a case in point. It is not uncommon to raise room rates during a period of peak demand and lower them when

Gerald E. Goll, DBA, is an Associate Professor and Chairman of the Hotel Management Department in the W. F. Harrah College of Hotel Administration, University of Nevada, Las Vegas. He earned his BA from Michigan State University, his MA in human resources from Pepperdine University, and his DBA in management from United States International University. He has published many articles, most of which deal with human behavior and management by values, and has received numerous awards for his teaching excellence.

demand lessens. After all, this is just common sense—economically. Room rates have become as complex as airline rates. What exactly is the significance of the rack rate when compared to the corporate rate, reduced rate, group rate, tour rate, or the Sunday–through–Thursday rate compared to the Friday–Saturday rate? Who is the unfortunate person reduced to paying the published rate?

It is perfectly legal to adjust rates. The American traveling public has even come to accept this practice as being "just the way it is." The public may not like it but accepts it. The public also maneuvers to become one of the chosen few who get a "special" rate. The justification would appear to lie in the economic laws of supply and demand and the reality that everyone does it. To be competitive, a hotel must ensure its room prices are fluid.

This practice, based on economic law, is legal. But is it ethical? Economic law, unfortunately, does not necessarily encompass, if it even addresses, ethical behavior, and this may be the nub of the problem. To be legal, one has only to stay within the parameters of the law. Ethical behavior, however, requires a moral judgment. It is a most distressing indictment of the American free enterprise system that ethical business behavior may come to be viewed by some as being analogous to naivete.

Too Much Law?

The idea of too much law and not enough justice appears to be the heart of this issue. Law is for collectives; it is for groups in the collective form. Justice relates to ethics. It is doubtful that ethical behavior can ever effectively be legislated.

It was former U.S. Supreme Court Chief Justice John Marshall who reminded us that we are a nation governed by the justice of laws, not of men. Of course, he said this early in the development of American society, at a time when the world was making the traumatic shift from feudalism to the Industrial Revolution. Justice of laws rather than of men was a value statement as an alternative to man's capriciousness.

Alexis de Tocqueville, the French philosopher who studied the United States in the 1800s, observed, "Americans see a problem and throw a law at it."[1] Today, we throw dollars as well as laws at problems, and they work no better because in most cases we are throwing them at symptoms of the problems, not at the problems themselves.

Bayless Manning, former dean of the Stanford Law School, said, "Too much law, too fast, is producing a gradual decline in the willingness of the public at large to assume voluntary compliance."[2] Legal scholar Grant Gilmore went even further, noting that laws reflect the moral worth of a society, and that a reasonably just society will reflect its values in reasonably just laws; likewise, an unjust society will reflect its values in unjust laws.

Law does not raise the moral standards of a society; it merely establishes the lowest acceptable level of behavior. Being legal or lawful merely entails adhering to the law. Being ethical requires a moral judgment.

The Social Responsibility-Business Ethics Dichotomy

In 1981, Peter Drucker attempted to come to grips with the issue of what constitutes business ethics:

Business ethics is rapidly becoming the "in" subject, replacing yesterday's social responsibilities. Business ethics is now being taught in departments of philosophy, business schools, and theological seminaries . . . not to mention the many earnest attempts to write business ethics into the law.[3]

But, should discussions of business ethics replace discussions of social responsibility as if a distinction should or could be made? Are they not one and the same?

Definition of Social Responsibility

Archie Carroll, also in 1981, provided a very workable model in his four-part definition of social responsibility:

1. Every business has its *economic responsibility* to provide goods and services that society wants and to sell them at a fair price in order to meet the owner's realistic expectations of return on investment. All other responsibilities will go for naught if this first responsibility is not met.

2. It is a business's *legal responsibility* to meet society's expectations that have been articulated in law.

3. It is business's *ethical responsibility* to meet society's expectations that, however, have not been articulated in law.

4. The gray area of *discretionary responsibility*—business actions not required by law or not even really expected by society. These are actions that may be the closest manifestations of an enterprise's values.[4]

It would appear that socially responsible business is ethical business and that social responsibility and business ethics are one and the same subjects—not to be separated. It is the balancing of the second and third parts of Carroll's definition that seems to cause the greatest potential for indecisive and misunderstood actions by business. An overly narrow and strict interpretation of legal responsibility may be seen by some planners and decision-makers as absolving them of personal accountability for their actions. "I do it because it's the law," may be the lament. This may be the case whether it is legislative law, judicial precedent law, or economic law. Too much law and not enough justice may result from an over-reliance on legal responsibility to rationalize, and in some cases justify, one's behavior.

It may be of some interest that there is little or no mention of values in Drucker's discussion of business ethics. Carroll, on the other hand, stresses that ethics and values are intimately related. Ethics is the moral principles or values that drive behavior, he claims. One's values shape one's ethics. This is, indeed, the case, whether it is an individual or an enterprise.

Management by Objectives

In 1954, Peter Drucker's book *The Practice of Management*[5] became a "must-read" for all students and practitioners of management. Management by objectives (MBO) as interpreted by management practitioners became a near-panacea for all management problems. The strength of MBO is that (1) these objectives are ostensibly jointly agreed upon by management and employees; (2) effective controls are established; and (3) feedback is provided on the progress being made. In MBO, *what* is to be done and *how* it is to be done are made very clear. Today's generation of students and practitioners ask how else can we manage without first setting objectives? However, the universal acceptance of MBO may pose a problem unto itself. It has become an almost automatic, knee-jerk approach without sufficient thought given to its mechanics. In the 1990s the need may not be so much management *by* objectives as it is to manage *the* objectives.

A narrow and possibly debilitating perspective can result when the focus is only on objectives and the means to achieve those objectives. The fast-talking, convincing manager may be able to get people to agree to almost anything. We have all experienced coming out of an objective-setting meeting asking the painful question, "I agreed to do what?" In such a situation, what may conspicuously be lacking is commitment. It is possible that a too-narrow application of MBO could be the very thing that exacerbates ethical uncertainties by creating an environment in which the "ends justify the means."

All workers want to know *what* it is that they are to do and *how* it is to be done. Management by objectives does, indeed, provide the *what* and the *how*. Possibly this was sufficient for most workers 40 years ago. It is doubtful that it is today. Today's employees also want to know *why*. In many cases they are demanding to know why. Knowing why enhances commitment. Answers like "Because I said so" or "Because we've always done it this way" simply will not cut it anymore, as if they ever did.

We have progressed from management by directing to management by objectives. We may now be at the next step in the evolution of management from an ethical point of view—management by values.

Management by Values

What is it that sets one organization in the hospitality industry apart from others providing essentially the same services and performing the same functions in the same geographic area? What gives one the competitive edge that causes certain people to become regular, repeat guests? On what basis may prospective employees, for whom the competition is so keen, select one organization over another? What is the basis for determining socially responsible and ethical business practices above and beyond the lowest levels of acceptable behavior associated with the limitations posed by mere legal compliance?

Management by values (MBV) represents an analytical approach to providing long-term responses to these questions rather than just settling for short-term expediencies. It is more than just a concept or a management style; it is a philosophy from which styles or concepts may flow. It represents a method employers may use to determine rather effectively the quality of the environment within the organization. As used here, it is an analytical tool.

The Analytical Model

The model is depicted in Exhibit 1. At its heart is the confluence of an organization's values, goals, and norms enclosed in the triangle—the "action triad."

Values. Values are the first and most critical element. Chester Barnard, president of New Jersey Bell Telephone in the 1930s, and later on the faculty of Harvard University,

Exhibit 1   Management by Values (The Action Triad)

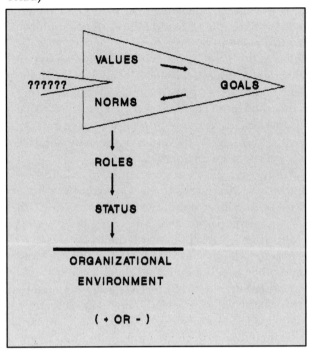

suggested that the real role of the executive is to manage the values of the organization. The primary responsibility of top management is not merely the setting of goals and objectives and establishing the means to reach those goals and objectives. Management's primary function is to establish, clarify, and disseminate the organization's values to each individual within the organization. In establishing and disseminating the organization's values, top management sets the tone for all that is done within the organization.

Values explain why an organization exists and give meaning to all that an organization does. An organization that lives according to, and up to, its values will have less to fear in meeting its legal responsibilities. An ethical organization has less need to be defensive of its actions in the face of the law. Such an organization will be less likely to justify its actions with the expediency of economic laws of supply and demand. Such an organization is less likely to have its behaviors adjudged by society as being unethical.

Of the 62 organizations that Peters and Waterman scrutinized in the research that led to their best-seller *In Search of Excellence*, two were within the hospitality industry—Marriott and McDonald's. The authors concluded that "excellent companies seem to have developed cultures that have incorporated the values and practices of the great leaders and thus those shared values can be seen to survive for decades after the passing of the original guru."[6]

Any attempt to understand the values of an organization and appreciate its competitive practices may be enhanced by studying the founder. In many cases, the values of the founder may be seen many years later within the organization. Looking at only four of the many examples available within the hospitality industry may help to clarify this point. These include the two whom Peters and Waterman examined, William Marriott and Ray Kroc, plus Conrad Hilton and Kemmons Wilson.

Conrad Hilton did not start out as a hotelier; he was a banker. He traveled from San Antonio, New Mexico, to Cisco, Texas, with the intention of purchasing a bank. When the deal fell through, he invested in the Mobley Hotel. To this day, Hilton hotels operate in the efficiency mode expected of a banker's mentality. It should come as no surprise that to this day the Hilton chain markets itself as the businessperson's hotel. In competing for this market, it accurately projects an image and attracts guests who are able to identify with this image. The values of the man with the banker's mentality may still be seen in the corporation he founded.

William J. Marriott had a different personality and value system. Raised in Salt Lake City and embracing the Mormon faith, he traveled to Washington, D.C., to open his first venture, an A&W Root Beer stand. Being an opportunist, he branched from that stand into the original Hot Shoppe and from that into providing food service for the airline industry during its post–World War II embryonic years. It was inevitable that he would venture into lodging shortly thereafter and ultimately into cruise ships, amusement parks, and other widely diversified activities in travel and tourism. The hallmark of any Marriott enterprise still bears the family-oriented values of the founder. Consistent with his basic values, cocktail lounges are discreetly offered to guests, not conspicuously displayed. Marriotts are still good places for families. Their image attracts a particular segment of the marketing population that identifies with this image.

Kemmons Wilson offers still another contrast. In a real sense, he created the motel industry as we know it today. He personally experienced the need while travelling with his family by automobile when such travel resumed after World War II. He experienced wide variances in quality among the tourist courts at which he stopped. Little, if any, provision was made for children, and obtaining food was a catch-as-catch-can proposition. As in the cases of Hilton and Marriott, Wilson saw a need. He rapidly constructed a network of motor lodges that featured consistency, on-property food service, the obligatory swimming pool, and free lodging for children under age 12 when traveling with their parents. His vision proved to be flawless when the corporation he founded soon boasted the greatest number of rooms under one name—Holiday Inn. To this day, the marketing pitch of "no surprises" bears the values of the man who sought the much-needed and desired consistency for travelers. There was a time when if you had seen one Holiday Inn, you had seen them all.

We turn to the fast-food segment of the food service industry for our fourth example, Ray Kroc. He detected a change in Americans' eating habits and in this change saw a need. The rapid growth of McDonald's is testimony to his vision. He completely changed the traditional image of the hamburger stand into an industry. Kroc aimed for the family, and particularly children. To this day, magazine racks, pin ball machines, pay telephones, or anything else that would encourage loitering will not be found in a McDonald's store. The image is projected and a major portion of the population is able to identify with this image.

The common denominator within these four examples is the values of the founder—not necessarily the same values, but values just the same. The personal values may still be seen within the corporations they founded. These men are identified as industry leaders, not industry managers. They had strong personal values and projected these values, and they were successful. They were leaders, and the corporations they founded continue to be leaders within their respective segments of the hospitality industry.

As already stated, competition for guests and the employees to serve these guests is keen. It may be said that marketing, specifically market segmentation, is the externalization of the internal values of an organization in order to attract a certain segment of the population that can identify with those values and become regular repeat guests. The same may be said in recruiting employees. The externalization of the internal values of the organization attracts a certain segment of the labor pool who can identify with those values and become productive and retained employees.

Indeed, the *quantity* and *returnability* of guests may be directly related to the *quality* and *retainability* of employees, as in a cause-and-effect relationship. A competitive edge in both of these critical markets may be gained by this realization.

Goals. Goals and their supporting objectives flow from an organization's values. Certain financial goals must be set and achieved or the organization will soon cease to exist. However, an organization does not market its profit and loss statement; it markets its image. It does not gain a competitive edge over its competition by its profits, although it surely will have a healthier budget with which to pursue its competitive goals. Certain goals, however, may be deemed unrealistic in the face of one's values. We achieve goals but we live by our values. The strength of the latter may be the more critical factor.

In *In Search of Excellence*, Peters and Waterman use the term "superordinate goals" as being analogous to organizational values. Their point is that successful organizations operate within certain parameters whether they are called values or superordinate goals. They state their belief that competitive decisions by good companies are shaped more by their values than by their dexterity with numbers:

> Their ability to extract extraordinary contributions from very large numbers of people turns on the ability to create a sense of highly valued purpose. Such purpose invariably emanates from love of product, providing top-quality services, and honoring innovation and contribution from all. Such high purpose is inherently at odds with 30 quarterly MBO projects, 25 measures of cost-attainment, 100 demeaning rules for production-line workers, or an ever-changing, analytically derived strategy that stresses costs this year, innovation next, and heaven knows what the year after.[7]

Norms. Norms are established within organizations as the means for achieving objectives and establishing standards of behavior leading toward goal attainment. More important, the organization's norms should enhance and protect the values, not only of the organization but the values of individuals within the organization. All too often, junior people allege that top management requires them to behave unethically. The norms of the value-related organization establish the parameters of accepted behavior. Definite limitations are placed on the number of options open for reaching an objective. Strategies are shaped by the values. When strategies are developed in the vacuum of goals, critical uncertainties may accrue.

An unfortunate but common example is offered to make this point. In my courses at both the undergraduate and graduate levels, students react the same to the following scenario. A business sets a goal of increasing profit through increased reve-nue. A strategy is adopted of hiring attractive, curvaceous young women to entertain male customers in order to encourage them to buy more. At this point in the scenario, the students' collective reaction is straight-faced with little apparent impact being made. When it is then added that the business is a religious supply house, the students erupt with laughter. Why is this? For illustrative purposes, the distasteful strategy just described represents a norm for achieving the goal. In our society, this strategy is not condoned because it is socially unacceptable and, in some situations, illegal. Although, unfortunately, it is not uncommon. The students accept it as such. They may not like it or condone it, but they accept it as reality. But, this strategy for a religious supply house? The image of what such an enterprise represents makes the strategy totally in-consistent with the perceived values. The norms are a contradiction. Such behavior does not meet society's expectations and is thus viewed as being unethical.

The contrast between the facades of hotels and restaurants and the locations of their personnel offices provides another example. At a time when the changing demo-graphics pose some uncertainties in the traditional labor pool for the hospitality indus-try, a critical look at the reception of potential employees is warranted. "Ours is a special world" is a value statement of the industry that is not always enhanced or pro-tected by the norms of individual properties. Out back, by the loading dock, behind the dumpster, at the end of a long, dark, dingy hallway, or at a local hiring hall are extreme examples of places where hiring sometimes occurs. Personnel or human re-sources offices should, instead, enhance and protect the industry's value statements. What are potential employees, the persons needed to provide services to guests, to think? How can first-class employees be expected when these very people perceive they are being treated as second-class citizens when seeking employment in "ours is a special world"?

The competitive edge is gained by proactive management that considers the possibility that prospective employees will sense this inconsistency. An inconsistency will be seen as just so many platitudes and so much hyperbole on the part of manage-ment. The prospective employee will see through the hypocrisy of the norms not sup-porting the values. Even if the person does accept employment after this questionable reception, the new employee has become prepared to look for more inconsistencies within the organization. In the face of such inconsistencies, employee turnover, not retention, is enhanced.

Ethical behavior results from norms that enhance and protect the values of the organization while meeting the expectations of society. We do not achieve values; we live by them. Ethical organizations live by their values while achieving their competi-tive goals. Their norms enhance and protect both values and goals because the two are not in conflict; they go hand in hand.

Roles. Roles are simply the expected behaviors of all individuals within the organiza-tion. The higher the degree of consistency between the values, goals, and norms of an organization, the greater the degree of certainty of the expected behaviors. In other words, employees know how to behave and they know why certain behaviors are en-couraged and others discouraged. When norms support values, people know their roles. When there is an inconsistency between the values and norms, they do not. "Do as I say, not as I do" is not a figment of one's imagination. Unfortunately, in some cases it is an organizational reality.

Status. Status is simply a ranking in a social hierarchy. In this model, status flows from roles. When people behave as expected and their behavior supports the organization's values while achieving its goals, a positive status is achieved. Of course, there is such a thing as negative status which may be analogous to being a "foul ball" or worse. Status that flows from an inconsistency between the elements in the "action triad" will be negative because people will not know how to behave.

Organizational Environment. Organizational environment is the bottom line. A positive environment reflects the degree of consistency among all elements of the model. Conversely, the higher the degree of inconsistency, the greater potential for a negative environment. Management must continuously assess the quality of the environment it has created because it is, indeed, management, not the employees, who creates the organization's environment. This may require a more introspective analysis than is common. It is far easier to attribute problems to someone else than to oneself. These problems may more often be the fault of management than the employee. Indeed, we have seen the enemy and the enemy is us.

At issue, of course, is distinguishing between a problem and the symptom of a problem. Low profit, the guest who does not return, high employee turnover, the unproductive employee, lack of competitive edge, allegations of unethical behavior, or accusations of unlawful actions are among the phenomena usually considered to be problems. Instead, they may be only symptoms of the problem. In most cases, the basic problem is an inconsistency between the organization's values and the norms that fail to enhance and protect those values.

The Manager as Teacher

An arguable point is that ethics cannot be taught, but we are able to learn what is ethical. Several years ago, Jerry Harvey raised the issue that teachers are not able to teach, but students are able to learn. His point was that the best that any teacher is able to do is to create an environment in which students may learn. Teachers, thus, become facilitators by creating an environment that enhances learning. Learning is really a very personal thing—we learn what *we* want or need to learn, not what someone else says we want or need to learn.

Effective teachers do not impose their own ethics on their students; rather, they shape the students' ethics. Effective teachers do not subordinate ethics to the rigidity of technique. Rather, they adjust the technique to mold and strengthen the ethic.

This learning process is closely related to motivation. We learn when we are motivated to learn. Using the late B. F. Skinner's operant conditioning, we are motivated to learn a behavior that has the greatest payoff. When the greatest payoff follows the most dubious behavior, the result is totally predictable. In the short run, too many of us opt for the quick return with very little thought given to the long-term consequences. Too many of us opt for the easy way. Rarely can ethical behavior be measured in the short term. And rarely will the easy way be the most ethical way.

In the more successful business organizations, management accepts teaching as one of its basic responsibilities. Does management teach or create an environment in which the employees can learn? The distinction is more than one of subtlety or semantics.

Conclusion

The proliferation of lodging and food service facilities in this country is being compounded by the impact of the changing demographics on the traditional labor supply. The United States is solidly ensconced in what the futurist Herman Kahn refers to as the tertiary, or service, activities, and its citizens enjoy increased leisure time to partake in such activities. This is forming an interesting paradox. The number of people seeking service is increasing while the number providing the services is decreasing.

The competition for guests, as well as for employees to serve the guests, has become critical. The ethics of such competition should be of major concern to the leaders of the hospitality industry. Most assuredly, the industry's guests and its employees are aware of this.

But, then, the contemporary American may be typified by his and her awareness. In spite of the criticisms of our education system, Americans today have been "educated" by the quantum improvements in communications and transportation.

Merely paying lip service to the problem of business ethics fails to recognize the reality that it may not be the problem but rather only one of several symptoms of a far deeper problem. Most of us are capable of developing the ability to solve problems, but it is doubtful that any of us will learn how to solve symptoms.

Until we at least attempt to really come to grips with what constitutes ethical behavior in business, we will continue to face the potential dilemma of the legal-ethical dichotomy. Indeed, the complexity of the American society itself may be the genesis of the legal-ethical dichotomy.

We achieve goals, but we live by our values. Ethical behavior begins with the organization's values. In competition, if we do not have values and live by them, what do we really have?

Endnotes

1. As quoted in Max Lerner, *America as a Civilization* (New York: Simon and Schuster, Touchstone Books, 1957), p. 437.

2. Bayless Manning, "Too Much Law: Our National Disease," *The Business Lawyer* 33, November 1977, p. 435.

3. Peter Drucker, "What Is Business Ethics?" *Across the Board*, October 1981, p. 22.

4. Archie B. Carroll, *Business and Society: Managing Corporate Social Performance* (Boston: Little Brown, 1981), p. 33.

5. Peter Drucker, *The Practice of Management* (New York: Harper, 1954).

6. Thomas J. Peters and Robert H. Waterman, Jr., *In Search of Excellence* (New York: Harper & Row, 1982), p. 26.

7. Ibid., p. 51.

Discussion Topics

1. To gain insight into a hotel chain's competitive practices, an analysis of the founder's personal values may be helpful. In addition to the examples presented in this chapter, consider some additional corporations for analysis.

2. Discuss the meaning of the statement that ethics flows from values. Discuss how consistency between an organization's values and its norms will provide guidance to employees for ethical behavior.

3. If an organization lives by its values, it will operate at a level above that required by the law. Discuss how an organization can achieve this.

4. A narrow approach to MBO may create an "ends justify the means" environment. Discuss the applicability of this statement and how practicing MBV may place limitations on an organization's "means."

Term Paper Topics

1. Compare and contrast several organizations with regard to their stated values and whether their competitive practices are consistent or inconsistent. Develop a hierarchy of effectiveness.

2. Compare the locations of human resources or personnel offices in several hotels and determine their impact on prospective employees.

20

Ethics in Hotel Appraising

Stephen Rushmore

The demise of the savings and loan industry presents an appropriate time to investigate ethics in hotel appraising. Many of the bank failures that plague the economy today can be traced to either inept or unethical real estate lending practices. Since appraisers had a significant role in reviewing many of these real estate transactions, industry observers and regulators are now questioning both the ability and moral integrity of these professionals.

This article discusses the various ethical issues involved with performing appraisal services. By understanding how appraisals are commissioned, performed, and ultimately used, you will easily see how the unscrupulous can benefit through unethical behavior. Because my personal background has been focused on hotel appraising, I will probably slant my viewpoint in that direction. However, ethics in hotel appraising will apply to all types of real estate. Lastly, the term "hotel appraisal" is intended to encompass a variety of professionals who perform consulting services for the hotel industry. While their products may be called feasibility studies, market studies, financial projections, or appraisals, they all have a common ethical bond—to render unbiased professional advice that can be relied on by lenders and investors.

Reasons for Appraisals

A hotel appraisal (or other similar study) is generally used to justify an investment in a hotel project. Because hotel developers and professional operators usually

Stephen Rushmore, CRE, MAI, CHA, is founder and President of Hospitality Valuation Services (HVS), the nation's leading real estate appraisal and consulting organization devoted exclusively to the lodging industry. He is a graduate of the Cornell University School of Hotel Administration and received his MBA in finance from the University of Buffalo. With well over 3,500 domestic and foreign consulting assignments in his career, Mr. Rushmore has written five authoritative texts on hotel/motel valuation and economic feasibility studies, including his most recent text, The Computerized Income Approach to Hotel-Motel Valuations and Market Studies. *An acknowledged appraisal expert within the industry, Mr. Rushmore lectures throughout the United States and contributes frequently to trade journals, including the monthly financial column "Investment Today" for* Lodging Hospitality. *He also publishes a quarterly newsletter,* The Hotel Valuation Journal.

have their own capability to evaluate potential opportunities, appraisals are looked upon as independent verification of preconceived conclusions performed to satisfy the needs of lenders and less sophisticated investors. For example, Baron Hilton does not need an MAI appraisal to tell him how much one of his hotels is worth. However, in order for him to obtain lender and investor financing, independent appraisal services become essential.

In most investment situations, the appraisal is commissioned after the hotel developer or purchaser has conducted extensive analysis and concluded that the opportunity exhibits economic viability. Once preliminary interest is shown by a suitable lender, the appraisal then becomes one of the final hurdles between conducting or not conducting the transaction.

You can imagine the stress involved in this process. The developer or purchaser has spent thousands and sometimes millions of dollars on research, legal fees, broker expenses, professional time, and so forth. The prospective lender or equity investor has been identified and shows interest. The fate of the entire deal rests on the appraiser. If there is going to be a breakdown of ethics, it will probably occur at this point.

Pressures

I have been in these situations many times and have experienced the various types of pressures exerted on appraisers. Sometimes these pressures are subtle and indirect, while occasionally the client's demands become obvious and abusive. In most cases, the pressure is monetary, but once I was threatened with physical harm.

As an appraiser, you become sensitive to the comments and innuendos used by some clients to influence your final value conclusion. A few of the pressure tactics and remarks I have heard over the years include the following:

- "Let's work together on this one, I have many projects coming down the line."

- "If we do this deal, I'll introduce you to all my partners."

- "Do you want to be added to our approved appraiser list?"

- "Do you want to remain on our approved appraiser list?"

- "We really want to do this deal."

- "I can find other appraisers who will give me the right number."

- "If you kill this deal, I'll sue you for the damages."

- "You better come up with the value or I'll file ethics charges against you."

- "You did not give me the value I needed so I will not pay your fee."

The ethical breakdown occurs when an appraiser yields to these pressures and places immediate monetary gain above long-term credibility. It might seem easy to just give in, please the client, get paid for the assignment, and line up future business. But in reality, this short-sighted approach will usually create long-term problems.

Need for Honesty

Appraisers are in the business of selling credibility. Lenders and investors depend on objective and unbiased findings. Knowledge and skill are important, but an appraiser's reputation for honesty and integrity is essential. Those who have sold out their reputations eventually begin to lose clients and friends. Since the nature of the appraisal profession requires the sharing of data and information, those who exhibit unethical behavior soon become ostracized by their peers. The downward spiral continues.

How can you spot an unethical appraiser? It is usually very difficult because there are so many components of a hotel appraisal that small adjustments at each step can ultimately result in a substantial change in the final value. Investors and lenders should carefully scrutinize each appraisal they receive and be alert to some of the techniques that unethical appraisers use to distort the final estimate of value.

Example

Let us assume that the purpose of the appraisal is to estimate the market value of a proposed hotel in order to justify a certain level of financing. The borrower/developer wants to "finance out" (i.e., not have to put any equity into the deal), so he attempts to influence the appraiser to produce a value that is approximately 25% above the total project cost so the amount of the mortgage would be sufficient to fund the entire development. Let us also assume that the proposed hotel has a marginal location, so to come up with the desired results the appraiser will have to push for additional value at every available opportunity in the appraisal process. Having performed thousands of hotel appraisals and reviewed the work of many other appraisers, I know the areas in which slight distortions of the data and conclusions will create an inflated valuation. This unethical practice is also cumulative so that each small and usually insignificant distortion will produce a higher final value.

Steps in the Hotel Valuation Process

Looking at the entire hotel valuation process, the following sections describe some of the techniques unscrupulous appraisers will apply to their analyses in order to pump up the final estimate of value.

Supply and Demand Analysis

The first step of a hotel appraisal is the supply and demand analysis in which the room night demand in the market is quantified and projected into the future. The existing and proposed supplies of hotel accommodations are then brought into the calculation based on the competitive attributes of each property. The final result of the supply and demand analysis is a projection of occupancy for the subject property out to a point where it reaches a stabilized level. Any overstatement of the existing demand or the expected demand growth rate tends to inflate the area occupancy levels and increases the market potential for any proposed lodging properties. Techniques to look out for include the following:

- **Increasing the size of the primary market area so that more hotels are included in the analysis**. By padding or inflating the base level of demand, the impact of additional proposed hotel rooms on the area's overall occupancy will be lessened. For example, assume the primary market area has five hotels with a total of 1,250 rooms. The area occupancy is 75%. Current room night demand is calculated as follows:

$$1{,}250 \times .75 \times 365 = 342{,}188 \text{ Room Night Demand}$$

If 300 new rooms were added to this market, the area-wide occupancy would decline to 60%:

$$1{,}250 + 300 = 1{,}550 \times 365 = 565{,}750 \text{ Room Night Supply}$$
$$\text{Occupancy} = 342{,}188 \div 565{,}750 = 60\%$$

An unscrupulous appraiser could lessen the impact of the new rooms on the area-wide occupancy by increasing the size of the market area to include hotels that would probably not be competitive. Assume that the primary market area was increased to include ten hotels totaling 2,500 rooms operating at an average occupancy of 71% (looks more conservative). The current room night demand is calculated as follows:

$$2{,}500 \times .71 \times 365 = 647{,}875 \text{ Room Night Demand}$$

If the same 300 new rooms were added to this market, the area-wide occupancy would decline to only 63%:

$$2{,}500 + 300 = 2{,}800 \times 365 = 1{,}022{,}000 \text{ Room Night Supply}$$
$$\text{Occupancy} = 647{,}875 \div 1{,}022{,}000 = 63\%$$

- **Using a higher demand growth rate**. Most hotel appraisals analyze the future and projected growth in hotel room night demand. Compounding the yearly increase in hotel demand by a slightly higher growth rate greatly inflates occupancy levels. For example, local economic and demographic trends indicate that hotel room night demand will probably grow at an annual rate of 2% per year. Exhibit 1 shows the impact of both a 2% and a more aggressive 4% growth rate on the area-wide occupancy.

Exhibit 1

	Year 1	Year 2	Year 3	Year 4
Room Night Demand 1,250 Rooms (2%)	342,188	349,032	356,013	363,132
Room Night Demand 2,500 Rooms (4%)	647,875	673,790	700,742	728,772
Area-wide Occupancy 1,250 Rooms	60%	62%	63%	64%
Area-wide Occupancy 2,500 Rooms	63%	66%	69%	71%

The combination of a wider, less diluted market area and an overaggressive demand growth rate produces seven additional points of occupancy by Year 4 that can greatly enhance the ultimate market value.

- **Inflating the competitiveness of the subject property**. Once an area-wide occupancy has been projected, the supply and demand analysis fits the subject property within the market based on its relative competitiveness. One of the techniques used to accomplish this analysis is known as penetration positioning. This process takes the area-wide occupancy and multiplies it by a penetration factor that represents the percentage of the area-wide occupancy the subject property is expected to achieve. For example, a new hotel in its first year of operation generally achieves an occupancy that is between 80% and 90% of the area-wide level. In the second year, a new hotel should normally produce an occupancy of between 95% and 105% of the area-wide level. In its third year of operation, this average hotel will probably reach an occupancy that is 105% to 115% above the area-wide. Using the area-wide occupancies calculated above, Exhibit 2 shows the impact of using aggressive penetration percentages.

Exhibit 2

	Year 1	Year 2	Year 3
Area-wide Occupancy 1,250 Rooms	60%	62%	63%
Realistic Penetration	85%	100%	110%
Projected Occupancy	51%	62%	69%
Area-wide Occupancy 2,500 Rooms	63%	66%	69%
Aggressive Penetration	95%	110%	120%
Projected Occupancy	60%	73%	82%

The total impact of the enlarged market area, aggressive growth, and competitive positioning amounts to 13 points of inflated occupancy by the third year.

Other techniques that are sometimes employed to create higher occupancy levels during the supply and demand analysis include: leaving out proposed hotels that have a good possibility of being developed; adding large amounts of latent demand; and including properties that are not competitive.

Forecast of Income and Expense

The next step in the hotel valuation process is the forecast of income and expense that uses as its basis the projected occupancy determined in the supply and demand analysis. Obviously, if this occupancy projection has been overstated as demonstrated previously, the forecast of income and expense will likewise represent these inflated assumptions. But even if the occupancy levels were realistic, there are many ways unscrupulous appraisers can juice up the bottom line during the forecast. Techniques to look out for include the following:

- **Using an unrealistic inflation rate**. Most forecasts of income and expense use inflated dollars that require certain inflation assumptions. The compounding effect of an aggressive inflation factor has been demonstrated previously with the use of the high room night demand growth rate. While sometimes it may be justified to inflate revenues at a rate greater than expenses, this technique is often used to increase the bottom-line profits.

- **Omitting certain expense categories**. Hotels' projections will normally follow the Uniform System of Accounts for Hotels and should include all categories of revenue and expenses. In addition, a reserve for replacement must be included as a normal cost of doing business. If the reserve is overlooked, the projected net income will be overstated.

- **Using insupportable operating ratios**. The technique that can easily create a substantial increase in bottom-line profit is to project unachievable operating ratios. Understating departmental expenses by three to five points will greatly inflate the net income. Just a little change in each expense category has a cumulative impact on the bottom line. Minor alterations in the operating ratios usually go undetected, particularly by those who are unfamiliar with hotel financial statements. Sometimes unusual effects can be created during the forecasting process. For example, a projection of income and expense for a hotel with a 15% food and beverage departmental profit will generally produce decreasing net income as the food and beverage revenue increases. Therefore, an unscrupulous appraiser can overstate the bottom line and create more value by merely decreasing the amount of food and beverage revenue projected.

Income Capitalization Approach

The last step in the hotel valuation process is the income capitalization approach that typically includes a ten-year discounted valuation model. The input for this calculation comes from the forecast of income and expense which by this point can be greatly inflated. In addition, more value can be created with some minor modifications to the model. Techniques to look out for include the following:

- **Using a high inflation rate**. Most appraisers will take the projection of income and expense and inflate the net income as of the stabilized year for as many as ten years using an overall rate of inflation. If this inflation factor is overstated, the final estimate of value produced by the model will also be overstated.

- **Using mid-year discounting factors**. Most valuation models assume that the net income is received at the end of each year so the proper discount factor would be an end-of-the-year factor. A higher value will be achieved if a mid-year or a beginning-of-the-year factor is used. This technique of creating value often goes undetected.

- **Using low discount and capitalization rates**. Low discount and capitalization rates produce high values. In fact, a small change will often produce a significant difference. For example, lowering an overall capitalization rate a single point from 11% to 10% will increase the value by approximately 10%. Since discount and capitalization rates are largely judgmental, unethical appraisers tend to hone in on this area when additional value is required.

Other techniques that are sometimes used during the capitalization process to create value include: extending the discounting period from five to ten years without increasing the discount rates; understating brokerage and legal fees; understating the cost of debt and equity capital; and failing to consider the age of the property at reversion.

As you can see, appraisers have many opportunities to adjust the inputs during the appraisal process in such a way that the ultimate value can be greatly increased. Likewise, in instances where a low valuation is required (i.e., property tax appeals), reverse techniques can be employed to deflate the final outcome. Unfortunately, since the hotel valuation process is so complicated and sophisticated, very few people can recognize when abusive practices are taking place.

As is the case with most unethical behavior, unethical appraisals are a means to an end. In most instances, appraisers resort to these practices to satisfy an unethical client and ensure that the appraisal fee for the assignment will ultimately be received. In addition, the threat of losing future business by not producing the desired results further entices those with low moral values to conform to the demands of the client.

A Possible Solution to Unethical Appraisals

Unethical behavior is self-imposed and cannot be condoned under any circumstances. However, it is hard to believe that an individual who has worked many years to learn the appraisal profession would become unethical without some persuasive, external motivating factors.

One of these external factors is an antiquated system whereby the party with the least financial exposure is usually the party who retains and pays for the appraisal. This inherently breeds corruption.

Basically, appraisals are used to protect someone from making an investment that exceeds the value of the property. This individual or entity is generally the money source that places at risk the major portion of the hard investment dollars. In many instances, this money source is not responsible for commissioning or paying for the appraisal. Rather, the deal-maker (i.e., general partner, syndicator, developer, etc.), who traditionally uses other people's money, finds the appraiser, commissions the study, and pays the bills.

This system is obviously prone to corruption. Because the deal-maker normally has little more than time invested in the deal, there is maximum incentive to take whatever steps are necessary to complete the transaction. The appraisal is considered a necessary evil that could kill the deal if a particular value is not achieved. Herein lies the basis for the monetary pressure applied to the appraiser. "Make my number or else" comes through loud and clear when some deal-makers commission their studies. In fact, in large transactions a few deal-makers will use several appraisal firms to maximize their chances of obtaining the desired result.

Looking further into the transaction, you will sometimes find lenders who seem to be more interested in doing the deal with an inflated appraisal rather than relying on an unbiased, objective study. In these instances, the bank's loan-originating department is probably receiving bonuses for the quantity of deals made rather than for their quality. This system also breeds corruption and provides additional incentive to unfairly influence the appraiser.

These are two examples of how people with motivations that are not exactly aligned with the transaction's money sources sometimes attempt to exert monetary pressure on appraisers. As stated previously, appraisers should never yield to these pressures. However, if the system were perfect, the appraiser could be isolated from these influences and would not feel compelled by any of these pressures.

Recommendations

It really does not take much to rid the appraisal system of adverse influences. Here are some ideas:

- Anyone who is investing money in a hotel transaction should independently select, retain, and pay for the appraiser. This may mean that several appraisers would be used on any one transaction, but the end result of multiple studies would highlight any disparities between these professionals. These studies enable the investor to reach a more informed investment decision.

- Any retainer agreement made with an appraiser should be structured so that the appraiser will be guaranteed of receiving full payment, even if the desired results are not achieved.

- Lenders should commission appraisal services through a totally independent appraisal department that is isolated from any of the bank's origination services.

- Lenders should not compensate employees based on the number or amount of loans made without factoring in the quality of the loans.

- Lenders should not require appraisers to look to any third party (i.e., the deal-maker) for payment of the appraisal fee.

- Lenders should not accept any appraisals commissioned by prospective borrowers.

- Lenders should have a screening procedure to ensure that only highly qualified appraisal professionals are used.

In addition to these suggestions for improving the way appraisals are commissioned, the appraisal profession should constantly monitor its members and enforce the code of ethics and standards of professional practice for those individuals who continue to perform in an unethical manner.

Conclusion

While the bad news is that it is too late to correct the abuses that ruined the savings and loan industry, the good news is that the banking regulators seem to now understand how the appraisal system was pressured by unethical parties and are starting to implement some of these suggested recommendations. Hopefully, ethical appraisal practices can be enhanced through these simple lender regulations, coupled with informed investors who understand the necessity of retaining their own, unbiased hotel appraiser.

Discussion Topics

1. Why is a high ethical standard such an important component of a hotel appraisal? What are some of the costs associated with a biased study?

2. Why do some appraisers produce biased studies?

3. What can be done to encourage ethical appraisal?

4. What other types of professionals are bound by ethical standards?

Term Paper Topics

1. Select an actual appraisal report and review its contents to determine whether any of the conclusions seem to have been biased in any way. Modify some of the calculations, particularly those that were based on subjective opinions, to determine their sensitivity relative to the final opinion of value or feasibility.

2. Develop a set of appraisal policies and standards that banks and other users of appraisal services could institute in order to eliminate biased appraisals.

21

The Ethics of Yield Management

Robert G. Cross

Yield management has become a buzzword in the industry. Although this is some recognition of the importance of the topic, the conversion of the concept to a buzzword trivializes the impact that yield management can have if properly implemented.

Yield management (or, more properly, revenue management) has been approached with alternating skepticism, awe, distrust, and hope for economic salvation. Even though its application can be quite complex, the concepts of yield management are simple. They have been practiced to a certain extent in the hospitality industry for years.

Yield management is the discipline of maximizing revenues from perishable assets (rooms) through a combination of pricing and inventory controls. It is an application of basic economic principles. With yield management techniques, hotels seek to balance the supply of rooms in their marketplace with the demand for rooms on any given night, using price and inventory controls as the levers to obtain the balance.

For example, if demand for a particular night is high, the property may reduce the number of rooms that it sells at a discount. Conversely, if the demand is weak, discounts, as a rule, will be made available.

Application of Yield Management

Essentially, there are only a few variables that hotels must control to practice effective yield management. These are rates, availability, overbooking, and length-of-stays. Using these control variables, the knowledgeable property manager can improve revenues and accomplish the following goals of yield management:

Robert G. Cross is President of Aeronomics, Incorporated, a company that specializes in systems consulting to the service industries. His primary thrust has been in the area of yield management. He holds a bachelor's degree in chemistry and a JD degree from Texas Tech University, and is a member of the Texas and Georgia Bar Associations. His yield management expertise has been recognized in many international publications, and he is a respected lecturer worldwide on the subject of revenue maximization. His concepts are currently being applied by many of the world's largest airlines and hotels.

- Forecasting rack rate demand and protecting enough inventory to accommodate late-booking, high-yield traffic

- Monitoring future arrival dates to ensure that discounts are available in periods of weak demand

- Imposing minimum stay requirements during high occupancy periods in order to help fill "shoulder" periods

- Overbooking to prevent undue room "spoilage" as a result of no-shows, cancellations, and early departures

As hotel firms have experienced more success in applying these principles, an evolution has occurred from selling room type to selling rate. Although physical room type will always remain a consideration, guests and hotels are focusing more on the price/quality ratio than on physical distinctions such as double, king, and queen.

Benefits and Risks of Yield Management

Using yield management techniques, hotels have seen average daily rate (ADR) increases occur simultaneously with occupancy increases as they use these methods to make more effective use of their capacity. For example:

- One luxury hotel increased its ADR by $16 without any decrease in occupancy.

- A hotel chain in the Southeastern United States saw its average rates increase $5 while occupancy climbed two points for properties installing yield management systems.

- A major hotel chain with numerous international properties saw significant share gains in its yield management hotels in contrast to flat performance in non-yield-management hotels.

Guests, as well as hotels, benefit from the proper practice of yield management. For example:

- Rooms will be saved and made available (although at a slightly higher rate) for late-booking guests during peak periods.

- More deeply discounted rate programs will be offered in off-peak periods.

- Guests who seek rooms after the hotel is booked to capacity will have an opportunity to make a booking if there is an historically high percentage of no-shows or early departures.

The benefits of yield management come with certain associated risks. For hotels, there is the risk of:

- Walking guests if the overbooking levels are too high

- Guests questioning why they pay more than other guests for similar rooms

- Hotels becoming overzealous in their pursuit of revenues so that they damage their image

Ethical questions are a significant underlying aspect of yield management. In the following section, we will explore ethical issues (both real and perceived) that may result from the implementation of yield management principles.

Ethical Considerations: Dealings Between Interacting Parties

Nebulous issues of right and wrong often transcend legal issues in business dealings between parties. We expect that the person with whom we are dealing adheres to the same moral values as we do.

Unscrupulous businesspeople can behave in a manner that is unethical but may not be illegal. In the short term, this may provide some competitive advantage, but in the long term such unjust behavior prevents others from dealing with the person at all.

Virtuous and honorable business dealings do not have to be weak or priggish. One can be tough and fair. The standard that should be sought is justice for all parties. In devising a set of rules, whether a code of conduct or a yield management process, it is important to consider the impact of the rules on all parties who are directly or indirectly affected by them.

Ethical standards should be established in the context of society at large. Too often, ethical situations are described for only the persons involved in the personal, face-to-face transaction of the moment. However, ethical conduct should be described in the broader context of persons, separated by time and space, who will be affected by the outcome of the issue.

For example, a pricing decision at a hotel affects not only the hotel and the guest seeking a reservation, but subsequent guests who may seek a room, previous guests who may have already booked, the GM's bonus, shareholders or other owners, and, ultimately, the employees at the hotel.

We will examine a variety of situations in which ethical questions could arise and view them from a number of different viewpoints.

The Hotel Vis-a-Vis the Guests

Price Discrimination

The essence of yield management is its ability to segregate anticipated future bookings based upon the willingness or ability to pay, so hotels are assured that room inventories are allocated to guests who will contribute the greatest net revenues.

If the hotel is projected to be full, and demand for the rooms exceeds supply, yield management techniques suggest a variety of means to ensure that the guests who obtain reservations are the ones generating the greatest revenues. These techniques include: closing the lowest rate categories; imposing minimum lengths of stay; and requiring guarantees for late arrivals.

One of the consistently observed phenomena about guest booking patterns is that the guests who are the most price-sensitive book their reservations the earliest. Therefore, in the absence of capacity controls, a hotel will fill to capacity before the price-inelastic demand asserts itself. If a hotel fills to capacity a number of days prior

Exhibit 1   High Yield Spill

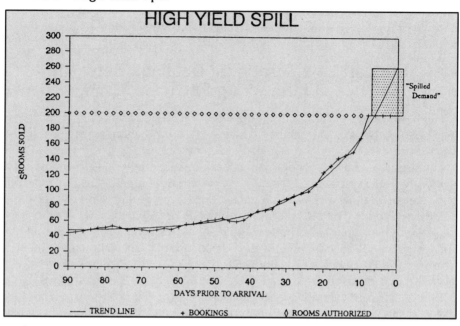

to the arrival night, it "spills" the high yield demand during the final few days. (See Exhibit 1.)

To prevent the loss of the highly valued (typically business) traffic during the final day prior to an arrival night, hoteliers will close discount rates while maintaining availability for rack rate guests.

Example: *A property near an airport will fill to capacity 10 days prior to arrival for Wednesday night stays if bookings are not constrained. The general manager has found that by closing off all discounts 25 days prior to arrival and imposing a 3-day minimum stay requirement, he can still fill his property while raising his ADR and improving his occupancy on Thursdays and Fridays.*

Do these restrictions violate the tried and true principle of first come, first served? Is it unfair or unethical to deny a potential guest a room on the expectation that a more valuable request for the room will materialize at a later date?

In considering the ethical implications of this situation, we must ask: "Who is harmed by this practice?" and "Who is harmed if this practice is not followed?"

Certainly, the guest requesting the discounted rate 25 days out is annoyed. Guests booking 30 days out were given the discounted rate, and the same physical rooms are available now at a much higher rate. Is this fair? We should consider the alternatives:

Make all of the rooms available at the lowest rate. This appears to be the equitable solution. Clearly, it is the easiest to implement. However, then guests will be denied bookings 10 days out when the property is full. Is it fair to a guest who cannot plan more than 10 days in advance to be denied a room if he or she is willing to pay a premium for last-minute availability?

The early-booking guest frequently has more alternatives than the late-booking guest. Payment of a higher rate is one alternative, as is shopping for alternative hotels at alternative rates. In addition, the early-booking guest might even be able to change dates, if necessary.

If we decide, nevertheless, that first come, first served is an equitable solution from the standpoint of the early-booking guest, the average rate (and accordingly, revenues) would be lowered if the discount levels remain the same. Is this fair to the investors who expect a certain return on their investment?

If all rooms must be made available at the lowest rate, then the hotel is likely to raise the lowest rate. Would this then be equitable to the guests who can book 30 days or more in advance?

Set one fair price that would fill the hotel without "spilling" high yield traffic. This would be the perfect solution if it could be accomplished. However, it is unlikely that the perfect price could be set for a room 180 days or more in advance. There are too many factors in the market that will change for the price to be perfectly established that far in advance.

Additionally, even if one had perfect knowledge of the price that should be charged for a room, it is unlikely that all of the diverse market segments for which the hotel is vying would agree that the price matched *their* perception of a fair price/value ratio.

If only one rate were offered at a hotel, then the hotel would seek the rate at which revenues were maximized. This would be at the level that generated the greatest number of guests at the greatest rate. (See Exhibit 2.) If we had a property consisting of 100 rooms, and we assumed the simplified demand curve below, the hotel could generate $2,500 from 50 guests at $50 each.

Exhibit 2   Revenue Potential—One Rate Offered

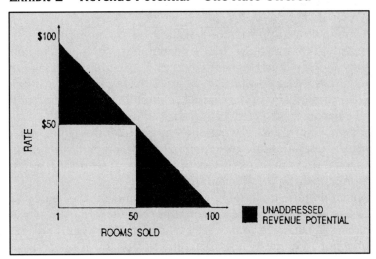

In this case, there are guests willing to pay less than $50, but rooms are not available at that rate. Similarly, there are guests who perceive the value to be above $50, but they pay only $50.

If the hotel offered four rates and controlled that capacity offered at any rate, then it could come closer to satisfying the demands of the market while generating $4,000 in revenues from 80 guests (20 × $80 + 20 × $60 + 20 × $40 + 20 × $20). (See Exhibit 3.)

Exhibit 3   Revenue Potential—Four Rates Offered

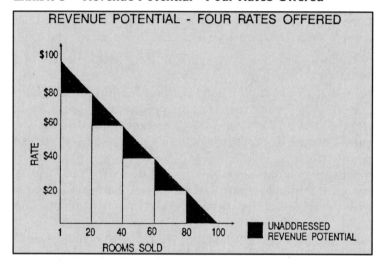

According to economic theory, the maximum revenues (and the maximum satisfaction of consumer demand) would occur if each room were priced individually. Theoretically, this would result in $5,050 in revenue to the hotel, more than twice the revenue if only one rate were offered! Also, an additional 50 guests would be accommodated, each at a rate they perceived to be a fair value. Although everyone who desired the lowest rate would not obtain it, more lower rates would be sold than if only one rate were offered.

Still, charging based upon a guest's willingness (or ability) to pay seems like a distasteful concept. Although rates could be extremely low for certain guests, others would be required to pay much higher than average rates. Even though the average rate paid by all guests might decline, is it ethical to have certain guests pay more than others for the same physical room? After all, a guest might discover that he or she is paying more than another guest for the same room.

If the guests were, in fact, paying different rates for the same product, then this would appear to be unethical price discrimination. However, is a room reservation 30 days prior to arrival when the hotel is half booked the same product as a room available at the last minute on a peak demand night?

An essential premise underlying yield management is the concept of demand-based pricing. Demand-based pricing recognizes the time-value of room inventory. As we know, the market value of a room varies by city, day of week, and season, as well as by competitive forces in the local market. In addition, the room's value varies over

Exhibit 4   Time Value of Room Inventory

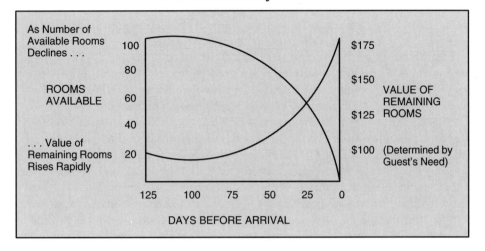

time. (See Exhibit 4.) Just as with any product, as the hotel fills and remaining rooms become scarce, the value of the remaining inventory increases.

The equitable way to allocate inventory to the various persons requesting rooms over time is to understand the ever-changing relationship between supply and demand. In this way, the hotel can ensure that discounts are plentiful in periods of low demand, and that there is last-minute availability for the rack rate guest. Although this will not necessarily please everyone, it will tend to satisfy the greatest number of guests while maximizing hotel revenues.[1]

Overbooking

Quite frequently, hotels find that a certain percentage of the guests are no-shows or cancel their reservations prior to arrival night. In addition, guests who checked in for multiple-day stays might check out early. These situations can cause the hotel to have a significant number of "spoiled" rooms. Hotels frequently overbook to prevent rooms from being empty as a result of guests failing to show up.

Example: *A downtown property that relies on a significant volume of convention business has a high cancellation rate prior to the arrival night and a high rate of early departures near the end of the week. The general manager has begun overbooking by a higher percentage as a result. This has improved his occupancy by two points, but it also has increased the instances in which guests are walked because of overbooking.*

Is it ethical for the general manager to sell more rooms than he or she physically has available?

A guest who is walked can be justifiably irate about not having a room available when he or she arrives. The person has an expectation that a reservation actually results in a room being reserved. Unquestionably, the walked guest is harmed by the practice of overbooking.

Should the ethical hotelier refuse to take any reservations beyond the physical capacity of the hotel?

If the hotel does not overbook, people who wish to make reservations are denied this opportunity, even if there is a high probability of rooms becoming available. In addition, the hotel can lose substantial revenue if spoilage is significant. Should that be considered a necessary cost of running an ethical business?

Certain hotels see as much as 10% to 20% attrition in bookings prior to arrival. No-shows can add another 10% to the number of vacancies. If hotels did not overbook in these situations, the financial viability of the hotel could be at stake. Is it ethical or fair to the employee group to allow such a situation to go unremedied?

The difficulty in managing spoilage is that the person causing the problem is often not the one who suffers the consequences of the problem. For example, guests departing a convention a day early may leave many rooms vacant. Other guests who would have liked to stay there were turned away, and the hotel loses substantial revenues. Few hotels impose a penalty on guests who check out early. The cost must be borne by the hotel or spread to all guests in the form of higher average rates.

The ethical issue in overbooking is not whether it should be done, but the extent to which it should be done. Sophisticated probability analysis can help a property understand no-show, early departure, and cancellation patterns so that the probability of walking a guest is significantly reduced. (See Exhibit 5.)

Exhibit 5   Walked vs. Spoilage Probabilities

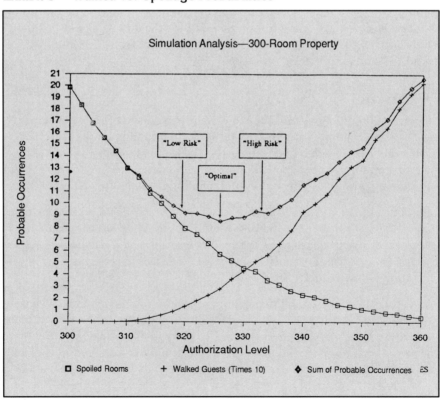

© 1990 Aeronomics Incorporated

In addition, the ethical hotelier must give consideration to the availability of suitable alternatives when setting overbooking levels and prepare procedures to assist the guests in the event a guest must be walked. If these are accomplished, the goal of fairness to all parties (current and future guests, employees, managers, and owners) is met.

Rate quotation

Hotel rate structures are becoming more complex and are changing much more frequently than in the past as capacity growth outstrips demand, and hotels must offer new rates that identify and target new market segments. Very frequently, there are numerous rates available for any given room type on any given day.

Example: *A large suburban property offers at least nine different rates which it capacity-controls for Friday arrivals: rack; corporate; SuperSaver (seven-day advance purchase); weekend (two-day minimum stay); SuperWeekend (three-day minimum stay); senior citizen; Godzilla (in conjunction with ticket purchases to local theme park); Drive Alive (joint promotion with rental car firm); and Vets Day Off (for veterans).*

What rate should be quoted first: the lowest, the highest, or the lowest available? Does the hotel have an obligation to explain all the programs up front to see if the guest making the reservation can qualify for any of them? What if the hotel has hundreds of rate programs rather than merely nine? Can it assume that the guest has been attracted by the existence of the program and, thus, will inform the person making the booking of the rate program he or she desires? If the person requesting the reservation asks only for a room for Friday night, is it incumbent on the hotel to investigate such things as the guest's military background, age, mode of arrival, and activities in the area in order to give the guest the best possible rate? Or is it the responsibility of the guest to uncover the existence of any rate programs for which he or she may qualify? What if rates change or new programs come into existence between the time the booking is made and the time the guest arrives at the hotel?

As with most ethical issues, there are no absolute black and white answers. For a small hotel with a very simple rate structure, full disclosure of all rates up front is probably the best policy. A hotel that is part of a typical major chain which has numerous local and national programs may expect that the person seeking the room will know if he or she qualifies for a particular program since the existence of the program may be the reason the person is making the booking.

In any event, the ethical hotelier should determine up front the particular wants of the guest. Guests who indicate they are very sensitive to the price quoted should be given the time to explore the various pricing options. Guests who are more concerned with availability might be satisfied with the rack rate. Although a lengthy investigation of the guest's itinerary or background might uncover an applicable discount program, the guest may or may not value that exercise, depending on his or her situation, the time it takes, and the depth of the discount. The exercise could create a loyal customer. On the other hand, a $2 discount after a half-hour discussion may not make sense to the hotel or the guest. Again, the interests of all parties (guests, employees, managers, and owners) should be balanced based on the particular circumstances of time and place.

Non-Refundable Rates

Under certain special situations (e.g., Super Bowl week), payment may be required in advance and would not be refunded in the event of cancellation. In addition, a minimum length-of-stay may be required. Is this fair?

In the absence of such requirements, speculative bookings might be made by individuals or travel agents to ensure they have space during those peak periods. If the rooms are not used, the hotel would absorb the cost of the empty rooms or pass the cost to the other guests in the form of higher rates. This would certainly not be fair.

What if the person canceling had a legitimate excuse? What excuses would authorize a refund? Illness or death in the family? What about a wedding or the inability to get time off from work? Would the hotel be put in the position of verifying the excuse? If so, what verification would be required? A death certificate and proof of relationship to the deceased? A note from the doctor or employer? In trying to be fair in establishing guidelines for refunds, could a hotel do more harm to its reputation than good?

The purpose of a non-refundable rate is to ensure that the hotel fills during peak times. If the hotel fills despite the cancellation of non-refundable bookings, is it unethical for the hotel to keep the money anyway, or should it be refunded? What if the property partially filled, or if it filled with discounted traffic? Is a partial refund in order? If so, how should the refunds be prorated among the persons canceling? Does it make sense to base a refund policy on the occurrence of a future event, i.e., whether the house will fill despite the cancellation?

During a hotel's existence, there are relatively few opportunities to really maximize its profit potential by providing the ability to sell the inventory more than once. Should it take advantage of the situation? What if the cash raised from keeping the payment for the earlier booking was enough to meet a critical bond payment? What if it went into renovations that entrenched the hotel in the local marketplace, thus securing the jobs for all of the employees at the hotel? What if the excess amount went to the general manager's bonus or as dividends to the owners? Does it make a difference?

Guests Vis-a-Vis the Hotel

Guests may make multiple bookings at multiple properties on multiple days in order to ensure availability or to protect themselves when their plans are uncertain. Is this ethical?

If the guest guarantees payment with a credit card, does it make multiple bookings any more palatable? Generally, even with guaranteed payments, the guest can cancel the booking up to or on the day of arrival. Thus, guarantees do not prevent the room inventory from being spoiled.

When guests make such speculative bookings, it not only hurts the hotel, but it also prevents other potential guests from making reservations. To a large extent, such inconsiderate guest behavior justifies the practice of overbooking. A vicious cycle could occur if guests made more multiple reservations to ensure availability, and hotels consequently overbooked even more, thus raising the risk of walking a guest and increasing the guest's need to protect him- or herself with multiple bookings!

Similarly, a guest may make a three-day booking in order to meet a minimum-stay requirement, even though the guest knows that he or she will check out after one night. Can this be justified ethically? Would it be appropriate for the hotel to charge for three days anyway? How about a non-refundable deposit for the last night? What if the hotel were not going to be full after all?

Is it ethical for a guest whose credit card was charged for a guaranteed night to call and threaten the hotel with the loss of future business if the charges are not removed? How does the ethical hotel respond and still be able to enforce guaranteed nights?

Unfortunately, the loudest, most obnoxious, and threatening guests seem to get privileges that ethical guests do not, such as refunds on non-refundable nights. By "greasing the squeaky wheel" are we encouraging guests to embrace offensive behavior?

The Hotel Vis-a-Vis Itself

As the practice of yield management becomes better known and more wide-spread, there is a chance that hotels misunderstand the need for balance in the practice. An overly zealous, near-term revenue generation program could injure the hotel's image and, ultimately, its long-term revenue growth.

Example: *A hotel company has set an ADR growth target of $5 for the following year in order to achieve revenue targets despite weakness in the market.*

If the hotel doggedly pursues a policy of increasing rates in a declining market, it will probably lose occupancy and market share. Even if the policy did not result in a loss of market share because of the strength of the product, the guests and travel agents might resent the short-term revenue-maximizing policies. This could hurt the hotel's ability to generate sustained, long-term growth.

Are there high-demand situations in which the hotel should offer discounts to everyone anyway, such as after a hurricane has left local residents homeless? In doing so, the hotel could generate an enormous amount of goodwill in the local community. However, if the housing shortage is severe, hotel rooms will be scarce as well. If so, what is a fair way to allocate the scarce room inventory? Should we employ a first-come, first-served approach? Should preference be given to employees or their families? If the rooms are to be discounted, should we give them to local business leaders and travel agents who might be in a position to help us recoup the investment in discounting the rooms? Should we treat the rooms the way we treat other scarce resources and raise the price so that demand no longer exceeds the supply?

Vendors Vis-a-Vis the Hotel

As yield management continues to be a hot topic in the industry, more vendors are professing to have yield management solutions. These solutions could take the form of seminars or software.

It is difficult for a hotelier to distinguish a responsible yield management provider from a huckster. Yield management solutions are part of an integrated program dealing with organizational issues, marketing programs, pricing policies, data analysis, property management systems, reservations systems, etc. Yield management software vendors and consultants have ethical obligations to inform the hotel management of the surrounding issues that must be addressed in order to implement an effective yield management program.

The benefits of yield management can be enormous. Some hotels have seen revenue increases of 7% to 11% as a result of initiating a comprehensive yield management program. However, the circumstances with each hotel group, and in fact at each property, vary tremendously. Hotel management should be wary of people promising extraordinary gains with little effort or claims that a methodology is universally applicable.

Unfortunately, some disservice to hotels has already been done by certain people in the name of yield management. Unsubstantiated claims have soured a number of hotels on the topic, as have simplistic approaches or software. In at least one case, the software solution made recommendations that were the antithesis of yield management.

Until ethical standards for yield management vendors evolve, yield management should be approached with prudent caution.

Employees Vis-a-Vis the Owners

In practicing yield management (or deciding not to practice yield management), employees can exercise a great deal of control over the revenues of the hotel. Is it ethical for a front office manager to refuse to practice yield management because he or she finds it more difficult to explain the concepts of demand-based pricing than pricing by room type? Is it unethical to refuse to overbook or to only overbook slightly in order to ensure there is never the inconvenience or hassle of walking a guest? What if the general manager thinks that the practices are bad policy or unethical?

In our North American culture, corporate executives are considered employees of the owners (shareholders). Ethically (and legally), the revenue the company derives belongs to the owners. The corporate executives often have discretion concerning how to spend those revenues, but the owners have a right to expect that the actions of the employees will be consistent with the owners' general desires to maximize profits while conforming to the basic tenets of society.

If a manager does not take the steps to maximize revenues through yield management techniques, he or she is giving away another person's income. Even if the manager's practice is in accord with his or her genuine belief of what is best for the guest, actions that reduce the return to the owners are the equivalent of spending the money of the owners without their consent. To the extent that the manager's aversion to yield management injures the hotel's profitability so that wages are reduced or jobs are slashed, then he or she has taken money from other employees.[2]

It could also be said that the failure of a manager to practice yield management techniques such as demand-based pricing and overbooking is unfair to the guest who might have deep discounts made available early in the booking cycle or a room available on a peak demand night.

Disclosure

Almost all of the ethical issues raised in this chapter can be easily overcome by a timely, forthright disclosure and discussion of the questions raised with the participating parties. For example, the ethical issues surrounding overbooking policies can be resolved by a plain statement of policies to guests and a clearly defined, equitable procedure in the event that the walking of a guest occurs.

It is important that the disclosure of any practice be made prior to any ethical issues arising. Not only does the practice of early disclosure help minimize the appearance of impropriety, but it also allows the parties to enter into the transaction in light of all the surrounding facts. With full disclosure, one party may elect not to enter into the arrangement.

For example, if promotional rates that are capacity controlled are clearly accompanied by a message such as: "The number of rooms available at this low rate are restricted, so be sure to book early," a guest who is denied the lower rate after all of the discount rooms are sold understands the rules by which the offer is made.

Conclusion

The ethical issues of yield management are in many ways similar to the other ethical issues faced in business on a daily basis. When we speak or write about ethics, we frequently mislead ourselves and others by the erroneous assumption that business ethics is a simple choice between good and evil. For yield management, as well as other business issues, this is almost never the case.

On each side of a question concerning ethics, there are countervailing choices between benefits and costs that fall alternatively on one party or another. In assessing the total costs and risks to the affected parties, the interests of all parties, directly and indirectly affected, must be considered. If each party's interest is dealt with fairly and justly, then an ethical resolution is assured.[3]

Endnotes

1. Alfred E. Kahn, *The Economics of Regulation,* vol. 1 (Cambridge, Mass: MIT Press, 1988), p. 131.

2. Milton Friedman, "The Social Responsibility of Business Is to Increase Its Profits," in *Business Ethics—Corporate Values and Society*, edited by Milton Snoeyenbos, Peter Almeder, and James Humber (Buffalo, N.Y.: Prometheus Books, 1983), pp. 74–75.

3. Paul Heyne, "What Is the Responsibility of Business Under Democratic Capitalism?" in *The Future of Private Enterprise*, vol. 2, edited by Craig Aronoff and John Ward (Atlanta, Ga.: Georgia State University, 1986), pp. 242–243.

Discussion Topics

1. An irate guest discovers that his rate is twice as great as a guest who has a similar room, but who booked 30 days prior to him. What are your options in handling this guest? Which option provides the most ethical solution?

2. Discuss the interests of the persons who are not direct participants in the above question, but who have an indirect interest in its outcome (e.g., other guests booking at the same time, future guests, the hotel's general manager, employees, and owners). Is your most ethical solution still the same in light of the interests of others?

3. You are beginning a yield management program at your property. What steps will you take to ensure that implementation is effective and ethical?

4. Discuss how the practice of the yield management techniques in this chapter might be used to actually enhance the hotel's image of quality in the marketplace.

Term Paper Topics

1. Many yield management techniques originated with the airline industry. Compare and contrast the ethical issues of how yield management has been employed in the airlines with how it should be approached in the hospitality industry.

2. Many major North American hospitality companies have instituted highly successful yield management programs. Interview three or four executives from these firms and write a paper about how the ethical issues raised in this chapter were addressed. Discuss the various approaches taken and which ones seem to be the most ethical as well as financially successful.

22

Ethics in Relationship with Community: An Overview

Linda K. Enghagen

The view has been gaining widespread acceptance that corporate officials and labor leaders have a 'social responsibility' that goes beyond serving the interest of their stockholders or their members . . . Few trends could so thoroughly undermine the very foundation of our free society as the acceptance by corporate officials of a social responsibility other than to make as much money for their stockholders as possible. This is a fundamentally subversive doctrine . . . The claim that business should contribute to the support of charitable activities . . . is an inappropriate use of corporate funds in a free enterprise society.[1]

—Milton Friedman

I maintain that business must change its priorities. We are not in business to make maximum profit for our shareholders. We are in business for only one reason—to serve society. Profit is our reward for doing it well. If business does not serve society, society will not tolerate our profits or even our existence.[2]

—Kenneth Dayton

Iron Law of Responsibility: Those who do not take responsibility for their power ultimately shall lose it.[3]

—Keith Davis and
Robert L. Blomstrom

Over the last two decades, the term "social responsibility of business" has become a common household phrase. For some, the words are a given—businesses are assumed to possess broad obligations to society. And it is not only the average citizen who has adopted this view; it is shared by many people engaged in business. For example, the first Earth Day celebration launched in the early 1970s was a political event

Linda Enghagen, JD, is an Assistant Professor in the Department of Hotel, Restaurant and Travel Administration of the University of Massachusetts. A pioneer in the teaching of ethics in the hospitality industry, she received her BA degree from the University of Wisconsin and her law degree from Suffolk University in Boston. She has published several articles and has written course materials in the areas of law and ethics in the hospitality industry. The author has been a member of the Board of Directors of the Western Massachusetts Food Bank since 1982.

spawned by radical environmentalists operating on a shoestring budget. Earth Day 1990, in contrast, was embraced by middle America with major corporations competing to be allowed sponsorship, as evidenced by logos on banners and advertisements. Nevertheless, there remain those who believe that the only social responsibility owed by a business is limited to maximizing the profits of its owners. Undoubtedly, the debate among the various schools will continue to rage.

Business Ethics and Community: Definitions

Before specifically examining the relationship between business ethics and the community, it is useful to provide some definitions for the purpose of establishing a framework for the discussion. According to the *American Heritage Dictionary*, one definition of ethics is: "The rules or standards of conduct governing the members of a profession." Similarly, a definition of ethical is: "Conforming to accepted principles of right and wrong that govern the conduct of a profession." Consequently, to the extent engaging in business qualifies as a profession, business ethics can be defined as the principles of right and wrong that govern the operation of a business.

The dictionary provides a number of definitions of community that are relevant to the business context.

One definition holds that a community is "a group of people residing in the same locality and under the same government." To the extent a business exercises control over its employees, it becomes a community in this sense.

Another definition of community focuses on location: "The area or locality in which such a group resides." This definition relates to businesses insofar as the impact of a business extends beyond its individual employees. For example, it has an impact on other businesses in the same geographic area by virtue of the fact that it does or does not do business with or compete with them. In a different vein, a business's impact on a geographic locale may be positive or negative, depending on whether the business pollutes the environment.

A third definition of community is "a group or class having common interests." In the business context this definition of a community highlights the fact that the influence of a business is not confined by geographical boundaries. Many businesses are national or international in scope. In fact, there are businesses seeking to expand their sphere of influence beyond the limited market of planet earth by anticipating the potential for interplanetary travel.[4] The common interests of national, international, and potentially interplanetary businesses are not, in any meaningful sense, confined to a geographic area. The common interests in this sense are more closely linked to other businesses and customers who are engaged in producing, providing, buying, and selling the products and services in question. Another way to think of "common interests" is to focus on society and the ways in which people co-exist and are interdependent with one another.

In the final analysis, given the variety of the possible meanings of "community," an examination of the relationship between business ethics and community permits a multifaceted discussion. On one level, the ethical responsibilities of a business to its employees may be discussed. On a second level, the responsibilities owed a community in the geographic sense may be examined. And, on a third level, the obligations of a business to others with shared interests is appropriate for inquiry.

Different Views on the Social Responsibilities of Businesses

Establishing the parameters of the social responsibilities of business is not an easy task. While it is easy to speak and agree in generalities (e.g., businesses should be run ethically), it is far more difficult to articulate clearly defined standards or rules that attract a consensus. For example, are the ethical responsibilities of businesses limited only by what the law prohibits? That is, if it is not illegal, is it then ethical? Is profit the legitimate controlling factor in all business decisions? A number of business management theorists have suggested models for defining the social responsibilities of businesses. The following material summarizes three models: the free-market model, the trusteeship model, and the social performance model.

The Free-Market Model

Adam Smith provided the classic statement of this model in his 1776 work *Wealth of Nations*. Simply put, the free-market model asserts that individuals are best situated to advance their own interests and should be permitted to do so without constraint.

Economist Milton Friedman is the modern protagonist of this view although he frames the theory somewhat differently. He asserts that the only social responsibility of business is to increase profits for the stockholders. Friedman does accept and assert, nonetheless, that businesses are obligated to conform to "the basic rules of society, both those embodied in law and those embodied in ethical custom."[5] However, he never explains what those ethical customs are; he only offers what they are not. According to Friedman, ethical custom does not include spending money on anything not required by law or otherwise in the best interest of the company. Consequently, in his view a company should not make expenditures for pollution control in excess of what is required by law or attempt to keep prices down for the purpose of preventing inflation in the economy. Friedman interprets these actions as imposing a private tax on businesses that is not within the proper purview of management's discretion because it inappropriately reduces the profits of the owners. In his characteristically outspoken style, Freidman finds businesspeople who speak of the social responsibilities of businesses are misled.

> The businessmen believe that they are defending free enterprise when they declaim that business is not concerned "merely" with profit but also with promoting desirable "social" ends; that business has a "social conscience" and takes seriously its responsibilities for providing employment, eliminating discrimination, avoiding pollution and whatever else may be the catchwords of the contemporary crop of reformers. In fact they are—or would be if they or anyone else took them seriously—preaching pure and unadulterated socialism. Businessmen who talk this way are unwitting puppets of the intellectual forces that have been undermining the basis of a free society these past decades.[6]

The Trusteeship Model

Adolph A. Berle, a law professor, was the first to suggest that a trusteeship model was the best approach to analyzing the responsibilities of management.[7] Although his framework is different from that of the advocates of a free-market model,

he reaches essentially the same conclusion. Berle asserts that managers held their powers in trust for the benefit of the owners of the corporation—the shareholders. Consequently, management's sole responsibility is to promote the best interests of the
shareholders. The public good is not their concern. In his view, the primary interest of
the shareholders is in generating the highest possible profit on their investment. Like
the advocates of a free-market model, management's duty is to conform to that end.

E. Merrick Dodd is another theorist who adopted the language of a trusteeship
model. However, similarity of language is the only agreement between Berle and
Dodd. Writing at the time of the Great Depression, Dodd asserted that the corporation
was a trustee (a person entrusted with the property of another for safekeeping) vis-a-
vis four groups: its shareholders, its employees, its customers, and the general public.[8]
In return, the owners (shareholders) were entitled to a fair return on their investment;
employees were entitled to fair wages; customers were entitled to good value for their
money; and the general public was entitled to expect the company to act as a "good
citizen."

The Social Performance Model

Archie B. Carroll is a contemporary theorist who offers a third model for
understanding the social responsibilities of businesses. Unlike the other models
discussed here, this model does not draw a distinction between business's economic
and social responsibilities. Rather, Carroll argues that the social responsibilities of
businesses can be evaluated on their performance in four areas: economic, legal,
ethical, and discretionary.[9]

Economic performance focuses on the delivery of goods and services at a profit.
Legal performance relates to achieving economic success without violating applicable
laws and regulations. While admitting it is not easy to define, Carroll claims that ethical performance is based on the principle that society has legitimate "expectations of
business over and above legal requirements."[10] His final category, discretionary performance, is the most ill-defined. Carroll argues that, while voluntary in nature, businesses have obligations beyond those in the other categories. According to this view,
these areas are all interrelated. For example, he points out that failing to meet an ethical
obligation today may result in it being required by law tomorrow.

Regardless of which, if any, of these theories one finds most convincing, the fact
remains that many businesses engage in activities that are not purely intended to increase profits or otherwise directly benefit the company. Whatever their mix of motives, businesses both small and large contribute to their communities in a variety of
ways.

The Contributions of Businesses to Their Communities

Essentially, businesses contribute to their communities in two ways. One is to
provide financial support to various activities and organizations. Another is through
volunteerism—that is, by providing the time and talents of the company's employees.

To date, there appear to be no specific studies of the ways in which businesses
in the hospitality industry contribute to their communities. However, the insurance

Exhibit 1   Community Projects Supported by Life Insurance Companies

(Percentage of responding companies that contributed)					
	1985	1984	1983	1982	1981
	%	%	%	%	%
Arts and cultural programs	89	84	86	86	86
Student and school activities	86	80	80	83	80
Local health programs	83	79	76	69	73
Youth activities	80	77	75	77	80
Neighborhood improvement programs	75	70	64	65	64
Race Relations	60	58	55	53	54
Programs for the handicapped	58	54	55	52	48
Drug or alcohol abuse programs	53	50	50	41	46
Activities for senior citizens and retired persons	46	45	42	41	41
Safety programs	41	44	42	36	39
Crime prevention	33	34	30	30	38
Housing programs	31	32	29	29	30
Transportation programs	23	25	33	30	32
Day-care programs	24	23	25	23	24
Anti-pollution programs	20	23	27	25	18
Number of Trend Companies (138)					

Source: Center for Corporate Public Involvement, *1986 Social Report of the Life and Health Insurance Business* (Washington, D.C., 1986), p. 4. Reproduced with permission.

Exhibit 2   Categories of 1984 Survey Contributions

Education	$561.7 million
Health and human services	$399.9 million
Civic and community activities	$271.6 million
Culture and art	$154.7 million
Other	$ 56.4 million

Source: Linda C. Platzer, *Annual Survey of Corporate Contributions,* 1986 ed. (New York: The Conference Board, 1986), p. 19.

industry has maintained a record of its activities and may be viewed as providing one example of the breadth of community projects supported by private business. (See Exhibit 1.)

Direct financial contributions are also given to a broad range of projects, activities, and causes. A 1984 study of 415 companies found they contributed a total of $1,444.3 million, broken down into the general categories shown in Exhibit 2.

Another survey of 1,600 companies (see Exhibit 3) provides a more specific delineation of the types of organizations, activities and causes supported by businesses through direct financial contributions.

Exhibits 1, 2, and 3 make it clear that many companies are involved in their communities in a variety of ways. What cannot be discerned from the exhibit lists, however, is what motivates companies to do so. In 1976, the results of a survey of 417 chairs and presidents of Fortune 500 companies were published which offer a number of reasons for corporate contributions:[11]

- Practice good corporate citizenship.

- Protect and improve environment in which to live, work, and do business.

- Realize benefits for company employees.

- Realize good public relations value.

- Preserve a pluralistic society by maintaining choices between government and private-sector alternatives.

- Commitment of directors or senior officers to particular causes.

- Pressure from business peers, customers, and/or suppliers.

- Practice altruism with little or no direct or indirect company self-interest.

- Increase the pool of trained manpower or untrained manpower or access to minority recruiting.

The Hospitality Industry Responds to Those in Need

The plight of the homeless and hungry in America has been one of the most compelling social issues of the 1980s. And although we have entered the decade of the 1990s, there is little long-term relief in sight.

> Today one percent of the population is homeless and, if economic, political, and domestic trends continue as they have throughout the last 15 years, the number of homeless people could grow as high as six percent of the population within the next 15 years.[12]

Even some of Hollywood's most popular figures have adopted the issue as their cause. It is a sad commentary that Comic Relief, as entertaining as it is, appears to have become institutionalized in American culture. But Whoopi Goldberg, Robin Williams, and Billy Crystal are not alone in their efforts to respond to the needs of the homeless and the hungry. Many businesses and organizations throughout the hospitality industry have contributed and are continuing to contribute in the effort to address the problems of homelessness. The following material explores the variety of ways in which businesses have contributed to this cause. Given the absence of any specific research on the contributions of hospitality businesses to their communities in general, this provides an example of what the industry has done and is doing in relation to one problem confronting most communities in America today. (This is not meant to be an exhaustive compilation of all contributions made by the hospitality industry to the plight of the homeless.)

Exhibit 3   Percentage of Companies Giving by Category

Category	Count	Percentage
Private Colleges	1,517	94.8%
General Education	1,491	93.2%
United Way	1,019	63.7%
Fine Arts Institutes	839	52.3%
Cultural Institutes	803	50.2%
Civic Programs	789	49.3%
Minority Programs	781	48.8%
National Organizations	688	43.0%
Youth Service	676	42.3%
Federated Campaigns	533	33.3%
General Arts	530	33.1%
International	519	32.4%
Public Colleges	506	31.6%
Scholarships	501	31.3%
Music	478	29.9%
Urban Problems	475	29.7%
Theatre	470	29.4%
General Health Care	456	28.5%
Economic Education	454	28.4%
Economic Development	443	27.7%
Welfare Programs	425	26.6%
Environmental	364	22.8%
Dance	358	22.4%
Hospitals	356	22.3%
Community Arts	348	21.8%
Rural Issues	347	21.7%
Medical Research	337	21.1%
Elem./Secondary Education	320	20.0%
Job Development	316	19.8%
Public Broadcasting	307	19.2%
General Charitable	305	19.1%
Children's Programs	280	17.5%
Women's Programs	269	16.8%
Vocational Ed.	251	15.7%
Legal Services	210	13.1%
Justice/Ex-Offenders	173	10.8%
Film	152	9.5%
Science	141	8.8%
Handicapped/Disabled	121	7.6%
Political	121	7.6%
United Way Agencies	118	7.4%
Legal Advocacy	116	7.3%
Community Organizing	114	7.1%
Equal Rights	109	6.8%
Scientific Research	74	4.6%
Continuing Education	63	3.9%
Science Education	63	3.9%
Neighborhood Based	58	3.6%
Senior Citizens	50	3.1%
Religious/Non-sect.	46	2.9%
Religious/Sectarian	46	2.9%
Writing and Poetry	33	2.1%
Family Life	32	2.0%
Humanities	31	1.9%
Redevelopment	26	1.6%
Alcohol/Drug Treatment	23	1.4%
Occupational Health	15	.9%
Sports	6	.4%
Veteran Programs	4	.3%
Non Tax-Exempt	3	.2%
Gay/Lesbian Programs	2	.1%

Source: Sam Sternberg, *National Directory of Corporate Charity* (San Francisco: Regional Young Adult Project, 1984), p. 8.

HA 590—Housing and Feeding the Homeless

In July of 1987 the School of Hotel Administration at Cornell University launched an experimental program designed to address the needs of the homeless as well as those who provide direct services to this segment of the population. Three major objectives were established:

1. To provide exposure to and understanding of existing housing and feeding delivery systems designed to assist the homeless, of organizations and individuals providing these services, and of the guests using these services.

2. To provide a structure for students to analyze, evaluate, and develop recommendations to improve the delivery systems in which they have been assigned for field placement by drawing on the knowledge and skills they have developed in other courses (organization and management, communication, food and beverage systems, operational analysis, financial planning, marketing, etc.).

3. To develop in students a comfort level and sense of confidence that they can apply their knowledge and skills in a tangible way to increase their interest in continued outreach and service beyond graduation.[13]

The results of the program have been very positive and have provided the impetus for further work in this area. For example, as a result of the program plans were made to write a series of articles or pamphlets targeted to service providers and hospitality industry professionals. The purpose of these materials is to provide information to each audience that will enhance their ability to be effective in their work with the homeless.

Jessie's House

Jessie Benoit is the former proprietor of the Red Lion diner located in the Smith College town of Northampton, Massachusetts. Prior to her recent retirement from the restaurant business, her establishment was a haven to many of the community's hungry and homeless, where a meal could be had without regard to one's ability to pay. In recognition of her generosity to the hungry and homeless, Jessie's House, a shelter for the homeless, was named in her honor when its doors opened in the spring of 1983. Since its opening, it has provided assistance to more than 500 families (including more than 2,000 persons). Presently, Jessie's House provides 20 beds for those in need of shelter. Housing is provided on a temporary basis with the goal of assisting the homeless in finding permanent housing. In addition, meals and other assistance (e.g., finding day care for children) are available.

Days Inn Responds to a Disaster and Seeks Long-Term Solutions

Days Inn has responded to the plight of the homeless in two different but significant ways. In one instance, a Navy fighter jet crashed into an apartment complex near Atlanta leaving 75 persons instantly homeless. The management of the Days Inn-Cumberland responded immediately by organizing a Red Cross relief station in the hotel lobby.

In a different vein, Days Inn has also contributed to the search for long-term solutions to the problem of homelessness. Toward this end, Days Inn of America instituted a program to offer jobs to the homeless. The original program was started in the reservations center in Atlanta. Realizing that it is extremely difficult to maintain a job if one is homeless, the organization offered more than a job. Individuals selected for this program are given not only a job but interim housing at a modest cost. In exchange, the employees in this program must agree to save a percentage of their paycheck toward a down payment on housing, to not have alcohol or drugs on the premises, and to not have more than one visitor at a time. After some initial problems in screening applicants, the program has been quite successful. The pilot program "graduated" 12 recruits. Since then, Days Inn expanded this program to another reservations center in Knoxville, Tennessee.

Best Western International and the American Society of Interior Designers (ASID)

Best Western International and ASID have joined forces with the National Alliance to End Homelessness to improve the shelters used to house the homeless. In this cooperative effort, Best Western hotels and ASID contribute interior design services, furniture, fixtures, and equipment to shelters designated by the National Alliance to End Homelessness.

Smith College's Meal Cancellation Program

Paul Garvey, director of dining services at Smith College, also serves as the president of the Board of Directors of the Western Massachusetts Food Bank (WMFB). The WMFB, like other food banks nationwide, is a non-profit organization whose purpose is to collect surplus food and distribute it to local non-profit agencies who, in turn, serve low-income families and individuals. In the early 1980s, Garvey worked with a group of Smith College students to develop strategies for helping the hungry and homeless of western Massachusetts. The Meal Cancellation Program is the result of their efforts. Formally established in 1983, Smith College dining services donates 10 cents to the WMFB for every meal canceled by a student. Students are apprised of the program early in the school year and then sign up for the meals they intend to miss. In the 1989–90 academic year, Smith College students cancelled 4,274 meals.

Taste of the Nation

Taste of the Nation is an annual fund-raising event sponsored by Share Our Strength (SOS). SOS is a national network of chefs and restaurants organized to combat hunger. The event itself consists of food and wine tasting activities held in major cities throughout the United States. In each city the area's top chefs and restaurants prepare and provide the food which guests enjoy for the price of a ticket. In 1988, SOS raised more than $700,000 with events in 47 cities. One hundred percent of the proceeds goes to hunger relief organizations, with 80% earmarked for domestic groups and 20% designated for international relief and development agencies.

Prepared Food Programs

There are a number of prepared food programs throughout the nation. These are programs that bring surplus prepared and perishable food from restaurants and banquets to agencies feeding the needy. Currently, there are programs in Atlanta, Chicago, Dallas, Kansas City, Memphis, Oklahoma City, Pittsburgh, St. Paul, Seattle, and Tucson. Generally, participating restaurants and caterers donate their excess prepared food to local agencies. Strict handling and packaging requirements must be met to ensure the safety of the food. Given estimates that as much as 20% of restaurant food is discarded, the quantity of food potentially available through this type of program is considerable.

Piece of the Pie

Piece of the Pie is another fund-raising event by which restaurants contribute to the nation's hungry. Sponsored by food banks, participating restaurants donate 10% of their gross receipts for the day to the local food bank. Traditionally, Wednesday nights are selected for these events because they are usually slow nights for restaurants. Piece of the Pie has been a successful event in Baltimore, New Haven, and western Massachusetts. For example, the 1989 Piece of the Pie in western Massachusetts generated approximately $15,000 for the local food bank. In addition, some restaurants reported that their business increased for the night to the point they exceeded their typical Wednesday night profit even after donating 10% of their receipts.

Conclusion

Regardless of one's view on the nature of the social responsibilities of businesses, it is clear that businesses and the communities they operate in have an impact on one another. It is also clear that many businesses have concluded, for whatever reasons, that contributing to their communities is desirable. For the hospitality industry, which is in the business of providing food and shelter, it is only fitting that many businesses, large and small, have directed their efforts to help those in their communities who lack these basic necessities.

Endnotes

1. Milton Friedman, *Capitalism and Freedom* (Chicago: University of Chicago Press, 1962), pp. 133, 135.

2. Kenneth Dayton, Seegal-Macy lecture, University of Michigan, Ann Arbor, October 30, 1975.

3. Keith Davis and Robert L. Blomstrom, *Business and Its Environment* (New York: McGraw-Hill, 1966), p. 174.

4. R. R. Craft Jr., "Space Law," *The National Law Journal*, June 15, 1987, p. 22.

5. Milton Friedman, "The Social Responsibility of Business Is to Increase Its Profits," *New York Times Magazine*, September 13, 1970.

6. Ibid.

7. A. A. Berle, "Corporate Powers as Powers in Trust," *Harvard Law Review* 44, 1931, p. 1049.

8. E. M. Dodd, "For Whom Are Managers Corporate Trustees?" *Harvard Law Review* 45, 1932, p. 1145.

9. A. B. Carroll, "A Three-Dimensional Conceptual Model of Corporate Performance," *Academy of Management Review* 4, October 1979, p. 497.

10. Ibid.

11. J. F. Harris and A. Klepper, *Corporate and Philanthropic Public Service Activities* (New York: The Conference Board, 1976), p. 16.

12. A. Hales, "First Semester Outcomes of an Experimental Program: 'Housing and Feeding the Homeless,'" *Hospitality and Tourism Educator,* Spring 1989, pp. 31–37.

13. Ibid.

Discussion Topics

1. This chapter offers three models of the social responsibilities of business—the free-market model, the trusteeship model, and the social performance model. In your view, which model most accurately defines the social responsibilities of businesses? Why?

2. The research done for insurance companies reveals a wide range of community projects that have gained the support of this industry. These projects include everything from crime prevention to day care centers. Which types of projects, if any, would you support? Why?

3. At least one hospitality chain has ventured into the long-term project of providing employment to the homeless. While this is laudable, isn't this really the job of the government? Why or why not?

4. Prepared food programs have been instituted in a number of cities throughout the nation. What quality control measures are necessary to ensure the safety of the food donated through this means?

Term Paper Topics

1. Research additional examples of the hospitality industry serving its communities, i.e., other than helping the homeless.

2. Develop a corporate policy regarding company involvement in philanthropic activities.

23

Hospitality, Travel, and the Theory of the Mean

Sven E. Jorgensen

My international hospitality management and consulting career spanned more than 40 years and included working with hundreds of governments, corporations, institutions, organizations, and associations. In short, I spent my entire professional life working in all sectors of the hospitality industry, all over the world.

At retirement I was Senior Travel Officer at the World Bank, responsible for negotiating the use of hotels by the bank's 7,000-plus officers and staff, as well as use of all required facilities and services for many international meetings, conferences, and workshops. This encompassed managing the annual use of approximately one-half million room nights worth about $30 million in more than 4,000 hotels in 156 countries. The total budget of this function included an additional $20 million per annum in expenses. In this position I was also concerned with ethics on a daily basis.

Ethics

As a youth, philosophy was a subject I studied with secondary interest while pursuing an undergraduate degree in hotel/restaurant management at Cornell University. During that time, I was more interested in escargot than Aristotle's teachings on ethics. Ethics really applied to students majoring in philosophy, politics, or the priesthood; I took it for fun. I next achieved graduate degrees in international marketing at Golden State University and international finance at the University of Minnesota. It was not until my career showed me the world that I took another look at ethics.

Sven E. Jorgensen is a graduate of the Cornell University School of Hotel Administration and has held several top management positions with the World Bank and leading hotel companies throughout the world, including Hilton Hotels International, Oberoi Hotels International, RockResorts, and Swiss Chalet Enterprises. Further, he has held posts as Director of New Business with the Pillsbury Company and with ITT Corporation. He has designed, developed, and opened two hotel schools, one at Golden Gate University in San Francisco, and the other for Oberoi International Hotels in India. He has lectured at various hospitality schools, and has conducted business seminars and lectured throughout the world in six languages.

In my work I began to see firsthand that not everyone has the same set of expectations. The more I traveled, the more I observed; the more I observed, the more my mind's eye cast itself back to what I had studied in that philosophy class. I remembered Aristotle had written about what he called the theory of the mean, in the book entitled *Nicomachaean Ethics*. I wondered if this was what I was experiencing and seeing time and again in everyday life.

The purpose of the theory of the mean is similar to that of a self-help book; it is meant to direct and assist the individual in acquiring virtue of character, and thus making the right decisions, taking the right actions, and doing well in life. Briefly, the theory states that virtue of character (i.e., ethos) results from habituation, hence the term "ethical." The theory explains that virtue of character is a mean between two vices, one of excess and one of deficiency. Some persons miss what is right because they choose the deficient, others because they choose the excessive; the virtuous individual finds and chooses what is intermediate. Most important, the intermediate is relative to each individual and his or her situation and therefore is not the same for everyone.

As an example, bravery on the part of a soldier would generally be considered virtuous. However, a soldier who chose to exhibit extreme bravery at an inappropriate time may unnecessarily sacrifice his life as well as those of his comrades, producing a victory for the enemy. In such a situation the soldier's decision and action would not be considered virtuous, but stupid. The right decision and action would be for him to contain his desire to show excessive bravery, waiting for a time when its display would assist in bringing about a victory for his compatriots. That would be the intermediate and virtuous decision and action.

Another example might be a hotel operator who so desired to treat his patrons well that the costs his operation incurred in doing so were far greater than what the guests were charged. While the operator's intention may be considered virtuous, his decisions and actions may not be, for his hotel would soon be bankrupt. Obviously, the intermediate and virtuous decision and action would be for him to balance his desire for quality with what the clientele were actually charged.

Hospitality

The hospitality industry is involved with providing accommodations, food, beverage, entertainment, and recreation for travelers away from their usual residences and normal surroundings. The industry also naturally concerns itself with meeting the traveler's needs for safety and support of their persons, property, modes of transportation, and even the very purpose of their travel, if so required.

Speaking generally, those who make use of hospitality services demand attainment of a professional level of quality consistent with world standards, although perhaps adjusted for local conditions. They anticipate the facilities will be clean, comfortable, safe, and secure. They expect to be furnished with hygienic accommodations and good, sanitary food and beverage at a reasonable rate. If there are shops or concessions on the premises, they expect these outlets to reflect the same standards as the main entity. Further, they look to the host for courtesy, friendliness, respect, and identification. Perhaps more important than anything else, they demand honesty, truth, and equity in their dealings with the operator and his or her employees.

The Theory of the Mean

What the customers may expect and what they ultimately receive are not always one and the same, whether they are aware of it or not. In my opinion, world standards appear to be averaged out, with American standards being very high on the technical side and very low on the guest recognition or service side.

The American hotel industry's smallest affront (which irritates me the most) is the reduced attention given to room service. American hotel operators claim this is done to save money. At worst, it can leave a traveler who is far from home in a health-threatening situation. At the very least, it seems to me all guests should have the opportunity to eat and drink in the privacy of their room, their home away from home. Moreover, because many hotel operators are insufficiently prepared in the art of service, they often choose to contract out food, beverage, and other vital services. As a result, the operator's responsibility and control over the evaluation, selection, quality, and price of services may be inadequate.

Ironically, American consumers tend to pay a great deal more attention to the quality of service and the ethics of hotel and restaurant management when traveling outside their own country. Coming from the wealthiest nation in the world, where society is based on laws that afford the individual inalienable rights, they sometimes assume all is fine and well at home, while everything foreign is subject to question.

Is the degree of sanitation in a commercial kitchen an ethical question? Most Americans would reply that it is, but try to teach foreign restaurateurs about sanitary food preparation, let alone the ethical ramifications associated with it, when they have lived their lives in environments quite unlike yours. As a consultant on food and beverage, I once assisted in opening a new, seven-star hotel in Sao Paulo, Brazil. The owners were extremely proud of their new enterprise, yet they had open sewer lines running through the kitchen! What's more, they refused to do anything about the situation even after numerous cases of dysentery among the patrons had been reported by the hotel doctor.

While a seven-star hotel is supposed to represent the zenith of quality, half the fun of traveling is going to the "little out of the way places" not attended by tourists. These are the places where one must really be concerned about dysentery. When living at the Maidens Hotel in Delhi, we used to go to an Afghan restaurant where the lamb was exquisite. We would also take the jitney over to eat at Moti Mahal, a wonderful Indian restaurant. During the many years I worked in India I never hesitated to visit a restaurant, but not many tourists frequented such local establishments. Although the food and atmosphere were superb, the sanitation was horrid. Since I had amoebic dysentery the entire time I lived in India, I was fortunate in not having to worry about it too much!

In the United States we have stringent enforcement of uniform health and safety codes designed to protect the consumer. When it comes to dining, American stomachs do not develop protection or immunity to the germs, microbes, and toxins one is exposed to in international travel. Any American hotel or restaurant suspected of maintaining slack sanitary conditions would quickly be set upon by the authorities, and its operator could possibly be taken to court by an angry customer. Our jury system is likely to favor a victimized plaintiff and award him or her damages. As a patron in the United States, you would likely have the opportunity to pursue legal recourse if you were to become ill.

While the ethics of sanitary food preparation is important, it is only one area of concern. During my years in hospitality I witnessed rank nepotism by some hotel operators, abuse of child and female workers, or dictatorial treatment of all employees as well as the guests. Yet despite these bad examples of quality and ethics in hospitality, and despite the tremendous differences in countries and cultures, the vast majority of individuals and groups I have worked with were completely honest and aboveboard. However, had I not bothered to become acquainted with their cultures, I probably would not have a positive impression of the persons I met, nor would they of me.

Even the best possible preparation and efforts at familiarity with the local etiquette will not prevent those unexpected situations which travelers and purveyors of hospitality alike must cope with on occasion. In Venezuela, one friend of mine was arrested for serving a sheriff what the sheriff considered a poor meal. Another friend was the manager of a hotel in Caracas, and was arrested and jailed overnight because there were no vacancies and some military general decided the manager's suite would be just fine for himself and his girlfriend!

One of the closest calls I had in my work was when I was assisting in opening the Hilton in Havana, Cuba, and brought undesirable attention to myself by refusing the wife of dictator Fulgencio Batista permission to roam freely through the kitchen and food storage areas. Her previously invisible entourage of special police easily persuaded me that it would be an honor to provide a complete tour of the facilities, or else I would be given a complete tour of their "facilities."

Any Western-oriented individual accustomed to democratic government will tell you that many countries in this world possess what appear to be archaic and rigid cultures, with absurd superstitions or traditions, and seemingly narrow histories with antiquated systems of law. However, having lived in several nations that were not governed by democratic principles, I can testify that there are those who hold a different opinion. The ethics of many cultures emphasize the value of self, family, ethnic group, and national group long before they recognize any obligation to others. Further, the less developed a society—by our standards—the more instinctive are their values likely to appear to us. Such societies may well consider the ethics of their politicians as well as their hotel and restaurant managers to be wholly appropriate, or at worst, necessary. If not properly informed or prepared, it can be a humbling experience for a Westerner to suddenly find himself or herself caught in such a society without recourse to the American systems of jurisprudence and the Bill of Rights we so take for granted.

There are places where ethics, law, and culinary tradition hold the very real potential for extremely perilous convergence. Cannibalism was still practiced in the jungles of Venezuela in 1958 when I resided there. The Amazon and New Guinea jungles are still home today to tribes I would not care to casually visit, for fear of ending up as a dinner entree. When in the Fiji Islands attending a government function, one of the chiefs reminded me that it was not long ago when they would breakfast on someone like me. My brother telephoned just recently to tell me a missionary was killed for patting a Fijian chief on the head, a dreaded insult there and in Thailand.

The Traveler

While avoiding serious tragedy, my family and I have had numerous experiences in travel and hospitality that caused us inconvenience, insult, and additional monetary expense. My automobile was stolen many times when I traveled. Our travelers checks and the postage on letters were regularly stolen by hotel staff and, in one case, even by my own consulting staff hired from the indigenous population. We have had our dogs poisoned and stolen. My wife has been propositioned and grabbed in an airport and a hotel lobby during broad daylight!

While some occurrences may be unavoidable, travelers still have an obligation to become familiar with and understand the customs of the cultures in which they are guests. When visiting unfamiliar places or foreign lands they should take responsibility for how they will interact with and fit into the cultural surroundings of the host country. It should be common sense to obtain more than just casual information about a destination before traveling, as well as about all points en route where there will be contact with a different way of life. Travelers of an earlier time were expected to know the essential political, religious, economic, and social mores. Unfortunately, today this is not the case. Travel is less expensive and more comfortable than it was in earlier times. Many who would never have traveled 50 years ago now do so regularly. Of these new travelers, too many are guilty of substantial *faux pas* due to their own ignorance and lack of circumspection.

The traveler should journey in a spirit of humility, realizing that the inhabitants of other countries will have not only different lifestyles, but also different ways of thinking that go hand-in-hand with their lifestyles. The traveler should have a sincere desire to experience and learn about another way of life. Also, the traveler should want to develop the skills of listening, observing, and asking questions, instead of exhibiting the stereotypical "I already know all the answers" attitude.

In addition, multinational hotel chains and resort developers should incorporate the same spirit into the operation of their firms. Some of these entities approach their work with little regard for the customs or concerns of the local community or country in which they seek to do business. They promise to cater to the culture, protect the environment, pump up the economy, and then proceed to ride roughshod over the long-term interests of the area and its inhabitants. One might think it obvious that shortsighted attitudes are practical only in the short-term, and ultimately have a negative impact on the profit margin. However, some developers and operators seem unable to resist the opportunism exemplified by short-term policies and practices.

Alexander

As an undergraduate I was not the most attentive student of Aristotle's teachings on ethics. The exemplary student of this celebrated Greek pedagogue is also one of history's most renowned and respected travelers: Alexander the Great. With Aristotle as his personal tutor during Alexander's youth, the young king of Macedonia went forth to travel the extent of the known world and beyond, becoming the only leader to rule the disparate peoples of Greece, Persia, Egypt, and India at one time.

Alexander's triumph of virtue lay not in his military conquest of these empires, but in his actions after victory—he made no attempts to conquer or subvert their cultures. His wish was not to eliminate, change, or ignore their customs and thought patterns, although they were quite unlike his own. He sought to unify the peoples of these regions, and to this end he made use of his formidable skills in inquiry, which had been whetted by his tutor. He desired to understand differing concepts and ways of life that he might discover reservoirs of human capability and potential to nourish his ideal of a vast, modern empire having universal citizenship and brotherhood.

Alexander the Great displayed virtue of character, made the right decisions, took the right actions, and did well in life. In this day and age, we consider ourselves to be modern men and women living in a modern world, yet we would do well as travelers and hosts to pay heed to the timeless teachings of Aristotle and the ancient example of Alexander.

Discussion Topics

1. Is there such a thing as a universal ethic that can be freely transmuted by and between societies, cultures, religious, ethnic and/or language groups?

2. What would be the underlying characteristics of such a universal ethical standard? Describe its elements and characteristics as well as priorities it imposes in taking care of self, family, tribal group, ethnic group, national group, religious beliefs.

3. What would such a universal ethical standard require from different societies that ascribed to it, such as a democratic society as found in the United States?

4. What societies would (a) freely accept such an ethical standard? (b) totally reject it? or (c) act some other way?

Term Paper Topics

1. How do standards of ethical behavior differ among the religious norms of societies practicing the following major religions?

    - Buddhism
    - Catholicism
    - Hinduism
    - Judaism
    - Islam
    - Protestantism

2. What would be expected today of (choose one of the following): (a) yourself, or (b) a young, white, Christian female from Charleston, South Carolina, or (c) a senior black Muslim male from Los Angeles, California, traveling alone on a world trip to any ten of the following destinations?

    - Chicago
    - Montreal
    - Reykjavik, Iceland
    - London
    - Paris
    - Sofia, Bulgaria
    - Moscow
    - Medina, Saudi Arabia
    - Tehran
    - Bombay
    - Ching Mai, Thailand
    - Hanoi
    - Lhasa, Tibet
    - Darwin, Australia
    - Suva, Fiji
    - Papeete, Tahiti
    - Havana
    - Puerto Vallarta, Mexico

24

Ethics, Value Systems, and the Professionalization of Hoteliers

K. Michael Haywood

Hoteliers and executives in other service industries should realize that the foundation of success in their businesses is based upon personal and corporate value systems and steady commitment to excellence. This chapter describes how ethical issues and manager morality are linked to and shaped by the values of executives and the organization, and how improved professionalism can only be achieved through the adoption of a value system that rewards contributions rather than the mere attainment of results.

Hoteliers invariably consider themselves professionals. The public with which they come into contact does not always agree. Incidents of overbooking, sanitation infractions, employment discrimination, indifference, and other discourtesies do not endear hoteliers to the traveling public or the community at large. Lack of integrity, honesty, and responsibility reveal value systems that are unacceptable. During early Greek and Roman times, such acts of inhospitality would have been considered uncivilized and dangerous. Not only was it unwise to offend a stranger or guest because he might turn out to be your enemy, but doing so would have incurred the wrath of the gods. Zeus sanctioned the stranger's right to hospitality. Religious sanction may be a throwback to yesteryear, but in its place we now find active governments eager to protect the unsuspecting traveler, zealous competitors eager to build market share and promising "no surprises," and vehement consumer groups who, if offended, will fight for their rights.

The time has come for hoteliers to examine their own standards of ethics, value systems, and professionalism. As Thomas Peters and Robert Waterman, Jr., contend in

K. Michael Haywood is an Associate Professor in the School of Hotel and Food Administration at the University of Guelph in Ontario, Canada. He is also President of Haywood, Bauer and Associates, Inc., a consulting firm specializing in hospitality and tourism management. He has published widely in the areas associated with the marketing of services, strategic management, and tourism. With reference to ethical issues, he has argued for a revision of the marketing concept as it applies to tourism and is a proponent of a more community-based approach to tourism development. He is Vice President of the International Academy of Hospitality Research and serves on the Board of Directors of the Tourism Research and Education Council at the University of Waterloo.

their book *In Search of Excellence: Lessons from America's Best-Run Companies*, the foundation of success in American corporations rests upon personal and corporate value systems and steady commitment to excellence.[1] Hoteliers must become value-driven. They must be committed to excellence both in actualizing their best potentialities and in excelling in all they do. In other words, the professionalization of the hotelier can be achieved through a high degree of self-control, internalized values, codes of ethics, and related socialization processes.

Serious ethical and legal issues exist for hoteliers as well as for many businesspeople and professionals in positions of responsibility. The acceptance of kickbacks and gifts from suppliers, the hiding of income from tax authorities, the lack of interest in installing and maintaining proper safety and security systems, and the raiding of competitors' staffs are common practices. Consider a recent case in Boston in which a hotel affiliated with a national chain was accused of blocking competitors' sales by making phony bookings. The case was reported in a local newspaper, picked up by a wire service, and given national media exposure.

Considerations

If a hotel or a hotel chain is to avoid such notoriety, questions about corporate and personal ethics must be asked and answered. Examples of such questions for the marketing of a hotel are listed below:

General Considerations

- Are customers satisfied with the marketing process?
- Are there existing mechanisms that can identify and evaluate whether ethical abuses occur in the marketing process?
- What philosophies, ideologies, and social expectations at the customer and societal levels can be used to help formulate ethical guidelines in marketing?

Product/Service Considerations

- Are inferior rooms, meals, and other services sold to customers as substitutes for the superior products and services that were promised?
- Are non-functional changes made only to stimulate repeat business?
- Are package offers needlessly proliferated and intentionally made confusing?

Promotion Considerations

- Are advertising claims based on unbiased research results?
- Are certain claims or benefits exaggerated or embellished?
- Do salespeople use questionable psychological pressure to close a sale?

Pricing Considerations

- Has management indirectly cut prices through unpublicized quality or quantity reductions?

- Are dissimilar prices to different customers attributed to lack of competition rather than actual costs?

- Are multiple pricing deals (e.g., two for the price of one) used to make it look as if rooms or meals are on sale when in fact they are not?

Distribution/Service Delivery Considerations

- Are travel agents and other channel members treated fairly when they provide business?

- Are services provided in a candid and hospitable manner?

- Are product/service problems encountered by guests corrected in a quick, fair, and equitable manner?

Few hoteliers set out to be intentionally unethical. However, situations occur in which ethical problems do arise. For example, a coercion and control problem may exist when some external force (head office, major customer) attempts to compel the hotelier to make a specific decision by using threats, extortion, or other sources of power. A conflict of interest situation may arise when the hotelier has more than one interest which, if mutually pursued, may result in injury to an individual or the hotel. A problem involving personal integrity may occur when a decision raises issues of conscience. These and other categories of ethical problems invariably generate a great deal of anguish and decision-making stress for most executives.

Morality of Managers Is Involved in Tradeoffs

Ethical problems seem to arise most frequently in the tradeoffs managers must make to maximize profits. The dominant question of hoteliers who seek to maximize profits is an economic one: Which course of action will make the most money? Theodore Levitt concludes that "the businessman exists for only one purpose, to create and deliver value satisfaction at a profit to himself" and the "cultural, spiritual, and moral consequences of his actions are none of his occupational concerns."[2] Similarly, Max Lerner says that "the business principle focuses on market sale for profit. It puts the making of money ahead of other craft and civilization values, gives privacy to the cultural and personal traits which lead to that end and tends to apply money values even to the human personality."[3]

Of course, not all hoteliers can be classified as "profit maximizers," willing to make as much profit as possible at any cost. Common sense and life experience suggest that there exists a wide variety of moral types of businesspeople. Michael Maccoby's typology of managers partially illustrates the diversity. Interestingly, though, Maccoby points out that while each of the four character types (craftsmen, jungle fighters, company men, and gamesmen) may not be in hot pursuit of profit, they invariably use their intelligence in order to plot their course toward winning their own respective prizes: quality, power, belongingness, and glory.[4] As such, Maccoby contends that successful managers manifest "qualities of the head"; in other words, their subordination of reason to the service of material and psychological values enthrones expediency as primary.[5]

Maccoby does not believe that successful managers demonstrate such "qualities of the heart" as compassion, generosity, and idealism. Indeed he sees such qualities as handicaps in moving up the corporate ladder.[6]

In contrast, empirical research of many well-known theorists (McGregor, Likert, Tannenbaum and Schmidt, Argylis, Schien, and Blake and Mouten[7]) suggests that the most effective manager must manage from the heart as well as from the head. In other words, the successful manager is self-actualized and is people-oriented. He or she sets the value norms of the organizational culture as a policy-making executive; believes that people are the most important resources of the corporation and its primary source of productivity; motivates by being a model for others, a living proof of how to be the best; and makes things happen with and through others, coupling business success with morality. The self-actualizing manager is dedicated to excellence in all he or she does.

Being able to achieve the self-actualized state whereby one actually determines values and renders more ethical decisions within an organization seems to represent an ideal state for many. First of all, values exist at a variety of levels: personal, professional, organizational, or societal. Secondly, there may be conflict between levels, and the influence among them can be varied. For example, the individual values of one department manager or employee have little impact on a company's values, but the company's values may have a considerable impact on the manager or employee. The exception lies with the values of key executives; they have a very powerful influence on the entire organization:

> When the chief executive's statements and his actions remain consistent with the established values of the company, people remain oriented to those values. When the pattern of his actions begins to diverge from those values people become confused, their own focus dissolves, and the drive born of the sense of shared values may simply evaporate.[8]

When an organization clearly defines, communicates, and acts on its values in a consistent way, values form a sturdy foundation for developing the mission and goals of a business. They silently give direction to the hundreds of decisions made at all levels of the business every day. Options that run counter to the value system are unlikely to be considered.

The existence of ethical questions and other conflicts over values in organizations and between individuals can be quite disruptive. It is relatively easy to manage different perceptions of a problem or proposed courses of action; but, when the difference is over a basic value, egos are more likely to become involved and defensiveness may cloud people's judgments. More energy goes into proving a point, assigning blame, and criticizing colleagues who differ than into seeking a simplistic solution.

The considerable cynicism and personal stress caused by a lack of shared values suggests the need for an increased dialogue about "what is really important around here."

Human and Corporate Excellence Can Be Realized

Values and ideals play a major role in the lives of executives and corporations; they measure the distance between success and failure. Michel de Montaigne, a sixteenth century French businessman and essayist, said in his *Essais* that "the greatest and glorious masterpiece of man is to know how to live to purpose; all other things, to reign, to lay up treasure, to build are just so many props and appendage."

Leading a life in conscious pursuit of a life-goal and having a corporation seek the fulfillment of its self-realizing value structure are purposeful and powerful existences. They allow both individual employees and the corporation to fully become what personal and corporate possibilities permit under the circumstances. The higher people aspire, the more meaningful their lives and the greater their worth and self-respect. Similarly, the higher level of excellence a hotel corporation aspires to, the more successful a business it will be, and the more exciting and self-actualizing a place for its employees. The worth of both individuals and corporations is ultimately measured not by bank accounts and buildings but by values. Personal and corporate degeneration are the fruits of inferior values.

Hoteliers can help shape the value system that characterizes their hotels in operating and in dealing with their many publics. A consistently applied right value scale leads to both personal and corporate success and happiness. Therefore, it is important not only in a personal but also in a corporate sense that executives attempt to be self-actualizing.

The contention of Peters and Waterman's *In Search of Excellence* is that the key to the history of success of American corporations is their value systems and steady commitment to excellence. Hospitality companies like McDonald's and Four Seasons Hotels are identified as self-actualizing organizations that reflect the value scale of their executives. The authors maintain that "as the excellent companies are driven by coherent value systems, so virtually all of them were marked by the personality of a leader who laid down the value systems."[9] Therefore, the examination of values and moral types is of practical significance for executives who wish to leave their mark of excellence on a company.

In aspiring to excellence, there is usually an attempt to identify with men and women of excellence. This is the process of what Peter Drucker calls "the ethics or aesthetics of self-development."[10] It is possible to classify and appraise the value of both people and corporations according to their heroes. The heroes of a corporation express the essence of its value system. By considering whom people or corporate cultures admire, we can understand them. For example, the aphorisms of founding fathers are often repeated in the corporate offices, boardrooms, and training seminars of Disney, McDonald's, Marriott, and Hilton. This admiration gives companies hope, strength, and enthusiasm to emulate excellence; helps them grow in the process; and transmits ideals which their heroes admired.

Ideals of excellence move employees and managers to aspire to self-actualization. However, nothing that exists in reality fully measures up to the ideal and never will. As Robert Browning remarked in *Andrea del Sarto*, "A man's reach should exceed his grasp, or what's a heaven for?" As successful hoteliers approach their ideal in practice, they constantly set newer and higher standards of excellence, for the ideal continues to evolve to still loftier heights.

To have a moral ideal is to have a conception of human excellence possessed by an ideal person or moral hero. In addition to the knowledge component in the concept of what an ideal person is like, there is a motivational force that spurs us to translate the knowledge of the ideal into externally observable behavior. The moral development of hoteliers and the institutional ethics of hotels are also helped by forces in the business environment that are likely to lead to rising levels of business ethics in the future. Among these forces John Steiner lists public indignation over unethical practices, increased professionalism of today's managers, consumerism, governmental surveillance, and growing interest in business ethics as a field of study. In comparing forces upgrading ethical business behavior with those downgrading it, Steiner optimistically concludes that the positive forces outweigh the negative ones and we can expect more ethical business practices.[11]

Ethical hoteliers, however, must be value-driven. They are committed to excellence both in actualizing their best potentialities and in excelling in all they do. These hoteliers must be leaders and managers in a truly professional manner.

Professionalism Is Hard to Achieve

From an academic point of view, it is unlikely that innkeeping or hotel management will ever become a pure profession because it does not meet all the conditions mentioned as necessary. According to Barber, these are:

- A high degree of generalized and systematic knowledge

- A primary orientation to community interest rather than individual (or corporate) self-interest

- A high degree of self-control through internalized codes of ethics and related socialization processes

- A system of rewards as symbolic of work achievement[12]

It seems that the first and last requirements are met by the activities of hoteliers. The second can only be achieved by a few despite the legal definitions of a hotel being a public place. The third, as evidence seems to suggest, is often not present, at least in a formalized way. Should hoteliers adopt a behavior mode as suggested in the third, however, they would be nearing a professional position.

If hoteliers want a revived sense of professionalism and vocation, not in the traditional or formal way, but in a modern context, they must come to an understanding of what their work is all about and what its social implications and consequences are. In addition, on the basis of that understanding they must accept those special responsibilities that rest with all those who work in the hotel industry. The concept of professionalism implies that hoteliers should consider how they can shift the emphasis of assessments from success in obtaining rewards to success in making contributions.

Success in making contributions requires embracing values. One of the most succinct and applicable sets of values is contained in Lawrence Miller's *American Spirit: Visions of a New Corporate Culture*; questions are posed regarding each of Miller's values in order to focus, shape, and organize management's attention to each.[13] By accepting, living, and acting on these values, it is anticipated that hoteliers can make extremely important contributions to the hotel industry and in the process achieve new professional heights.

The Purpose Principle

To be successful, a hotel must establish a well-defined sense of purpose, a definitive idea, a basic philosophy or set of beliefs that provides each individual in the company with a point of reference and direction in producing the products offered, performing the services required, and satisfying the needs and wants of customers.

Question: Do your employees understand the mission of your hotel and do they consider that mission worthy? Effective leadership creates the energy in the company by instilling and communicating this sense of purpose. Success can only be defined and measured in terms of accomplishment of the business purpose—the success of the product or service. This will inspire and motivate all employees of the hotel to do their best. It is up to the hotelier to ensure that all individuals in the company achieve their personal and highest values by contributing to the achievement of company purpose.

Question: Are management decisions made with consideration of the mission or purpose of the hotel or do they tend to be primarily expedient?

The Excellence Principle

Every company must promote the pervasive spirit of excellence by providing the right climate for reinforcing and increasing the probability that more of its members will achieve excellence. This is partially achieved through the belief that the ways in which things are accomplished today will be inadequate tomorrow—a system of creative dissatisfaction.

Question: Are managers generally satisfied or continually dissatisfied with today's performance? The three ingredients that result in excellence are standards, motivation, and feedback. Standards need not be formal guidelines but rather examples of excellence, reference points, and virtues that are easily understood, accepted, and rewarded. Hoteliers, or someone associated with the organization, could be used as a role model or mentor in order to promote these ingredients of excellence. Motivation is achieved by setting a few objectives that are of consequence to the hotel and the accepted responsibility of the individual, by measuring performance, and by rewarding behavior based on achievement.

Question: Is there an understanding that every employee is responsible for self-evaluation and accepting responsibility for change? To create the climate for excellence, it is the hotelier's job to set the right example and to continually communicate and reinforce the values and virtues that the company deems important.

Question: Are employees and managers engaged in a continual process of value clarification, education, and improvement?

The Consensus Principle

Management should attempt to steer away from command leadership and move toward a more positive type of leadership: consultative and consensus. If the goal is to achieve more determined and united action, individuals within the firm must feel as if they contributed to and are part of the decision-making process. Through improved communication and listening, the gap between personal and organizational value systems can be narrowed.

Question: Do managers have the skills necessary to facilitate consultative and consensus decision-making?

The Unity Principle

More consensus can occur when the differences and barriers between "we" and "they" are broken down. It is necessary to establish a unity of purpose and ownership. All individuals working for a hotel, for example, should feel as if they are the hotel. This means that hoteliers must openly share responsibility for achieving objectives and provide more responsibility at the lower levels of the company. For this to work, hoteliers must be seen as more trusting.

Question: Are employees working toward goals which they believe will contribute to the hotel achieving its goals?

Question: Do managers assume that employees are capable of making a meaningful contribution to the decision-making process?

The Performance Principle

Hoteliers must reinforce and reward good performance. When rewards are granted without regard to performance, productivity suffers and individuals will abuse the system and turn to unethical means to accomplish their own goals. Only when rewards are tied to good performance and good work will individual and corporate performances improve.

Question: Are the rewards that have the highest motivational force achieved by performance or length of tenure?

Question: Is there a system for sharing in the rewards of performance that normally accrue to the hotel?

Question: Do individuals clearly understand the relationship between rewards and their performance?

The Empiricism Principle

The future of a business depends on the ability of all individuals within the firm to think clearly, critically, and creatively. It is necessary that every individual be given the tools to help think through a problem or decision rationally, and be given the skills to measure or determine his or her own performance.

Question: When problems arise and decisions must be made, are people given access to the right data and provided with the best tools to evaluate that data?

The Intimacy Principle

Individual employees display loyalty for the hotel when they know that management respects and is concerned about them as people. This bond between the individual and the corporation occurs when people feel as if they truly are part of a group and are making an important contribution. With this closeness comes increased commitment and greater creative performance.

Question: Do employees believe the hotel is committed to their individual development?

Question: Is management concerned with employee welfare and well-being?

Integrity Principles

Faith and commitment to a business is based on the integrity displayed by executives. Integrity does not refer only to simple honesty; it also embodies a consistency and predictability built over time that simply says, "I will do exactly what I say I will do when I say I will do it. If I change my mind, I will tell you well in advance so you will not be harmed by my actions." Such a statement is partly a matter of ethics, but even more a question of vital practicability. This kind of integrity builds trust. From trust comes security. So integrity is a core element in keeping large, amorphous organizations from collapsing in their own confusion.

A hotelier's integrity is manifested by actions. For example, any employee will know the priorities of managers by observing what they say and do. Integrity, therefore, is demonstrated by ensuring that any decisions made do not compromise the hotel's basic purpose and long-term objectives; that promises are kept; that talk and action are consistent; that attention to the product and service is given top priority; that the person is honest, trustworthy and trusting; that the concerns and ideas of others are listened to sincerely; and that all actions are guided by the spirit of ethical conduct.

Question: Has management developed and communicated a code of ethics or a clearly understood value system?

Question: Is the long-term interest and purpose of the hotel ever compromised?

Question: Is the behavior of all executives, managers, and employees beyond reproach in dealing with each other, with guests, or with the public in general?

Conclusion

The professionalization of innkeeping or hotel management is the responsibility of all hoteliers. Their values shape the companies they manage and the ethical behavior of individual employees. Since business ethics is largely a question of corporate character, it is vital that hoteliers carefully and thoroughly assess their own values and the values that ought to be important to their companies.

Endnotes

1. Thomas J. Peters and Robert H. Waterman Jr., *In Search of Excellence: Lessons from America's Best-Run Companies* (New York: Harper & Row, 1982), p. 280.

2. Theodore Levitt, "Are Advertising and Marketing Corrupting Society?" *Advertising Age,* October 16, 1958, p. 16.

3. Max Lerner, *America as Civilization* (New York: Simon & Schuster, 1958), pp. 311–312.

4. Michael Maccoby, *The Gamesman* (New York: Simon & Schuster, 1976), pp. 178–179.

5. Ibid.

6. Ibid.

7. Douglas McGregor, *The Human Side of Enterprise* (New York: McGraw-Hill, 1964); R. Likert, *The Human Organization* (New York: McGraw-Hill, 1964); R. Tannenbaum and W. Schmidt, "How to Choose a Leadership Style," *Harvard Business Review,* 1958. pp. 95-101; Chris Argylis, *Personality and Organization* (New York: Harper & Row, 1957); Edgar H. Schien, *Organizational Psychology* (Englewood Cliffs, N.J.: Prentice-Hall, 1965); R. R. Blake and J. S. Mouten, *The Managerial Grid* (Houston: Gulf Publishing, 1964).

8. Julian R. Phillips and Alan A. Kennedy, "Shaping and Managing Shared Values," *McKinsey Staff Paper,* December 1, 1980, p. 4.

9. Peters and Waterman, pp. 285–286.

10. Peter Drucker, *Management* (New York: Harper & Row, 1974), p. 429.

11. John F. Steiner, "Major Upgrading and Downgrading Business Ethical Behavior," in *Issues in Business and Society,* edited by George A. Steiner and John F. Steiner (New York: Random House, 1977), pp. 255–257.

12. Bernard Barber, "Some Problems in the Sociology of Professions," in *The Professions in America,* edited by K. A. Lynn (Boston: Beacon Press, 1967), p. 18.

13. Lawrence M. Miller, *American Spirit: Visions of a New Corporate Culture* (New York: Morrow, 1984), pp.15–20.

Discussion Topics

1. Quality is often used to signify excellence of a product or service. Major hotel firms are all attempting to assess and improve the quality of their offerings. To what extent are corporate ethics and value systems related to quality and the process involved in meeting the true requirements of guests?

2. Identify some thorny ethical issues and the tradeoffs managers frequently face, particularly with respect to enhancing their career and/or to maximizing profits. What guidelines would you suggest for helping the decision-making process?

3. Indicate appropriate procedures for the development and effective implementation of a code of ethics for a company interested in having such a code.

4. Attempt to answer the questions that are asked with respect to the value-related principles mentioned in the chapter (purpose, excellence, consensus, unity, performance, empiricism, intimacy, and integrity). Base your answers on your own experience working for a company.

Term Paper Topics

1. Research the topic of professionalism and identify the relevant criteria by which to assess whether occupational groups such as chefs, purchasing agents, salespeople or managers qualify. Then, based on actual interviews with one of

these groups, measure their performance against the criteria. Identify ways to close the gap between the ideal model and actual performance.

2. Write a case study that identifies and details a major ethical dilemma facing a senior executive. Interview a variety of industry professionals to obtain their views on how this executive might or should resolve the dilemma. Summarize their views and conclude with a commentary of your own.

Bibliography

Alvarez, Roy, and Heinz Klein. "Information Systems Development for Human Progress." In *Systems Development for Human Progress.* Edited by H. K. Klein and K. Kumar. North-Holland, Amsterdam, 1989.

American Express Travel Related Services Company, Inc. *The Contribution of the World Travel and Tourism Industry to the Global Economy: Executive Summary,* 1989.

Andrews, Kenneth R. "Ethics in Practice." *Harvard Business Review* 67, no. 5, September/October 1989.

Argylis, Chris. *Personality and Organization.* New York: Harper & Row, 1957.

Bally's Casino Resort. *Management Ethics II Seminar.* Las Vegas, Nev., 1989.

Barber, Bernard. "Some Problems in the Sociology of Professions." In *The Professions in America.* Edited by K. A. Lynn. Boston: Beacon Press, 1967.

Barnard, Chester. *The Functions of the Executive.* Cambridge, Mass.: Harvard University Press, 1968.

Berle, A. A. "Corporate Powers as Powers in Trust." *Harvard Law Review* 44, 1931.

Bernstein, Charles. "Unified Effort Vital to Women's Advancement; Stereotypes Remain Barrier to Executive Suite." *Nation's Restaurant News,* June 18, 1990.

Bhide, A., and H. H. Stevenson. "Why Be honest If Honesty Doesn't Pay." *Harvard Business Review* 68, no. 5, 1990.

Blake, R. R., and J. S. Mouten, J. S., *The Managerial Grid.* Houston: Gulf Publishing, 1964.

Blake, Robert B., and Deborah Anne Carroll. "Ethical Reasoning in Business." *Training and Development Journal,* June 1989.

Blanchard, Kenneth, and Norman Vincent Peale. *The Power of Ethical Management.* New York: Morrow, 1988.

BNA Editorial Staff. *Grievance Guide.* 7th ed. Washington, D.C.: Bureau of National Affairs, Inc., 1989.

Bowen, Ezra. "Ethics: Looking At Its Roots." *Time,* May 25, 1987.

Bower, J. L., and T. M. Hout. "Fast-Cycle Capability for Competitive Power." *Harvard Business Review* 66, no. 6, November/December 1988.

Bowie, Norman E., and Ronald F. Duska. *Business Ethics*. 2d ed. Englewood Cliffs, N.J.: Prentice Hall, 1990.

Brennan, Steven N., and Earl A. Molander. "Is the Ethics of Business Changing?" *Harvard Business Review*, January/February 1977.

Buchholz, Rogene A. *Fundamental Concept and Problems in Business Ethics*. Englewood Cliffs, N.J.: Prentice Hall, 1989.

Carroll, Archie B. *Business and Society: Managing Corporate Social Performance*. Boston: Little, Brown, 1981.

—————. "A Three-Dimensional Conceptual Model of Corporate Performance." *Academy of Management Review* 4, October 1979.

—————. "In Search of the Moral Manager." *Business Horizons*, March-April 1987.

Casey, John L. "Teaching Ethics." In *Business in the Contemporary World* 2, no. 4. Waltham, Mass.: Bentley College, 1990.

Cavanagh, Gerald F., and Arthur F. McGovern. *Ethical Dilemmas in the Modern Corporation*. Englewood Cliffs, N.J.: Prentice Hall, 1988.

Center for Corporate Public Involvement. *Social Report of the Life and Health Insurance Business*. Washington, D.C., 1986.

Chase, David R. "The Corporate Challenge." In *Ensuring Minority Success in Corporate Management*. Edited by Donna Thompson and Nancy DiTomaso. New York: Plenum Press, 1988.

Cooke, Robert A. *Ethics in Business: A Perspective*. Arthur Anderson and Company, 1988.

Craft, R. R. Jr. "Space Law." *The National Law Journal*, June 15, 1987.

Dahl, J. "Congress Passes a Bill Likely to Force Many Hotels to Install Room Sprinklers." *The Wall Street Journal*, September 11, 1990.

D'Aprix, Roger. *Communicating For Productivity*. New York: Harper & Row, 1982.

Davis, George. "The Changing Agenda." In *Ensuring Minority Success in Corporate Management*. Edited by Donna Thompson and Nancy DiTomaso. New York: Plenum Press, 1988.

Davis, K., and R. L. Blomstrom. *Business and Its Environment*. New York: McGraw-Hill, 1966.

Dayton, K. *Seegal-Macy Lecture*. Delivered at the University of Michigan, Ann Arbor, October 30, 1975.

DiTomaso, Nancy; Donna Thompson; and David Blake. "Corporate Perspectives on the Advancement of Minority Managers." In *Ensuring Minority Success in Corporate Management*. Edited by Donna Thompson and Nancy DiTomaso. New York: Plenum Press, 1988.

Dodd, E.M. "For Whom Are Managers Corporate Trustees?" *Harvard Law Review* 45, 1932.

Drucker, Peter. "Ethical Chic." *Forbes*, September 14, 1981.

—————. *Management*. New York: Harper & Row, 1974.

—————. *The Practice of Management*. New York: Harper & Row, 1954.

—————. "What Is Business Ethics?" *Across the Board*, October 1981.

Durant, Will. *The Story of Philosophy*. New York: Simon & Schuster, 1961.

Elkouri, Frank, and Edna Asper Elkouri. *How Arbitration Works.* 4th ed. Washington, D.C.: Bureau of National Affairs, Inc., 1989.

Enghagen, L. K. "Ethics the Response." *Lodging* 15, no. 3, 1989.

Farrell, Paul V., ed. *Aljian's Purchasing Handbook.* 4th ed. New York: McGraw-Hill, 1982.

Firnstahl, T. W. "My Employees Are My Service Guarantee." *Harvard Business Review* 67, no. 4, 1989.

Freudberg, David. *The Corporate Conscience—Money, Power, and Responsible Business.* New York: American Management Association, 1986.

Friedman, Milton. *Capitalism and Freedom.* Chicago: University of Chicago Press, 1962.

———. "The Social Responsibility of Business Is to Increase Profits." In *Business Ethics, Readings and Cases in Corporate Morality.* Edited by W. Michael Hoffman and Jennifer M. Moore. New York: McGraw-Hill, 1984.

Fritzche, David J., and Helmut Becker. "Linking Management Behavior to Ethical Philosophy—An Empirical Investigation." *Academy of Management Journal*, 1984.

Fromm, E. *Escape from Freedom.* New York: Avon Books, 1967.

Garret, Thomas M. *Business Ethics.* New York: Appleton-Century-Crofts, 1966.

Gellerman, Saul. "Why Good Managers Make Bad Ethical Choices." *Harvard Business Review*, July-August 1986.

Goll, G. E. "Management by Values: Consistency as a Predictor of Success." *Hospitality Research Journal* (Professional Journal of the Council on Hotel, Restaurant and Institutional Education), 14, no. 1, 1990.

Goodpaster, Kenneth E. "The Concept of Corporate Responsibility." In *Just Business: New Introductory Essay in Business Ethics.* Edited by Tom Regan. New York: Random House, 1984.

Goodpaster, Kenneth E., and Thomas R. Piper. *Managerial Decision Making and Ethical Values: A Course Module.* Boston: Harvard Business School, 1989.

Hales, A. "First Semester Outcomes of an Experimental Program: 'Housing and Feeding the Homeless.'" *Hospitality and Tourism Educator*, Spring 1989.

Hall, Jay, PhD. *The Competence Connection: A Blue Print for Excellence.* The Woodlands, Texas: Woodstead Press, n.d.

Hall, Stephen S.J. "Ethics in Hospitality: How to Draw Your Line." *Lodging* 15, no. 1, 1989.

———. "National Survey on Hospitality Ethics." Unpublished manuscript, Harvard Divinity School, 1988.

———. *Quality Assurance in the Hospitality Industry.* Milwaukee, Wis.: ASQC Quality Press, 1990.

———. The Role of Ethics in Quality. Unpublished master's thesis, Harvard Divinity School, 1988.

Haney, W. V. *Communicating and Interpersonal Relations.* 5th ed. Homewood, Ill.: Irwin, 1986.

Harris, J. F., and A. Klepper. *Corporate and Philanthropic Public Service Activities.* New York: The Conference Board, 1976.

Haywood, K. Michael. "Ethics, Value Systems and the Professionalization of Hoteliers." *Florida International University Hospitality Review* 5, 1987.

Haywood, M. K. "Revising and Implementing the Marketing Concept as It Applies to Tourism." *Tourism Management* 11, no. 3, 1990.

Heyne, Paul. "What Is the Responsibility of Business Under Democratic Capitalism?" *The Future of Private Enterprise.* Georgia State University, 1986.

Hogner, Robert H. "Ethics in the Hospitality Industry: A Management Control System Perspective." *Florida International University Hospitality Review* 5, 1987.

Hosner, LaRue Tone. "Chapter 3, Managerial Ethics and the Rule of Law." In *The Ethics of Management.* Homewood, Ill.: Irwin, 1987.

Hospitality Law 3, no. 3, March 1988.

Hulbert, Terry, and Elaine Ingulli. *Law and Ethics in the Business Environment.* St. Paul, Minn.: West Publishing Co., 1990.

Hunt, Shelby D.; Van R. Wood; and Lawrence B. Chonko. "Corporate Ethical Values and Organizational Commitment in Marketing." *Journal of Marketing* 53, July 1989.

"Inventory of Ethical Issues in Business." *Ethics: Easier Said Than Done* 2, no. 1, n.d.

Jefferies, Jack P. *Understanding Hospitality Law.* 2d ed. East Lansing, Mich.: Educational Institute of the American Hotel & Motel Association, 1990.

Johnston, William B., and Arnold Packer. *Work Force 2000, Work and Workers for the Twenty-first Century.* Indianapolis, Ind.: Hudson Institute, 1987.

Jones, Donald G. *Doing Ethics in Business.* Oelgeschlager, Gunn & Hain, 1982.

Kahn, Alfred E. *The Economics of Regulation.* Cambridge, Mass.: MIT Press, 1988.

Kahn, Herman. *World Economic Development: 1979 and Beyond.* New York: Morrow, Quill Paperbacks, 1979.

Kanter, Rosabeth Moss. *The Change Masters.* New York: Simon & Schuster, 1984.

————. "Ensuring Minority Achievement in Corporations." In *Ensuring Minority Success in Corporate Management.* Edited by Donna Thompson and Nancy DiTomaso. New York: Plenum Press, 1988.

Kappa, Margaret M.; Aleta Nitschke; and Patricia B. Schappert. *Managing Housekeeping Operations.* East Lansing, Mich.: Educational Institute of the American Hotel & Motel Association, 1990.

Kenny, John J. *Primer of Labor Relations.* 23d ed. Washington, D.C.: Bureau of National Affairs, Inc., 1987.

Klein, H., and Roy Alvarez. "Information Systems in the Hotel Industry: Part of a Problem or Part of a Solution?" In *Computers and Democracy.* Edited by Gro Bjerknes, Pelle Ehn, and Morten Kyng. Avebury, England, 1987.

Kohlberg, Lawrence. *Psychology of Moral Development.* New York: Harper & Row, 1984.

Kristol, Irving. "Ethics, Anyone? Or Morals?" *Wall Street Journal,* September 15, 1987.

Lacey, M. "Instilling Ethics by Example." *Food Management* 22, no. 11.

Laczniak, G.R., and P. E. Murphy, eds. *Marketing Ethics: Guidelines for Managers.* Lexington, Mass.: Heath, 1985.

Lammermeyer, Horst V. *Human Relations—The Key to Quality.* Milwaukee, Wis.: ASQC Quality Press, 1990.

Lane, Harold E. "The Corporate Conscience and the Role of Business in Society." *Cornell Hotel and Restaurant Administration Quarterly* 23, 1982.

Bibliography 283

Lawrence, W. Sherman, and Jody Klien. *Major Lawsuits Over Crime and Security: Trends and Patterns, 1958-82.* Washington, D.C.: Security Law Institute, September 1984.

Lerner, Max. *America as Civilization.* New York: Simon & Schuster, 1958.

Levitt, Theodore. "Are Advertising and Marketing Corrupting Society?" *Advertising Age,* October 16, 1958.

Lewis, R.C., and Chambers, R.E. *Marketing Leadership in Hospitality.* New York: Van Nostrand Reinhold, 1989.

Lewis, R.C., and C. Roan. "Selling What You Promote." *Cornell Hotel and Restaurant Administration Quarterly* 27, no. 1, 1986.

Likert, R. *New Patterns of Management.* New York: McGraw-Hill, 1961.

————. *The Human Organization.* New York: McGraw-Hill, 1964.

Logsdon, Jeanne M., and David R. Palmer. "Issues Management and Ethics." *Journal of Business Ethics,* no. 7, 1988.

Ludeman, Kate. "Instilling the Worth Ethic." *Training and Development Journal,* May 1990.

Lundberg, Craig C. "Working with Culture." *Journal of Organizational Change Management* 1, no. 2, 1988.

Lundberg, Craig C., and Robert H. Woods. "Modifying Restaurant Culture: Managers as Cultural Spokespersons, Assessors, and Facilitators." Unpublished manuscript, Cornell University, July, 1989.

Maccoby, Michael. *The Gamesman.* New York: Simon & Schuster, 1976.

McGregor, Douglas. *The Human Side of Enterprise.* New York: McGraw-Hill, 1960.

McKay, P.S. "Do the Right Thing." *Enroute,* October, 1990.

Miller, Lawrence M. *American Spirit: Visions of a New Corporate Culture.* New York: Morrow, 1984.

Molanphy, M.L.; A. S. Lee; K. Rudoph; and E. P. Hartmann. "Pricing Structure Analysis of Selected Hotels in Springfield, Massachusetts." Unpublished monograph, University of Massachusetts/Amherst, 1990.

Moshowitz, A. *The Conquest of Will: Information Processing in Human Affairs.* Reading, Mass.: Addison-Wesley, 1976.

Nash, Laura L. "Ethics Without the Sermon." In *Executive Success: Making It in Management.* New York: Wiley, 1983.

National Fire Protection Association. *Fire at the Dupont Plaza Hotel and Casino.* Quincy, Mass.: NFPA, 1987.

Novak, Michael. "The Judeo-Christian Values That Characterize Economic Freedoms." In *The Future of Private Enterprise.* Georgia State University, 1986.

Olafson, Frederick A. "The Idea of Progress: An Ethical Appraisal." In *Progress and Its Discontents.* Edited by Gabriel A. Almond, Marvin Chodorow, and Roy Harvey Pearce. Berkley, Calif.: University of California Press, 1982.

Parker, Linda Bates. "Dealing with Diversity." *The Black Collegian,* March/April 1990.

Pastin, Mark. "Lessons from High-Profit, High-Ethics Companies: An Agenda for Managerial Action." In *The Hard Problems of Management: Gaining the Ethics Edge.* San Francisco: Jossey-Bass, 1986.

Peters, Thomas J., and Robert H. Waterman Jr. *In Search of Excellence: Lessons from America's Best-Run Companies.* New York: Harper & Row, 1982.

Phillips, Julian R., and Alan A. Kennedy. "Shaping and Managing Shared Values." *McKinsey Staff Paper*, December 1, 1980.

Platzer, Linda C. *Annual Survey of Corporate Contributions*, 1986 ed. New York: The Conference Board, 1986.

Porter, Elias. *Manual of Administration & Interpretation: Strength Deployment Inventory.* Santa Monica, Calif.: Personal Strengths Publishing, 1985.

Rankin, Robert A. "Changing Demographics May Make Affirmative Action Moot in 1990's." *The Philadelphia Inquirer*, July 1, 1990.

Reitzel, Lyden, Roberts, and Severance. *Contemporary Business Law, Principles and Cases.* 4th ed. New York: McGraw-Hill, 1990.

Rion, Michael. *The Responsible Manager: Practical Strategies for Ethical Decision Making.* New York: Harper & Row, 1990.

Rue, Leslie W., and Phyllis G. Holland. *Strategic Management: Concepts and Experiences.* New York: McGraw-Hill, 1989.

Sandroff, Ronni. "Sexual Harassment in the Fortune 500." *Working Woman*, December 1988.

Sathe, Vijay. *Culture and Related Corporate Realities.* Homewood, Ill.: Irwin, 1985.

Schering, Eberhard E. *Purchasing Management.* Englewood Cliffs, N.J.: Prentice Hall, 1989.

Schien, Edgar H. *Organizational Psychology.* Englewood Cliffs, N.J.: Prentice-Hall, 1965.

Selekman, Benjamin M. "Cynicism and Managerial Morality." *Harvard Business Review*, September/October 1958.

Serpa, Roy. "Creating a Candid Corporate Culture." *Journal of Business Ethics* 4, 1985.

Shafritz, Jay M., and J. Steven Ott. "The Organization Culture School." In *Classics of Organization Theory*. Chicago: Dorsey Press, 1987.

Shames, Laurence. *The Hunger for More: Searching for Values in an Age of Greed.* New York: Random House, Times Books, 1989.

Sharpin, Arthur. *Strategic Management.* New York: McGraw-Hill, 1985.

Shaw, Bill, and Art Wolfe. *The Structure of the Legal Environment: Law, Ethics and Business.* Boston: Kent Publishing, 1987.

Sherwin, Douglas S. "The Ethical Roots of the Business System." *Harvard Business Review*, no. 61, November\December 1983.

Skinner, B.F. *Contingencies of Reinforcement.* East Norwalk, Conn.: Appleton-Century-Crofts, 1971.

Steele, Shelby. "A Negative Vote on Affirmative Action." *The New York Times Magazine,* May 13, 1990.

Stefanelli, John. *Purchasing Selection and Procurement for the Hospitality Industry.* 2d ed. New York: Wiley, 1985.

Steiner, John F. "Major Upgrading and Downgrading Business Ethical Behavior." In *Issues in Business and Society.* Edited by George A. Steiner and John F. Steiner. New York: Random House, 1977.

Stephenson, S. "A Sense of Right and Wrong." *Restaurant & Institutions* 98, no. 22, 1988.

Sternberg, S. *National Directory of Corporate Charity.* San Francisco: Regional Young Adult Project, 1984.

Stone, Christopher. "The Place of Enterprise Liability in the Control of Corporate Conduct." *Yale Law Journal* 90, 1990.

Sturdivant, Frederick D., and Heidi Vernon-Wortzel. *Business and Society*. Homewood, Ill.: Irwin, 1990.

Tannenbaum, R., and W. Schmidt. "How to Choose a Leadership Style." *Harvard Business Review*, 1958.

Thompson, Donna, and Nancy DiTomaso, eds. *Ensuring Minority Success in Corporate Management*. New York: Plenum Press, 1988.

U.S. Merit Systems Protection Board. *Sexual Harassment in the Federal Government: An Update*. Washington, D.C., 1988.

Vallen, Jerome J., and James R. Abbey. *The Art and Science of Hospitality Management*. East Lansing, Mich.: Educational Institute of the American Hotel & Motel Association, 1987.

Van Doren, C. *The Idea of Progress*. New York: Praeger, 1967.

Velasquez, Manuel; Dennis J. Moberg; and Gerald F. Cavanagh. "Organizational Statesmanship and Dirty Politics: Ethical Guidelines for the Organizational Politician." *Organizational Dynamics*, Autumn, 1983.

Virts, William P. *Purchasing for Hospitality Operations*, East Lansing, Mich.: Educational Institute of the American Hotel & Motel Association, 1987.

Vogel, David. "Ethics and Profits Don't Always Go Hand in Hand." *Los Angeles Times*, December 28, 1988.

Westin, Alan F., and Alfred G. Feliu. *Resolving Employment Disputes Without Litigation*. Washington, D.C.: The Bureau of National Affairs, Inc., 1988.

Whitney, David L. "Ethics in the Hospitality Industry: with a Focus on Hotel Managers." *International Journal of Hospitality Management* 9, no. 1, 1990.

Woods, Robert H. "More Alike than Different: The Culture of the Restaurant Industry." *Cornell Hotel and Restaurant Administration Quarterly* 30, no. 2, August.

Woods, Robert H. "Restaurant Culture: Congruence and Culture in the Restaurant Industry." Unpublished doctoral dissertation, School of Hotel Administration, Cornell University, 1989.

Woods, Robert H. "Surfacing Culture: The Northeast Restaurants Case." Unpublished paper, Michigan State University, June 4, 1990.

York, Kenneth M. "Defining Sexual Harassment in Workplaces: A Policy-Capturing Approach." *Academy of Management Journal* 32, no. 4, 1989.

Zack, Arnold M., and Bloch, Richard I. *Labor Agreement in Negotiation and Arbitration*. Washington, D.C.: The Bureau of National Affairs, Inc., 1983.

About the Editor . . .

With the publication of *ETHICS: A Book of Readings,* yet another achievement is added to Stephen S.J. Hall's already long and diverse list. His accomplishments and his career are quality-oriented and international in scope. He developed the American Hotel & Motel Association's "Quest for Quality" program; the "Quality Index" system; and the first college curriculum on quality assurance for hospitality at Cornell. He conducted the first American hotel survey on ethics and morality; developed the first means of analyzing the cost of error for service industries; instituted quality assurance programs at many properties in the United States and abroad, and implemented a 15-property QA program for the Bermuda Hotel Association; developed the "Graph Factor System of Energy Control" which has reduced utility costs for hotels; and developed engineering management systems which have helped hoteliers schedule and control maintenance operations for many years.

He is the author of *Quality Assurance in the Hospitality Industry* (published in 1990 by the American Society of Quality Control and Quality Press) and many articles and feature stories in American and French hospitality publications. He has conducted quality assurance seminars throughout the world.

Mr. Hall is a graduate of the Cornell University School of Hotel Administration and holds an MBA from Michigan State University as well as a master's degree in divinity from Harvard University. Following thirteen years of service with ITT Sheraton Corporation, he spent five years as Vice President for Administration of Harvard University, leaving in 1976 to form his own companies.

He is Executive Director of the International Institute for Quality and Ethics in Service and Tourism (IIQEST), which he formed in 1988, and he is founder, owner, and President of Crescent Industries, Inc., and Stephen Hall Associates. Additionally, he is a part-time pastor at Beechwood Congregational Church in Cohasset, Massachusetts, and is an adjunct professor of quality and ethics at the Institut de Management Hotelier International in Cergy-Pontoise, France.